BOOK SALE

More Praise for *The Leadership Capital Index*

"Much needed! Leadership has always been the X factor in gauging the health of any organization—we know it's vitally important, but we haven't had a way to think about it objectively. Now we can compare apples to apples."
—**Cheryl Bachelder, CEO, Popeyes Louisiana Kitchen, and author of *Dare to Serve***

"All investors who take their job seriously will want to read this book. Ulrich has closed a critical gap in risk mitigation with this comprehensive 360 for assessing leadership capability throughout an organization."
—**Sandy Ogg, Operating Partner, The Blackstone Group**

"Long-term-oriented investors understand that 'people lead, financial numbers lag.' Thanks to Dave Ulrich's leadership capital index, we now have a more rigorous way to evaluate the people who lead and can make much better investment decisions."
—**Fred Trigueiro, founder and CEO, Archipelago Partners, Brazil**

"It is a remarkably comprehensive model. *The Leadership Capital Index* will be an important and immensely useful book not only for investors but for anyone needing to better understand the nature of leadership."
—**Hermann Hauser, cofounder and Partner, Amadeus Capital Partners**

"Dave Ulrich has written a foundational book. He has introduced the concept of the leadership capital index and brought together eight key elements of the index. Each element is carefully developed and ultimately put into a format designed for practical usage. As the CIO of an investment management firm specializing in publicly traded stocks, I am tasked with making investment decisions based on publicly available data. This means my investment team and I have to carefully choose only a few critical items to discuss with each corporate management team. We also hold our stocks for long periods of time; our approach is significantly dependent upon superior corporate leadership. Dave's book will help us select the one or two key index elements for each potential investment and ask the pertinent questions. Refreshingly, Dave has left the door wide open for improvements in the index."
—**Frederick K. Martin, CEO and CIO, Disciplined Growth Investors**

THE
LEADERSHIP
CAPITAL
INDEX

Also by the Author

Dave Ulrich has written 30 books and more than 200 articles that shape managerial thinking and action in organizations, leadership, and human resources. Key books include:

ORGANIZATION INSIGHTS

Justin Allen and Dave Ulrich. 2013. *Talent Accelerator: Secrets for Driving Business Growth in Asia*. RBL Group and Ministry of Manpower (Singapore).

Dave Ulrich and Wendy Ulrich. 2010. *The Why of Work: How Great Leaders Build Abundant Organizations That Win*. New York: McGraw Hill.

Ron Ashkenas, Dave Ulrich, Todd Jick, and Steve Kerr. 1995. *The Boundary-less Organization: Breaking the Chains of Organization Structure*. San Francisco: Josey-Bass.

Dave Ulrich and Dale Lake. 1990. *Organizational Capability: Competing from the Inside/Out*. New York: Wiley.

LEADERSHIP INSIGHTS
Defining the Outcomes and Practices of Leadership

Dave Ulrich and Norm Smallwood. 2013. *Leadership Sustainability: Seven Disciplines to Achieve the Changes Great Leaders Know They Must Make*. New York: McGraw Hill.

Dave Ulrich, Norm Smallwood, and Kate Sweetman. 2008. *Leadership Code: Five Rules to Live By*. Boston: Harvard Business Press.

Dave Ulrich and Norm Smallwood. 2007. *Leadership Brand: Developing Customer Focused Leaders to Drive Performance and Building Lasting Value*. Boston: Harvard Business Press.

HUMAN RESOURCE INSIGHTS

Dave Ulrich, William Schiemann, and Libby Sartain. 2015. *The Rise of HR*. HR Certification Institute.

Dave Ulrich, Jon Younger, Wayne Brockbank, and Michael Ulrich. 2012. *HR From the Outside In: Six Competencies for the Future of Human Resources*. New York: McGraw-Hill Publishing Company.

Brian Becker, Mark Huselid, and Dave Ulrich. 2001. *The HR Scorecard: Linking People, Strategy, and Performance*. Boston: Harvard Business Press.

Dave Ulrich. 1997. *Human Resource Champions: The Next Agenda for Adding Value and Delivering Results*. Cambridge, MA: Harvard Business Press.

*Realizing the
Market Value
of Leadership*

THE

LEADERSHIP
CAPITAL
INDEX

Dave Ulrich

BK

Berrett–Koehler Publishers, Inc.
a BK Business book

Berrett-Koehler Publishers, Inc.
1333 Broadway, Suite 1000
Oakland, CA 94612-1921
Tel: (510) 817-2277 | Fax: (510) 817-2278 | www.bkconnection.com

ORDERING INFORMATION
Quantity sales. Special discounts are available on quantity purchases by corporations, associations, and others. For details, contact the "Special Sales Department" at the Berrett-Koehler address above.
Individual sales. Berrett-Koehler publications are available through most bookstores. They can also be ordered directly from Berrett-Koehler: Tel: (800) 929-2929; Fax: (802) 864-7626; www.bkconnection.com.
Orders for college textbook/course adoption use. Please contact Berrett-Koehler: Tel: (800) 929-2929; Fax: (802) 864-7626.
Orders by US trade bookstores and wholesalers. Please contact Ingram Publisher Services: Tel: (800) 509-4887; Fax: (800) 838-1149; E-mail: customer.service@ingram publisherservices.com; or visit www.ingram publisherservices.com/Ordering for details about electronic ordering.

Berrett-Koehler and the BK logo are registered trademarks of Berrett-Koehler Publishers, Inc.

Printed in the United States of America.

Berrett-Koehler books are printed on long-lasting acid-free paper. When it is available, we choose paper that has been manufactured by environmentally responsible processes. These may include using trees grown in sustainable forests, incorporating recycled paper, minimizing chlorine in bleaching, or recycling the energy produced at the paper mill.

Library of Congress Cataloging-in-Publication Data

Ulrich, David, 1953–
  The leadership capital index : realizing the market value of leadership / Dave Ulrich.
— First edition.
      pages   cm
  Includes bibliographical references and index.
  ISBN 978-1-62656-599-9 (hardcover)
  1. Leadership.   2. Organizational effectiveness.   3. Corporate culture.
4. Corporations—Valuation.   5. Performance.   I. Title.
  HD57.7.U45795   2015
  658.4'092—dc23   2015022816

First Edition

20 19 18 17 16 15 | 10 9 8 7 6 5 4 3 2 1

Produced and designed by BookMatters, edited by Kristi Hein, proofed by Janet Blake, indexed by Gerald Van Raavensway, and cover designed by Richard Adelson

To investors and leaders
who seek common ground

CONTENTS

PART FOUR | **APPLICATION AND ACTION**

FOREWORD

All of us in the investment world are continually challenged to find that single best share investment that will produce excellent profits and not result in losses for ourselves and our clients. More important, we strive to do that consistently not only for one company stock that we have purchased but for all of the shares in our portfolios. We therefore spend a great deal of time studying companies listed in stock markets all over the world. We pore over company audited accounts, examining the profit and loss figures as well as the balance sheets. The profit and loss numbers give us clues to the company's history of earnings and what kind of trends they may reveal. By calculating such ratios as return on assets, return on equity, net profit margin, and so forth, we also gain insight into the profitability of the company.

The company's balance sheet reveals how safe the company is in terms of any possible debts that could result in bankruptcy. Of course, those profit and loss figures as well as balance sheet accounts are not sufficient to really understand what is happening, since the business environment changes from one report date to another. There could be dramatic changes in the company's sales, the competition, the debts acquired, and so forth. For that reason we try to get updates regarding the company's activities by visiting the company and having follow-up calls.

Despite all of these efforts, however, our investments still are vulnerable to events both internal and external to the company. For this reason we need to depend on the company's management—the most important element on the firm's viability. Who is in charge and what are their capabilities? If we can identify those firms whose managements are capable of confronting the challenges facing the company and, more important, capable of making it grow, then our chances of good investment returns rise dramatically.

But how can we make this assessment of the company's management? Up to now it has been done on a very subjective basis without any systematic approach. This is a major challenge, since we are dealing with intangible variables such as strategy, brand, and operational capabilities. The key is to assess the firm's leadership. An interview with the firm's top management often is not comprehensive and is colored by personal biases.

The good news is that someone has finally developed a systematic and logical way to measure the elusive variable of company leadership that plays such a key role in determining company success and market value. Dave Ulrich has found a way to measure this variable, so critical to investment success. For investment professionals like me, this book is long overdue.

Anyone interested in improving investment performance should not only read but also carefully study this book. By realizing the market value of leadership through a leadership capital index, investors will be able to reduce their overall investment risk and improve their chances of investment success.

—Mark Mobius, Executive Chairman,
Templeton Emerging Markets Group

THE
LEADERSHIP
CAPITAL
INDEX

INTRODUCTION

The Market Value of Leadership

You're considering investing in a firm; how do you know what it's really worth? Helping investors answer this question has occupied a good part of my past decade. I've drawn ideas from the vast and multifaceted financial literature, the emerging and complex intangibles literature, and the broad literature of leadership. This book shifts investor attention from financial measures to intangibles (like strategy, brand, operations, and customer service) to leadership. This book integrates theory and research to address the question of how to add leadership to your view of firm valuation.

The results will be useful to many audiences. Looking at leadership through investors' eyes—the main thrust of the book—will of course benefit investors themselves, but it will also benefit the rating agencies who create indices to report value, the government monitoring bodies who work to ensure that business standards are maintained, the trade associations who promote the interests of their members, the boards of directors who steward and oversee value-creating firm behavior, the executive teams who succeed by delivering value, and the leadership development professionals and human resource professionals and others who build value through leadership and organization processes.

In much of my writing, I tackle large and messy problems, like defining how human resources can be adapted to deliver business performance (*HR Champions, HR Transformation, HR Value Proposition, HR from the Outside In, The Rise of HR*), how organizations can change their culture and create new capabilities (*Organization Capability, GE Workout, Boundaryless Organization, Learning Organization*), how leadership can be codified, improved, and tied to customers (*Results Based Leadership, Leadership Code, Leadership Brand, Leadership Sustainability*), and how employees can find more meaning from their work setting (*Why of Work*). My goal has been to shape future conversations that solve relevant business questions through integrating innovative and complex ideas in a simple way.

Leadership matters, and most acknowledge that leaders affect an organization's value. Almost every activist investor recognizes the importance of leadership for firm success and can point to iconic leaders who have created great value. However, just by observing that a particular leader is visionary or inspiring, by focusing only on the person at the top and ignoring the larger leadership team, or by failing to assess whose leadership capability is woven into the organization's DNA, investors make simplistic and intuitive assessments of leadership value. The main title of this book, *The Leadership Capital Index,* draws on a useful metaphor for how to include, conceive, and audit leadership in the assessment of firm value. A leadership capital index is like a financial confidence index—Moody's or Standard & Poor's. Rather than assessing a firm's likelihood of paying its debts, however, the leadership capital index offers a more thorough way to assess a firm's present and future leadership. The subtitle of this book, *Realizing the Market Value of Leadership,* promises a more comprehensive and rigorous way of evaluating leadership as part of a firm's overall value.

One reason this book has taken a decade to write is the difficulty of articulating a simple solution to the complex task of judging leadership quality as an outside debt or equity investor. I started by trying to help investors go from instinctive to rigorous leadership assessments. I wanted the leadership capital index in this book to take investors from a present 5% confidence in their assessment of leadership to a 90% confidence level, but I eventually concluded that this goal was naïve on my part.

Instead, I have chosen to write an MVP—minimum viable process—book, picking up a concept from software development. In software, innovators get started, go public, share ideas, receive critiques, experiment, and continually improve. In the same vein, my leadership capital index is not yet perfect—but it offers a simple and already helpful approach to the question of assessing genuine value. This MVP logic is like software version 1.0, knowing that 2.0 and 3.0 will follow. But 1.0 becomes the critical first draft that will define and shape the conversation. Creating this rigorous way to define and assess leadership through the eyes of investors is a significant step forward.

My hope is to frame a dialogue about something that investors and others will use in a disciplined way. The leadership capital index will be used to assess firm value, but it will also become part of conversations about risk, social responsibility, governance, mergers and acquisitions, and leadership selection or development. This is a lot to ask of one book, but the ideas presented will make real progress on this journey.

Most popular business books start with stories of beloved companies and try to uncover insights from those exemplars. These insights might come from in-depth narrative on a few companies or from research on many companies designed to discover what respected companies do. I have written a number of such books. The benefit of this approach is that the stories (and the research) are compelling and interesting, offering details that bring the insights alive. The downside is that the stories and research reflect a point in time. However excellent or great they are now, companies may not continue to be so in the years (or even months) to come. Starting with stories, either as individual cases or as research based on lots of cases, runs the risk that events will overtake the author's insights and lead readers to doubt the inferences the author has drawn.

While not focused on specific companies, we wanted to figure out how active investors can better assess leaders, so my colleagues and I wanted to get inside the investor's mind. Norm Smallwood and I interviewed dozens of thoughtful investors around the world; ran a number of focus groups with four to eight investors in Brazil, Singapore, Canada, Norway, Germany, the United Kingdom, the Middle East, and the United States; and surveyed more than four hundred investors (and published these results). We found that investors were intrigued with the concept of leadership, acknowledged it as a missing ingredient (some said the holy grail) of investment assessment, but were unsure how to approach it with more than casual observations.

I also looked at dozens of studies by consulting firms and experts who attempted to put substance behind the assessment of leadership. Very talented colleagues have approached the challenge of assessing how leaders can be more effective. In general, these studies offered deep insights on one piece of the leadership puzzle. Some focused on compensation practices, others on personal style, and still others on organization governance and design. None attempted to prepare a comprehensive approach to leadership capital as a whole.[1]

It's just as well that I abandoned the idea of starting with stories of investors' successfully assessing leadership—such stories are rare, and those that exist are often incomplete or even more transitory than the usual story of business excellence. Instead, my focus is on stimulating ideas that will deliver investor rigor in assessing leadership capital. Throughout the book, I refer to insights from investor interviews, focus groups, and surveys, but concentrate on the ideas and frameworks rather than the stories. I put myself in the place of an investor who has done financial and intangible analytics and is now seeking insights on leadership that will inform the final decision.

When I discuss this leadership capital index, people often demand, "Show me the measures on the existing balance sheet and income statement." I struggled for years to do this, but then the obvious hit me: current income statements and balance sheets were designed to give investors financial information to assess a firm's value—not information on leadership capital. Nonetheless, investors and others who are serious about long-term value creation will seek the additional insights that come from a thorough assessment of leadership—the sort of assessment this leadership capital index begins to provide. The measures of this index come from more in-depth observations, interviews, surveys, and other data about leadership. The value of this book is that it provides you with the right questions to ask and the right indicators to track.

So this is an ambitious and sweeping book. When you see leadership through the eyes of investors, you will build new insights into how you can better realize the full market value of a company. The proposed leadership capital index offers a rather simple (but not simplistic) approach, with ideas, tools, and diagnostic questions that can be used with increasing amounts of granularity (one could audit two domains of leadership, ten elements, or fifty-nine items). Using this leadership capital index, investors can hope to move from 5% to 30% or even 40% confidence in their assessment of leadership. By offering a leadership capital index, I will take a major step forward to shape the discussion to realize the market value of leadership.

The book is divided into four parts. Part 1 (Why and How Leadership Matters to Investors), in Chapters 1 and 2, provides the context for the leadership capital index. These chapters summarize previous work on firm valuation and leadership, present the rationale for leadership as an increasingly important part of market value, and define a leadership capital index to advance and assess quality of leadership with two domains: individual and organizational elements of leadership. Part 2 (The Individual Elements of the Leadership Capital Index), in Chapters 3 through 7, presents five elements of individual leader behavior that investors can monitor, then identifies specific competencies and indicators for these five elements. These five chapters will help investors determine the quality of individual leaders within an organization. Part 3 (The Organization Elements of the Leadership Capital Index), in Chapters 8 through 12, presents five elements of organizational systems that shape leadership that investors can monitor and identifies specific dimensions and indicators of these five human capital systems. These five chapters will help investors realize the value of the organization that creates leadership. Part 4 (Application and Action), in Chapters 13 and 14, pulls together all of the ideas and show how investors, regulatory agencies, boards of directors, C-suite executives, and leadership development professionals can apply these ideas to improve the quality of leadership of companies they assess or work in.

I am deeply indebted to many colleagues who have shaped the ideas in this book. My insights draw on exceptional thought leaders in diverse disciplines including finance, market valuation, organization systems, human capital, human resources, and leadership. I am particularly indebted to those who have worked to bring investment-level rigor to the assessment of traditionally "softer" organization issues. The list of these colleagues is too long to mention, but they are cited in Chapters 1 and 2. I have learned firsthand about the elements of leadership capital and organization capability from working with hundreds of clients over many decades. I am grateful to these clients for allowing me to observe and co-learn with them. My personal intellectual guides on this work include remarkable insights from cherished colleagues including Justin Allen, Dick Beatty, John Boudreau, Wayne Brockbank, Bob Eichinger, Allan Freed, Peter Goerke, Marshall Goldsmith, Lynda Gratton, Gordon Hewitt, Steve Kerr, Dale Lake, Ed Lawler, Mark Nyman, Jeff Pfeffer, CK Prahalad, Ray Reilly, Norm Smallwood, Pat Wright, and Jon Younger. Each has directly contributed to my understanding, and I clearly have assimilated their ideas.

I am indebted to Hilary Powers for her extraordinary assistance in developmental editing. She has an incredible gift for making abstract ideas accessible. None of my books would be the same without her remarkable editing. I am very grateful for Steve Piersanti and his amazingly talented team at Berrett-Koehler, who are not only professionally gifted but also show personal care. Clearly, this book and other work-related activities would not happen without the incredible support of Ginger Bitter, my assistant for over twenty-five years, who not only manages unwieldy logistics but is also a dear personal friend. Yet my most heartfelt appreciation and gratitude goes to my wife, Wendy, who continues with positive patience to support and shape my professional and personal lives in ways that I could not begin to imagine without her: *plus que hier, moins que demain.*

PART ONE

Why and How Leadership Matters to Investors

Sometimes, new ideas completely disrupt traditional thinking. More often, new ideas emerge from synthesizing previous thinking, then evolving to fresh insights. This present work builds on outstanding work in the study of market value and leadership. Each of these separate disciplines has vast reservoirs of ideas, studies, and tools. In Chapter 1, I want to acknowledge this previous work but then show that by connecting market valuation and leadership, each discipline moves forward. Market valuation with leadership insights becomes more complete and accurate. Leadership through the lens of market valuation brings more discipline to the study of what effective leaders know and do. In Chapter 1, I also report on how the most prominent investor of our day (Warren Buffett) continually reflects on management as part of his decision making, and I report our research from investors about the importance of leadership in their decision making. Leadership matters to investors, but they can be comprehensive in their assessment.

In Chapter 2, I show that now is the time to propose a *leadership capital index* that offers investors a much more comprehensive way of assessing leadership as part of their firm valuation process. While investors recognize the importance of leadership, they often lack rigor in assessing it. The proposed leadership capital index identifies two domains of leadership (individual behavior and organization capabilities) and five elements in each domain that investors can access to move beyond superficial and casual leadership observations. This leadership capital index will also inform those interested in understanding governance, risk, social responsibility, and other organization processes. The domains and elements of this leadership capital index synthesize and extend multiple strands of excellent work into the next step of realizing the market value of leadership.

CHAPTER 1

When Leadership Matters to Investors, It Matters More

"How much is that doggie in the window?" asked Patti Page in a 1952 novelty song. Investment analysts and others have asked essentially that same question since companies have been publicly traded: "How much is this company?" (With a strong subtext of "How much is this company worth to me?")

A dog's value comes from its recognizable traits (breed, age, health, temperament), but also from its personal value to the owner (relationship, history, companionship). Similarly, a company's value comes from its tangible assets like products, receivables, technology, and facilities—the assets that show up on the balance sheet and are as easy to see as the surface of a dog. Company value also includes intangibles such as strategy, brand, intellectual property, and reputation, which are more subjective and less likely to show up on the balance sheet but have been recognized as being just as essential to determining a company's desirability as an investment.

Underlying the intangibles, each organization has a level of leadership capital—an established pattern of both individual leader characteristics and organization and human capital processes—that can and should be included in determining firm value. Investors often have a strong feeling about the importance of a particular leadership trait, but their opinions tend to be superficial because they don't recognize or have ways to fully evaluate all the elements that underlie effective leadership. They make judgments with only one or two pieces of a leadership puzzle, not the entire puzzle.

The leadership capital index in this book will help investors and others improve their approach to firm valuation. When leadership capital becomes a factor in investor judgments, it will naturally receive more emphasis in day-to-day corporate life, to the benefit of many.

Audiences for Leadership Capital Insights

The insights from this book should prove useful for stakeholders committed to understanding leadership and value: investors, rating firms, proxy advisory firms, boards of directors, senior executives, and HR and leadership specialists.

INVESTORS

The primary audience for this book is investors looking to value the quality of a company's leadership. Interested investors include equity and debt investors, long-term and short-term investors, and relational and transactional investors. Investors who value and assess the quality of leadership will make more informed decisions about the future value of a company. Most thoughtful investors recognize that leadership matters, but they are not clear on how to rigorously assess leadership.

A major private equity group held an annual conference for the CEOs of companies it had acquired, where it would share advice on what these independent CEOs should focus on in the next year. In 2009, soon after the market collapse, this conference focused for two days on leadership. The group executives had discovered that it often took five to seven years to turn around a distressed company—and that in 60% to 70% of the cases, the biggest challenge was the quality of leadership. Often the leaders who'd gotten the company into a position where it was purchased by the private equity group were not able to make the bold changes needed to turn around and transform their company to prepare it to be repositioned in the marketplace. The group leaders felt that if they could prepare acquired-firm leaders to be more capable, they could turn the companies faster. The group decided to hire a talent czar, someone who could assess leadership talent in companies likely to be acquired and then develop leadership in acquired companies to be better able to transform their company and prepare it to be resold. These private equity investors recognized that leadership mattered—and that they were not in a position to perform thoughtful or thorough assessments of leadership. So they retained a specialist to do so.

As this private equity group recognized, valuing leadership comes from and extends the work on intangibles. Two firms in the same industry with the same financial results may have dramatically different market valuation. This differentiated market valuation is often attributed to intangibles, which show up in business by boosting—or undercutting—investors' confidence in a firm's performance. Leaders architect intangible value. When investors accurately assess leadership, they are indirectly but accurately assessing the future intangible value of a firm. Thus investing in leadership capital may result in a leadership premium or discount, depending on the outcome of the assessment.

RATING FIRMS

Standard & Poor's (S&P), Moody's, and Fitch issue about 95% of the creditworthiness ratings based on their view of a company's ability to pay back its debt. Credit rating has been a staple of measuring firm financial performance since the early 1900s, and a firm's credit rating influences both its cost of capital and its ability to access capital. While critics sometimes challenge the details of risk assessments, these ratings continue to have great influence.

Just as credit ratings reflect the likelihood of continued financial effectiveness, a leadership capital rating could be created to reflect the likelihood of leaders' making the right choices to drive firm performance. If universally accepted, a leadership capital index would have implications for numerous stakeholders. For example, in 2011, S&P very publicly downgraded U.S. securities from AAA to AA because of the budget deficit and rising debt burden. This downgrade influenced borrowing costs for the U.S. government, companies, and consumers. However, the underlying reason for this downgrade was not just the debt burden itself but the inability of leaders in Congress to collaborate well enough to face and solve the deficit problem. A leadership capital index that assesses the quality of leadership would complement a report on the symptom (debt burden and ability to repay), but go beyond it to assess the underlying problem (quality of leadership).

Likewise, in the 2008–2010 recession, many Western banks were "bailed out" by government support. The problem with this metaphor is that bailing water out of a boat only relieves the symptom. If the hole in the boat is not fixed, water will keep leaking in. The "hole in the boat" may be defined as poor leadership. Unless and until leaders behave differently, similar results will occur. Even after financial bailouts, leaders who spent excessively at executive retreats or on executive compensation continued to place their firms at risk. To avoid future bank risks, regulators formed bank stress tests that focused on risky assets, balance sheet quality, and the amount of capital on hold. Unfortunately, none of the bank stress tests in the United States (by the Federal Reserve Board), Asia (by the International Monetary Fund), or Europe (by the European Banking Authority) include an assessment of leadership. Perhaps this is why financial stress tests are somewhat discounted and do not receive the confidence they were intended to inspire.[1]

PROXY ADVISORY FIRMS

Proxy advisory firms, including Institutional Shareholder Services (ISS), Egan-Jones Proxy Services, Glass, Lewis & Co., and Institutional Investor Advisory Services (IIAS) in India offer shareholders advice on how to vote their shares. These firms issue reports on how a firm's governance practices relate to firm performance based on public financial data. For example, ISS reports four pillars of governance practices: board structure, executive compensation, shareholder rights, and audit-related activities. While all are related to leadership, none of these four pillars rates leadership capital directly. They report the alignment of total shareholder return over one, three, and five years with CEO pay and compare this to an industry peer group to measure pay for performance, but they do not offer further insights on leadership. Including more refined indicators of leadership would enable these proxy firms to offer more thorough recommendations.

BOARDS OF DIRECTORS

As trustees of a firm's assets and shareholder interests, boards of directors have fiduciary responsibility for its performance. To fulfill this responsibility, boards review strategic plans, financial performance, firm policies, and operating choices. A primary task of a board is to select a CEO who can make astute decisions to lead the firm. In addition, the board determines compensation for the CEO and other key executives. Through these actions, boards recognize the importance of leadership capital for firm success—especially in settings like government agencies, not-for-profits, privately held companies, or countries where market value may not be a dominant logic.

A leadership capital index could help the board manage succession against a set of criteria that informs and bolsters confidence from investors and others. Executive succession is not just about the person who moves into a key position—it is about how the individual qualities instill confidence in others, particularly investors. In addition, boards sometimes invite in financial advisers to help determine how to increase total shareholder return. Often these advisers examine industry trends (to see if the firm has a strategic advantage) and financial performance (to see if it meets financial expectations). Less often do boards invite in leadership advisers to examine intangible value to see if their firm trades at a premium or discount to the industry. Boards might use the leadership risk assessments proposed in this book to review their firm's quality of leadership, which in turn would give investors more confidence.

THE C-SUITE

C-suite executives and senior leaders want to demonstrate excellent leadership skills. Often leadership excellence is defined by the personal characteristics of the leader (authenticity, charisma, communicator, and so forth). But unless these personal leadership characteristics build confidence with investors, they are not contributing all they could to sustainable value. CEOs are also committed to building future human capital—their number one priority, according to a recent survey.[2] Having a leadership capital index would help senior leaders know what to expect of themselves and other leaders so that investors would be more likely to invest in the company because of what leaders know and do.

HR AND LEADERSHIP SPECIALISTS

HR and leadership development specialists who design and deliver leadership improvement efforts could also be well served by a leadership capital index. Recently, my colleagues and I were in a consortium of leading companies, most of which had teams or HR professionals in attendance. One question we asked these groups to consider was, "What would you like investors to know about your quality of leadership that would increase their confidence in your future earnings and market value?"

Almost none of these senior HR professionals had considered this question, even as they worked to improve leadership in their company. Indeed, one of the consortium teams happened to be investors from one of the large global sovereign wealth funds, and these investor participants talked about what they look for in leadership when they make significant investment choices. But as they were presenting their list of desired leadership attributes, I noticed that none of the HR participants in the workshop were paying much attention.

I stopped the discussion at that point. "Do you realize what you are hearing?" I asked. "Guys from one of the largest investors in the world are sharing what they are looking for in leadership in your companies— or your rivals in the investment market. No one is taking notes. What you should be doing is rigorously writing down what they say, then sharing this with your CEO and chief investment officer so that they can communicate these messages in conference calls and investor discussions. And you should be rethinking leadership investments to ensure that you have or develop these traits."

With some embarrassment, these HR professionals starting taking notes! And some later told me they could now engage in more business-oriented discussions with their business leaders.

Using a leadership capital index that focuses on how investors view leadership can help sharpen leadership improvement efforts. If nothing else, it will bring the concept to the table and allow it to be considered.

Logic of Leadership Capital Index

A leadership *index* differs from a leadership *standard*. Standards define what is expected; indices rate how well an activity performs. For example, consider the *Economist*'s Big Mac index, which measures the cost of a Big Mac in various countries in terms of its difference from the average Big Mac price in the United States. The index doesn't try to tell you how much a Big Mac should cost—rather, it is a crude but useful assessment of the cost of living around the world.

An index guides investors to make more informed choices. When a rating agency like Moody's or S&P downgrades a company, it is not saying the company did or did not meet financial reporting requirements. It is offering an opinion about the firm's ability to repay loans in the future. Likewise, a leadership capital index would inform investors and others about the readiness of the firm's leadership to meet business challenges.

I am not proposing some sort of leadership equivalent of generally accepted accounting principles (GAAP)—this is not an attempt to codify all leaders in the same way. Developing such a leadership standard would be nearly impossible because leadership is inevitably both personally subjective and contingent on the unique needs of the company. Defining a leadership standard would be like defining the perfect basketball player. Both Michael Jordan and Bill Russell were enormously successful, but they had very different skills, played in different eras, and had different roles on their teams. Likewise, it is silly to ask who was or is the best leader—Bill Gates, Richard Branson, Indra Nooyi, Ratan Tata, Carlos Ghosn, Warren Buffett, Zhang Ruixin, Steve Jobs, Larry Page, Oprah Winfrey, or Jack Welch? In fact, each was very successful using unique skills appropriate for the circumstance. In the near future, no uniform standard of leadership is at all likely, but an investor who recognized the quality of leadership in each of these leaders and thus invested in them early on would have been well served. A leadership capital index can give investors and other interested parties a set of guidelines to assess leadership.

When my colleagues and I share our aspiration to develop a leadership capital index, almost everyone agrees that this would be a marvelous resource. Some call it the holy grail for both firm valuation and leadership development, but most are skeptical that it can happen. However, the timing is now right, because both firm valuation and leadership improvement efforts have evolved to a stage where such an index can actually be created.

My current proposal for a leadership capital index follows the logic of the *minimum viable product* for innovation in high-tech.[3] According to this logic, web applications and lean start-ups continually experiment to learn how to improve. The product is not wholly defined in advance; it develops as it is tested, used, and improved. In valuation and leadership, a number of initial efforts have been made to establish an investor view of leadership. By combining these separate but thoughtful initiatives, we can now create a more rigorous and holistic leadership capital index. Leadership capital index 1.0 is to build the case for the index and establish a framework and baseline for the index, which is the purpose of this book.

Valuation Evolution:
From Financial to Intangible to Leadership

The definition of an organization's value has changed over the years, and I believe it is still changing. Once it was mainly the physical stuff that could be removed and sold; then it expanded to include the intangible assets that made it a going concern. Leadership looks like the next step.

It's worth tracing the development in more detail. Historically, the accounting profession received a major challenge after the stock market crash of 1929. Many argued that stock prices misrepresented firm value because the public information available to investors did not accurately reflect the extent of a firm's assets. In 1934 the Securities and Exchange Commission was formed to create standards and regulate how public companies report their financial performance to investors. The large accounting and audit firms at the time (called the "Big Eight": Price Waterhouse & Co.; Haskins & Sells; Ernst & Ernst; Peat, Marwick, Mitchell & Co.; Arthur Young & Co.; Lybrand, Ross Bros. & Montgomery; Touche, Niven & Co.; and Arthur Andersen & Co.) established a set of standards and principles through the Financial Accounting Standards Board (FASB). The rules define uniform standards in an effort to communicate accurate information to investors so they can better measure firm value (generally accepted accounting principles—GAAP—in the United States, or international accounting standards—IAS—outside the United States).

The intent of these accounting standards is to offer investors comparable, public, and transparent data that will enable them to make accurate valuation decisions. The ingredients, or financial data, from the accounting standards can then be combined to define a firm's value. An entire industry has been created and evolved to define approaches to the increasingly complex task of measuring a firm's value.[4] Income approaches to valuation focus on capitalization of current net income or cash flows and discounting of future cash flows. Cost approaches to valuation emphasize the cost of replacement of an asset to determine its value. Market approaches value assets because of their current value based on competitive pricing. Again, each of these broad approaches to valuation combines the ingredients from the accounting standards data to determine a value of the firm.

IMPORTANCE OF INTANGIBLES FOR VALUATION

In recent years, due to changes and uncertainty in markets, information, and globalization—and despite the constant attention reported in the preceding section—the financial data publicly reported by firms has not reflected their value accurately.[5] Earnings reported in a variety of forms (net income, operating earnings, core earnings, and more) have become ever more suspect.[6] As a result, efforts at firm valuation have turned from financial results toward a deeper understanding of the intangibles that influence these results.

Baruch Lev, an accounting professor who is a thought leader of the intangibles movement, has shown the importance of intangibles as indicated through *market to book value*—suggesting that for every $6 of market value, only $1 occurs on the balance sheet.[7] This means that the balance-sheet number—which is what traditional accounting measures—represents only 10% to 15% of the value of these companies.[8] This data shows that the value of many firms comes as much from perceived value as from hard assets. Firms like Coca-Cola and Gilead have high market value from brands and patents. Technology-based firms like Amazon and Google have high market value with relatively little in the way of cash flow, earnings, hard assets, or patents. And even traditional companies like 3M and IBM are increasing market value by focusing on brands, leveraging the Web, and restructuring. Professor Lev further recommends that managers learn to win investors over by finding ways to more clearly communicate intangibles with them.[9]

Harvard professor Robert Eccles and his colleagues at Pricewaterhouse Coopers (PwC) call for a "value reporting revolution" by changing financial reports to include more intangible information. They find that only 19% of investors and 27% of analysts "found financial reports very useful in communicating the true value of companies." They argue for changing the performance measurement game to better allocate capital and assess the true value of firms. In identifying better measures of firm performance, they focus on "key performance measures—both financial and non-financial, and how they relate to each other, that they are measured and reported on, and that they create real value."[10] They propose a model they call "Value Reporting Disclosure" with enhanced business reporting where firms report information on business landscape (industry, technology trends, the political and regulatory environment, social, and environmental trends), strategy (mission, vision, goals, objectives, portfolio, governance), resources and processes (physical, social, organizational capital and key processes), as well as GAAP-based performance.[11] By reporting these more intangible factors, they give investors better information for determining a firm's true value. Analysts perceive the benefits of better disclosure when they help long-term investors have greater confidence in future earnings.

Accenture's finance and performance management group also reports that intangibles are an increasingly important part of a firm's value.[12] Its classification of assets still includes monetary and financial assets, but also intangible assets of relationships, organization process, and human resources, and it proposes measures to track these intangible assets.

Ernst & Young's Center for Business Innovation has also attempted to find out how investors use non-financial information in valuing firms.[13] It concludes that non-financial criteria constitute, on average, 35% of an investor's decision. Sell-side analysts use non-financial data, and the more non-financial measures analysts use, the more accurate their earnings forecasts prove to be.

Because of studies like those just cited,[14] in recent years intangibles have received more attention as a source of value.[15] Generally intangibles have been listed as intellectual capital or knowledge as evidenced in patents, trademarks, customer information, software codes, databases, business or strategy models, home-grown processes, and employee expertise.[16] Investors have worked to classify lists of intangibles that include intellectual capital but are more expansive. Baruch Lev categorizes intangibles into R&D efforts (such as trademarks, patents, copyrights), brand value (such as image, reputation), structural assets (such as business systems, processes, and executive compensation, human resources), and monopoly position.[17]

In our earlier work, Norm Smallwood and I synthesized the work on intangible value into four domains called the *architecture for intangibles* (see Figure 1.1). We found that intangibles could be clustered into four broad categories—making and keeping promises, having a clear strat-

Figure 1.1. Architecture for Intangibles

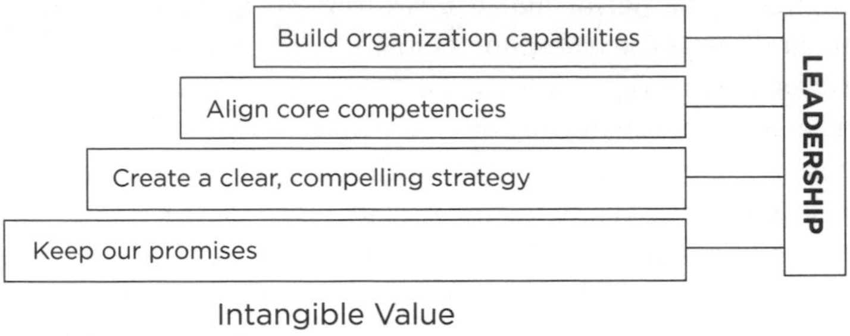

Intangible Value

Source: Dave Ulrich and Norm Smallwood, *Why the Bottom Line Isn't: How to Build Value Through People and Organization* (New York: Wiley, 2003).

egy for growth, managing core competencies, and building organization capabilities—all of which depend heavily on the behavior of leaders.[18] To elaborate:

- *Keeping promises* comes when leaders build relationships of trust by doing what they say to employees inside and customers and investors outside, often measured as risk.

- *Creating a clear, compelling strategy* comes when leaders have strategic capital to define the future and work with customers to deliver value through brand identity and reputation.

- *Aligning core competencies* increases when leaders invest in R&D and the intellectual capital that comes from patents, copyrights, trademarks, and the like. Creating core competencies also comes when leaders access functional expertise in technology, manufacturing, and operations.

- *Building organization capabilities* comes when leaders have the ability to create a corporate culture consistent with its mission, which could mean a culture of innovation, collaboration, efficiency, risk management, or information asymmetry.

In this current work, I emphasize the point that leadership is a key underlying factor in an organization's ability to keep promises, set clear and compelling strategies, align core competencies, and build organization capabilities. When leaders at all levels of a firm guide these four domains, they create sustainable intangible value. Therefore investors who assess leadership will be more able to fully value a firm's intangible assets and overall market value.

As I've said, this is the right time for this book. Nearly every interested investor has access to publicly reported data, so essentially, each investor knows what every other investor knows about a firm's financial position and, increasingly, about its intangibles. Investors need to dig deeper to find new insights, and this is not easy to do. For example, the New York State Attorney General recently required BlackRock (the world's largest asset management company) to stop surveying Wall Street analysts to find out their collective views on a company's financial performance and likelihood of being taken over.[19] The argument was that financial data should be public, transparent, standardized, and shared so all investors have the same access to it. When financial data is widely shared, however, investors have to find other information, such as leadership, to inform and differentiate their investment choices.

LEADERSHIP: THE NEXT STEP

When New York University researchers administered a questionnaire to a hundred venture capitalists, exploring the criteria for fundability of new ventures, they found that the most important factor is the quality of the entrepreneur or management.[20] Similarly, when Boris Groysberg and his colleagues at Harvard surveyed analysts to find out what they valued in making their investment decisions, they found that quality of management was among the top factors.[21] However, they also found that analysts lack consistency in rating this dimension.

Research among joint ventures and venture capital firms has also found that information that has not traditionally been incorporated in the due diligence process, such as the quality of management and culture, can be critical to the future success or failure of the acquisition. The success of many companies can be traced to a few prominent managers who provided the required leadership. Without auditing intangible assets such as management, it is not possible to conduct a correct valuation of a potential investment.[22]

These studies show that work on valuation is moving toward an assessment of the quality of leadership—the leadership capital—that underlies and creates intangibles and leads to financial results. Figure 1.2 traces the s-curves in the history of valuation, showing how intangibles move beyond financial information and proceed almost inevitably to the inclusion of leadership.

These days investors are creating metrics for intangibles (like brand recognition, strategic clarity, innovation index). Investors who do a better job of assessing leadership will create information asymmetry for themselves and make better investment decisions. However, man-

Figure 1.2. Evolution of Firm Valuation

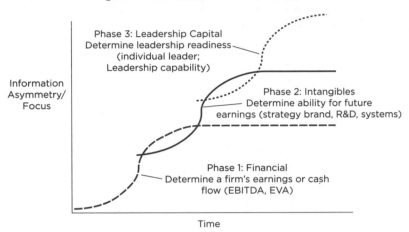

agement practices and leadership vary enormously across firms and countries.[23] Financial valuation sets the accepted baseline that levels the playing field, but leadership valuation differentiates how investors can determine long-term firm value.

Leadership Evolution: From Personal Style to Organization Impact to Investor Value

"What makes effective leadership?" That is the dominant question when it comes to the study of leadership, and its exploration has filled count-less books, many thicker than this one. Nonetheless, it is useful to review the overall development of the idea. The answer to what makes effective leadership has evolved over time, each new stage building at least in part on its predecessors.[24] Some firms have celebrity leaders or an individual leader who gains notoriety. While these charismatic individuals become important to a firm's success, more often it is the depth of leadership talent throughout the organization that builds long-term success. When my colleagues and I talk of *leadership*, we mean the collective group of leaders throughout a company, not just the CEO or another individual senior executive. Thus, while individual leaders matter, increasingly the entire cadre of leaders, the *leadership*, matters more.[25]

Assessments of effective leadership have moved from a stance of believing that leaders excelled by first leading themselves, then being the sort of people others follow. Later assessments examined how leaders looked to others by leading in the organization, and the more modern view has them looking outside by creating value for external stakeholders.

WHO YOU ARE

Early leadership theorists tried to identify a core set of demographic traits that characterized an effective leader: height, gender, heritage, speaking style. They also tried to identify personality traits and backgrounds that made leaders more effective.

All to no avail.

It turned out that successful leaders could come from a variety of backgrounds and display a variety of physical and personality traits. The only trait that seemed to consistently differentiate better leaders was being somewhat (not too much) smarter than their followers.[26] Traits eventually combined to form a leadership style, often a trade-off between people and task. Generally, leaders exhibited a preferred style, but the best leaders could be both soft and hard, caring about people and managing tasks.

Defining effective leadership by looking inside a leader is still an active field, with some useful observations to offer. The focus is now on the core competencies—the knowledge, skills, and values—of successful leaders.[27] My colleagues and I have synthesized this competency-based work into what we call the *leadership code,* suggesting that leaders master five competency domains to be effective (strategy, execution, talent, human capital, and personal proficiency).[28] I discuss these domains in more detail in Chapter 2 and throughout the book.

While many leadership theorists and advisers emphasize one competence area (for example, authenticity, emotional intelligence, strategy, execution, talent management, or human capital development), my colleagues and I have found that effective leaders master all five competency domains to be effective. Personal approaches to leadership primarily focus on helping leaders become more attuned to who they are and who they can become to be effective.

WHAT YOU DO FOR OTHERS IN YOUR FIRM

Leadership theorists eventually recognized that looking inside the leader was not enough to define effective leadership. Leaders also had to deliver results according to the task at hand. Part of this effort was to determine which leadership approaches worked in which situations. In this view, effective leadership depends on the requirements of the situation. Situations may vary by maturity of team members, complexity of the tasks at hand, time horizon for doing the work, or uncertainty in predicting outcomes of the work. Any individual leadership style will work better in some situations than in others, and truly effective leaders can tailor their style to the needs of the moment.[29]

The other part of looking to others means that leadership effectiveness is less about a personality trait and more about how leaders help make organizations more effective. Leaders can drive organization effectiveness through employees, organization cultures, or financial performance.[30]

The impact of leadership on employee performance has been studied extensively.[31] Leaders' actions shape employee sentiment at work, a phenomenon that may show up as satisfaction, commitment, and engagement—or the reverse. Thousands of studies have shown that leaders drive employee response to work.[32] Leaders also create strategies that differentiate their firms for long-term success.[33] In addition, leaders shape an organization's culture or identity. *Culture* has often been represented as the values, norms, beliefs, and unwritten rules of an organization, and it tends to take on the personality of the leader.[34] Leaders create culture through managing people, performance, information, and work practices.[35] Culture in turn drives financial performance.[36]

Leaders also drive financial performance within a firm. Many studies have shown that leadership has about a 12% to 14% impact on firm performance.[37] In one study, extraordinary leaders doubled company profits.[38] Strategic leaders help make choices that help position their organizations for success.[39] For example, in her research, Alison Mackey wanted to find out how much CEOs affected firm performance. She looked at fifty-one firms over ten years with ninety-two CEOs. She was able to show that the CEO affected a 29.2% variance in firm performance, which was somewhat higher than corporate impact (7.9%) and five times the industry impact. In particular, in smaller and faster-growing firms, CEOs have more impact.[40]

Both the personal and organizational approaches to leadership effectiveness find that leaders' ability to match skills to situation enables them to deliver success within the organization.

WHAT YOU DO FOR EXTERNAL STAKEHOLDERS

More recently, in a further step in leadership thinking, the definition of leadership effectiveness has gone beyond the person or the organization outcomes and addresses what happens outside the walls of the organization.[41] Effective leadership in these terms is not merely what leaders know and do but also how their actions shape the experiences of customers. If customers choose to buy Lexus because of the quality and design, then leaders inside Lexus should make sure their actions drive quality and design to new and yet more attractive heights.

Leadership matters not just because employees are more productive, organization cultures are more conducive to strong results, or financial outcomes are better, but because external stakeholders receive value from what leaders do within the firm. For customers, leaders are effective when they link internal organization processes in ways that deliver on customer expectations. Culture becomes less focused on the norms and values inside the company and more on making the external identity of the firm (its brand) consistent with the internal culture.[42] For leaders, this means not only creating an internal culture consistent with an external identity but also building a leadership brand. Such a brand exists when leaders ensure that the behaviors of employees reflect the expectations of customers outside the company.[43] Work has begun to define leadership effectiveness through the expectations of customers.

Linking leadership actions to investor expectations would be part of measuring what this book calls *leadership capital*.[44] Chapter 2 reviews how people have approached the connection of firm valuation and leadership, but to highlight the importance of this connection here, I offer some snippets from Warren Buffett's annual letters to his shareholders. (Warren Buffett is among the most influential and successful investors of all time, and his annual letters highlight his philosophy and approach. Similar sentiments appear every year, but these are some of the most vivid from the past decade.)

Selected Quotes from Warren Buffett Annual Shareholder Letters

- **2007**

    "A terrific CEO is a huge asset for any enterprise. . . . At Berkshire . . . their abilities have created billions of dollars of value that would never have materialized if typical CEOs had been running their businesses."

    "But if a business requires a superstar to produce great results, the business itself cannot be deemed great."

- **2010**

    "An outside investor stands by helplessly as management reinvests his share of the company's earnings. If a CEO can be expected to do this job well, the reinvestment prospects add to the company's current value; if the CEO's talents or motives are suspect, today's value must be discounted. The difference in outcome can be huge."

- **2011**

    "The primary job of a Board of Directors is to see that the right people are running the business and to be sure that the next generation of leaders is identified and ready to take over tomorrow."

- **2014**

  "For good reason, I regularly extol the accomplishments of our
  operating managers. They are truly All-Stars, who run their businesses as if they were the only asset owned by their families. I believe
  the mindset of our managers to be as shareholder-oriented as can
  be found in the universe of large publicly-owned companies."

As definitions of leadership effectiveness move from inside the person
to inside the organization to beyond the organization's borders, it is
important to recognize the emerging connection between leadership
and investors. Leaders are more effective if and when they meet investor
expectations. Investors are effective if and when they understand and
realize the market value of leadership.

Investors Value Leadership: Research Results

To answer the question of how investors value firms, my colleagues and I
interviewed twenty-five investors, had twelve focus groups with forty-five
seasoned investors, and reviewed research on the topic (summarized in
subsequent chapters).[45] From this preliminary work, we defined three
broad domains of information most important to investors: industry
favorableness, company performance, and quality of leadership.

- *Industry favorableness* refers to the characteristics of the industry,
  such as its growth potential, barriers to entry, competitiveness,
  social trends, customer opportunity, regulatory opportunities, and
  so forth. Industries may be more or less favorable (for example,
  twenty-first-century demographics favor care of the elderly and are
  less favorable to traditional printing).

- *Firm performance* refers to consistency of financial results as
  indicated by a variety of metrics. Firm performance also refers
  to the intangibles related to strategy, technological advantage,
  and organization capabilities such as speed to market, degree of
  innovation, customer service, and so forth.

- *Quality of leadership* refers to the confidence investors have in the
  leadership capability of the company. Investors are more likely to
  invest in companies with leaders who have a strong track record
  and have more ability to set and execute strategy, to manage
  current and future talent, and to develop future leaders.

Next, we determined the relative weight of each of these three
domains for investor decisions by asking them to divide 100 points across
the three domains and their confidence in assessing each domain. We
received 430 responses from portfolio managers, institutional investors,

Table 1.1. Relative Importance to Investors and Investor Confidence to Assess

Domain	Importance (Standard Deviation)	Confidence to Assess (Standard Deviation)
Firm performance	38.5% (15)	4.47 (0.58)
Industry favorableness	33.1 (16)	4.33 (0.66)
Quality of leadership	28.4 (14)	3.75 (0.96)

Note: To rank importance, survey participants were asked to divide 100 points based on how important each domain is for investment decisions. To evaluate confidence in ability to assess, they were asked to rate themselves on a scale of 1 to 5 (highest) for each domain.

mutual and hedge fund managers, private equity investors, and venture capitalists. These investors each had, on average, more than fifteen years of professional investment experience.

Table 1.1 reports the relative importance of each domain, along with investors' confidence in their ability to assess each area.

Investors consider company performance the most important domain for making investment decisions (38.5 percent) and also have the highest confidence in their ability to assess it (4.47). The standard deviation of 0.58 is the lowest of any domain. This result is not surprising; performance is the most objectively measurable of the domains, and it is comparable across firms and consistent with most investor training.

Industry favorableness also matters (33.1 percent) to investors, and they have high and consistent confidence in their ability to track it (average score of 4.33 with a standard deviation of 0.66).

Although ranked lowest among the three domains, quality of leadership clearly matters to investors (28.4%) in a consistent way (standard deviation of 14). But investors have much less confidence in their ability to assess quality of leadership (3.75) and they sense a much higher risk (standard deviation of 0.96) associated with their evaluations. Their comments reflect these findings:

- "Quality of leadership is important but . . . if high quality of leadership is required for an investment to succeed, then there may be other investments out there . . . with fewer hurdles to success. . . . At the end of the day, it always comes down to people."
- "We care a *lot* about this. This is what drives a firm to capture opportunity. Nearly all the pathologies of leadership are easy to find if you know where to look. Too many CEOs are such great toadies (some seem to be sociopaths) that you can't depend on just meeting

them—they will charm you, and they'll figure out what you want to hear. So, you have to get out into their operations and walk around. If you know what real leadership is and what real integrity is, you will find it or the absence of it out on the front lines where products and services are being forged and delivered to customers."

- "Leadership is one of the most important considerations that our fund makes when considering a potential investment. If we are not comfortable with the management team, we will usually not invest until changes are made."

- "This is a leading nonfinancial indicator, yet all information systems and research services are designed to provide financial metrics. Quality of leadership, culture, quality of relationships with core stakeholders are critical to understand but are also difficult to gauge. We've spent four years trying to get better in this area."

Clearly, leadership matters to investors, but they often find it difficult to define, measure, or track. Investors vary more in how much confidence they have in their ability to assess leadership. This tells me that investors would indeed be glad to have a usable leadership capital index.

In our interviews with investors, my colleagues and I almost always heard a resounding "of course" to whether leadership mattered in valuing a firm, but then we heard skepticism about how to accurately assess leadership. Most investors have spent their careers studying spreadsheets and computer programs, not dealing with the more subjective and behavioral assessments of individuals. But there is a body of knowledge on assessing leadership that can be accessed by investors to help them make more informed decisions.

Conclusion

In a nutshell, here is the logic. Firm valuation has evolved from increasingly granular financial metrics to intangibles to leadership (Figure 1.2). Quality of leadership has evolved from personal leader traits to how the leader delivers to others within the organization to creating value outside the organization. Leadership can inform the valuation effort to create information advantages for investors and to deliver sustainable intangibles within the firm. The intersection of firm valuation and quality of leadership benefits creates leadership capital.

It is time for a leadership capital index that would benefit investors and others interested in both valuation and leadership.

CHAPTER 2

Creating a Leadership Capital Index

The valuation of any firm improves with an accurate view of its leadership—but such a thing is hard to come by. However, it is now possible to construct an index to assess a company's leadership capital, or quality of leadership. This chapter, building on studies both of how investors currently assess leadership and of leadership itself, recommends a leadership capital index that investors and others can use to realize the market value of leadership.

How Do Investors Assess Quality of Leadership?

Some investors focus on financial returns or intangibles (or both) and ignore leadership altogether. Wise long-term investors recognize that leadership matters. A colleague reports working in an energy company whose price/earnings ratio was consistently below industry average. When queried, investors said that the firm was too reliant on one key leader, and they weren't confident in his health, his willingness to stay at the company if he received a better offer elsewhere, and his ability to build successor candidates. In this case, investors looked at the senior leader's personal commitment as a surrogate for leadership and discounted the company's value.[1]

Another firm regularly invites investors to management briefings that go beyond the publicly available financial data or summaries reported by advisory services. This firm also invited significant investors to visit one of its operations and spend a few hours talking to employees in unscripted conversations. These investors got a real sense of the extent to which stated goals were shared throughout the organization, which gave them more confidence in the firm's future than they would have derived from formal presentations by senior management.

An investor from a large investment fund shared its three-step decision-making process:

- Pick an industry, based on likely growth of a particular market because of demographics, social conditions, or technology.
- Identify three to five leading firms in the industry, based on the financial returns indicated on income statements and balance sheets.
- Learn about the leaders of these industry front-runners.

While the firm had sophisticated analytics to test projections of industry growth and to evaluate financial performance, its assessment of leaders was much more subjective. After some discussion, the investor finally said that the favorite ploy was to invite the CEOs of the selected firms into an uncomfortable situation—take them out sailing, for instance, one at a time—to see how they responded. The analysts could then watch how the CEO handled the uncertainty. It was hard not to laugh: *sailing* as a test of whether or not a leader can make choices that help a company continue to outperform its industry? It seems odd that this successful fund follows a very sophisticated industry and financial analysis by a "finger in the wind" assessment of leadership—but even that has proved useful.

These cases, and countless others, show that many executives recognize the importance of helping investors become more acquainted with and aware of company leaders, and many investors are equally eager for the insight. But they also highlight how frequently the exposure of investors to company leadership is haphazard and episodic, often focused on a few leaders with limited information. The decision-making process resembles shopping for a house on the Internet and making a choice based on pictures, property tax, age, and so forth—without visiting the house to get a feel for the neighborhood, the condition of the house, and the flow of living in it. While few would buy a house that way, investors often buy into a firm without a thorough or thoughtful leadership assessment. When investors define leadership only as the CEO, when they examine only one aspect of effective leadership, or when they assess haphazard views of leadership, they are working in the right direction but with limited information.

Requirements of a Leadership Capital Index

A leadership capital index enables investors and others to systematically and predictably determine the quality of leadership within a firm. As noted in Chapter 1, an index is not a standard for leadership; rather, it is a rigorous and replicable set of guidelines that investors can use to improve their assessment of leadership capital as they make investment decisions.

Today, the components of a leadership capital index often come with confusing concepts and murky language. Would the index refer to

- Ability to make decisions?
- Authenticity?
- Charisma?
- Style?
- Ability to meet expectations?
- Emotional intelligence?
- Ability to build effective teams?
- Experience in the industry?
- Personal reputation?
- Personal attributes?
- Use of power and influence?
- The leadership pipeline?
- Talent in general?
- Competence or commitment of people throughout the organization?
- Organizational culture?
- Pay philosophies of the organization?
- Investment in management or human resource practices like staffing and training?
- Organizational structure and governance processes?

To condense the broad domain of leadership, organization, talent, culture, and human capital into an index that investors can actually use to determine leadership readiness, these complex and at times confusing concepts need to be simplified into a practical framework.

At first glance, it may sound impossible, but this sort of thing has been done before. Consider the credit ratings index, for example. Standard & Poor's (S&P) created an analytic framework in structured finance securitization that includes five domains:

- Credit quality of the securitized assets
- Legal and regulatory risks
- Payment structure and cash flow mechanics
- Operational and administrative risks
- Counterparty risk

Once these five domains are identified, S&P then creates a credit ratings index with specific factors and metrics within each domain.

Likewise, a leadership capital index will need to synthesize the various and muddled concepts related to leadership capital and provide a discipline to rigorously track them. As discussed in Chapter 1, I am beginning the development with a minimum viable process (1.0) that

Figure 2.1. Synthesis of Leadership Capital Domains

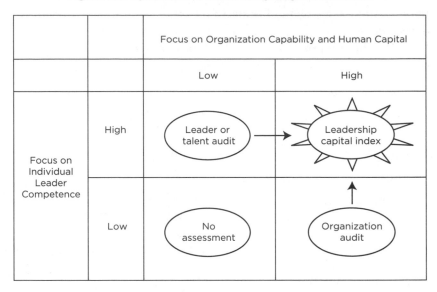

focuses attention on leadership issues and synthesizes previous work, yet has room for improvement over time. Based on this intent, a leadership capital index has two dimensions, or domains: individual and organizational (see Figure 2.1). *Individual* refers to the personal qualities (competencies, traits, characteristics) of the top leader and key leaders in the organization. *Organizational* refers to the systems (often called human capital) these leaders create to manage leadership throughout the organization, as well as to the application of organization systems to specific business conditions. Using these two domains, existing leadership and human capital work can be synthesized into an index that investors can use to inform their leadership valuation decisions.

Domain 1: Individual Leader Competencies

The individual dimension of leadership capital focuses on the personal qualities of leaders within an organization. Leadership obviously begins with the CEO, but it extends to the top team and even the middle managers who assume leadership responsibilities throughout an organization.[2] Too often investors look only at the CEO to represent overall quality of leadership, relying on either personal interactions or reports like the extensive analysis of CEO pay (correlation of CEO pay to performance, CEO base versus at-risk pay, ratio of CEO pay to next highest officer, and CEO pay versus peers) published by the ISS. This information is easy to compile because it is publicly reported in SEC reports, but it does not really cover the entire topic.

Investors can look at the individual attributes of leaders throughout the organization, and they can assess personal leadership competencies through observations, interviews, surveys, general reputations, and demonstrated behaviors. Their real challenge is not *how* to assess but *what* to assess. What makes a leader effective? Sometimes, isolated experiences with leaders may not give investors a full view of the leaders' overall abilities, and a given leader may have strengths in some areas and not in others.

APPROACHES TO INDIVIDUAL LEADER COMPETENCY

Many studies of leadership acknowledge the general importance of people and overall leadership as the driver of organizational value.[3] Some have focused on the individual skills of the top and senior leaders as inputs to key investment decisions. A sampling of approaches to examining personal leadership competencies is captured in Table 2.1.

Based on studies like those in Table 2.1, thoughtful investors interested in long-term investing (portfolio managers, institutional investors, mutual and hedge fund managers, private equity investors, and venture capitalists) are all likely to recognize that leaders matter in valuing the firm. But when asked about leadership, analysts emphasize more how to get information than what information to seek. Without a guiding framework for what makes an effective leader, each analyst draws on personal assumptions. This is no surprise. Most analysts who drive investment decisions are proficient in accessing and assessing financial information. They have little experience, training, or guidance on how to define and assess the quality of individual leaders. While their instinct for assessing leadership may be accurate, they need tools to bring rigor and repeatability to their results. Returning to the real estate metaphor, they may like living in a house, but they do not fully appreciate the architectural design and infrastructure that makes it livable.

For analysts to move from novice to informed observers of individual leadership, research suggests three themes that will enable better assessment:

Look at leadership rather than leaders: It is convenient to assume that the CEO or another top leader represents the collective leadership within an organization. More realistically, valuing leadership requires looking at not only current but also future leaders. Future leaders will be the ones to respond to forthcoming opportunities.

Table 2.1. Examples of Studies on Individual Leader Competencies and Financial Results

Study Author or Sponsor	Key Question	Key Findings
Geoffrey Smart[a] and colleagues[b]	What are the leadership skills investors should look for in private equity (PE) deals?	Leadership has major impact on success of financial deals.[c] Harder skills (persistence, efficiency) were more important than softer skills (teamwork, listening). The more time PE firms spend on leadership issues, the more successful the deals.
Deloitte[d]	What do investors look for in individual leaders?	By interviewing 450 analysts, they concluded that leadership gives a firm a 15% premium or 20% market discount. Leaders need skills in strategic clarity, strategy execution, culture for innovation, and moral courage. Analysts did not have strong consistency in what to look for in leadership.
McKinsey Consulting[e]	How do investors include management evaluation in due diligence and after acquisition?	Management assessment is a key to operational value creation when PE firms make acquisitions. PE firms generally act too late to assess management. Management may be assessed through many tools (structured interviews, personality profiling, observations, surveys).
Spencer Stuart and National Venture Capital Association[f]	How do venture capitalists consider management team?	Based on 200 surveys, venture capitalists said that management was the most important consideration to fund a venture (37% of the decision). Leaders should have ethics and integrity, manage talent, set visions, and know industry. About 65% of venture capitalists assess management before acquisition.
Bruce Avolio and Susan Dunn[g]	What is the impact of leadership on stock price?	Based on surveys of 350 analysts, top management team affected stock price 16% (3 years of organic growth).
Corporate Branding LLC	How much would analysts want to pay attention to leadership?	Analysts pay attention to trade record, reputation, and presence. 80% of analysts said they would like more accurate information on leadership to make decisions.

Study Author or Sponsor	Key Question	Key Findings
Ted Prince[h]	How does personal style of leader affect financial results?	Different personality styles (e.g., Myers-Briggs, Hartman Personality Profile, and the Herrmann Brain Dominance Instrument) enable leaders to be more effective. Conscientiousness affects financial performance more than openness to experience.[i]

a. Geoffrey Smart, "Management Assessment Methods in Venture Capital," *Frontiers of Entrepreneurship Research* (1998): 600–612; Geoffrey Smart, "Management Assessment Methods in Venture Capital: Toward a Theory of Human Capital Valuation" (doctoral dissertation, Claremont Graduate University, 1998); Geoffrey Smart, "Management Assessment Methods in Venture Capital: An Empirical Analysis of Human Capital Valuation," *Journal of Private Equity* 2, no. 3 (1999): 29–45; Geoffrey Smart, "What Makes a Successful Venture Capitalist," report, ghSmart and The Ignite Group, 1999, http://www.ghsmart.com/media/press/what_makes_a_vc.pdf; see more at http://www.iijournals.com/doi/abs/10.3905/jpe.2013.16.3.057#sthash.d7h4X2j6.dpuf.

b. Roshan Tantirimudalgie, "Human Capital Valuation by Private Equity Firms" (master's thesis, Swiss Federal Institute of Technology, Zurich, 2012).

c. Geoff Smart and Randy Street, *Who* (New York: Ballantine Books, 2008); Brad Smart and Geoff Smart, *Topgrading: How to Hire, Coach, and Keep A Players* (Dallas: Pritchett, 2005).

d. Simon Holland and Margot Thom, *The Leadership Premium: How Companies Win the Confidence of Investors* (Deloitte, 2012).

e. McKinsey, *Perspectives on Merger Integration* (2010), http://www.mckinsey.com/Client_Service/Organization/Latest_thinking/-/media/McKinsey/dotcom/client_service/Organization/PDFs/775084%20Merger%20Management%20Article%20Compendium.ashx

f. Spencer Stuart and National Venture Capital Association, *Emerging Best Practices for Building the Next Generation of Venture-Backed Leadership* (2010), www.spencerstuart.com.

g. Susan Dunn and Bruce Avolio, "Monetizing Leadership Quality," *People and Strategy* 36, no. 1 (2013): 12.

h. E. Ted Prince, "The Fiscal Behavior of CEOs," *Sloan Management Review* 46, no. 3 (2005): 22–26; E. Ted Prince, *The Three Financial Styles of Very Successful Leaders: Strategic Approaches to Identifying the Growth Drivers of Every Company* (New York: McGraw-Hill, 2005).

i. Mark A. Ciavarella, Ann K. Buchholtz, Christine M. Riordan, Robert D. Gatewood, and Garnett S. Stokes, "The Big Five and Venture Survival: Is There a Linkage?" *Journal of Business Venturing* 19, no. 4 (2013): 465–483.

Likewise, while it is convenient to look at a single great leader, it is more important to look at collective leadership and next-generation leaders.

Remember that the situation can define the type of leadership needed: One of the most common succession planning mistakes is to expect future leaders to require the skills that past leaders needed. As situations change, leadership must change. While my colleagues and I do believe in the existence of a core set of skills that all leaders must master, those skills are not enough. Leaders must also have the bandwidth to adapt to changing situations. Investors need to look at the business requirements before defining desired leadership competencies.

Don't try to specify a single strength or trait as the one that matters: No single strength or trait characterizes every effective leader. Leadership requires multiple skills. It's easy to become enamored with a particular strength, be it communication, planning, or execution. However, wise investors see individual leadership assessment as multidimensional and examine many characteristics of leaders.

Out of the myriad studies that have attempted to define the qualities of an effective leader, my colleagues and I have defined the metaphor *leadership brand,* which consists of the core leadership code and a number of differentiators.

The leadership code addresses the question of whether leaders in a firm can accomplish their basic duties. Then the leadership differentiator addresses the question of the extent to which leaders engage in behaviors that are uniquely suited to the firm, given its external brand. (My colleagues and I have found that about 60% to 70% of effective leadership consists of doing the basics well; 30% to 40% involves making sure that a leader's actions inside a company reflect customer expectations outside the company.)

The leadership capital index addresses five factors from the individual leader domain—four from the basic code and a fifth from the differentiator:

1. Personal proficiency: To what extent does the leader demonstrate the personal qualities required for effectiveness? (See Chapter 3.)

2. Strategic proficiency: To what extent does the leader articulate a point of view about the future and strategic positioning? (See Chapter 4.)

3. Execution proficiency: To what extent does the leader make things happen and deliver as promised? (See Chapter 5.)

Figure 2.2. Individual Leader Elements

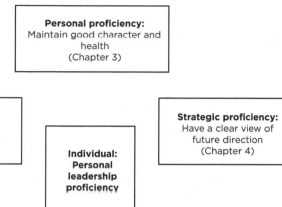

Personal proficiency:
Maintain good character and health
(Chapter 3)

Leadership brand proficiency:
Act as outside stakeholders expect
(Chapter 7)

Individual: Personal leadership proficiency

Strategic proficiency:
Have a clear view of future direction
(Chapter 4)

People proficiency:
Build and maintain an effective workforce
(Chapter 6)

Execution proficiency:
Get things done
(Chapter 5)

4. People proficiency: To what extent does the leader build the competence, commitment, and contribution of their people today and tomorrow?[4] (See Chapter 6.)

5. Leadership brand proficiency: to what extent do leaders inside a company act in ways customers expect? (See Chapter 7.)

These five elements offer a framework for what investors should pay attention to in assessing individuals as leaders. Investors who assess leaders at the top and throughout an organization will know if they have the personal qualities that define effective leadership. These five elements, outlined in Figure 2.2, provide a graphic roadmap for Part 2, Chapters 3 through 7.

Finally, with these five elements in mind, investors can do a more rigorous job of assessing leadership capital. Investors who are serious about leadership can perform a leadership audit through interviews, observations, and surveys of potential investments. Of course, it is difficult to extract this sort of information. Investors can do such leadership audits themselves or use an advisory service that specializes in that type of work. While such audits may take more time than relying on financial advisory services, they offer investors a clear advantage. The information asymmetries they create can mitigate investment risks and increase the probability of success.

Domain 2: Organizational Capability and Human Capital

Besides the quality of the individuals currently holding leadership positions, a firm's leadership capital includes its investment in cultural development and HR practices designed to build future leaders. Studies have shown a relationship between a firm's investment in human capital practices and its financial performance. A number of consulting firms have worked to create assessments focusing on basic HR practice areas (staffing, training, compensation, succession planning), generally emphasizing the strengths of their consulting firm.[5] At times these assessments show the relationship between a single practice and financial performance, but more recently efforts have been made to create human capital indices showing how integrated HR investments affect business performance.[6]

APPROACHES TO HUMAN CAPITAL ANALYSIS

It is useful to take a look at some of the human capital analyses currently available, as aspects of what they cover may be included in a leadership capital index. Examples of these studies are summarized in Table 2.2.

What investors want are insights into the organizations in which they invest that help them improve their chances of success. Of course, they could choose to ignore leadership altogether in their firm valuation assessments, or they could continue to assess leadership through a haphazard gut-feeling approach. Conversely, they could choose to use this leadership capital index. The idea and ideal of standards may emerge when investors want to have more replicable and consistent information. At this stage, investors would be happy to have unique information that gives them preferential insights into their choices without taking so long to assemble that the opportunity disappears in the process.

ORGANIZATION CAPABILITY AND HUMAN CAPITAL SUMMARY

As with the personal competencies of effective individual leaders, the domain of human capital is very broad, ranging from specific HR practices like executive compensation and training investments to broader issues like culture. This domain generates a fourth theme for consideration:

Pay more attention to capability than to management structure: An organization's capability represents what the organization is good at doing and is known for. The capability concept synthesizes work on

Table 2.2. Examples of Studies on Organization Capabilities/ Human Capital and Financial Results

Study Author or Sponsor	Key Question	Key Findings
Human Resource Accounting[a]	How can issues around people be put onto balance sheet?	Costs of labor (compensation, hiring, training costs) can be calculated.
		Opportunities for labor may be calculated.
		Some human resource practices create more value or utility than others.[b]
Mark Huselid and colleagues[c]	How do human resource (HR) practices affect firm performance?	Based on data from over 900 firms, HR practices create high-performing work systems (HPWS).
		Firms with HPWS had better financial performance.
		Based on data from 590 U.S. firms, firms with progressive HR practices had 30% better financial performance.[d]
Laurie Bassi[e]	How do people practices show up in market valuation?	Firms that invest in human capital practices have a 4.7% per year greater increase in market returns than firms that do not make human capital investments.
		Firms can prepare a human capital report to highlight what they should focus on to be more effective.[f]
Mark van Clieaf[g]	How can the gap between tangible and intangible value be measured and managed?	There is a large gap between tangible value ($3.37 trillion) and intangible value ($12.64 trillion).
		Intangible value can be managed through strategic governance (boards, levels of work, pay for performance).
Mark Ubelhart Aon Hewitt	How much do pivotal employees (top 20%) impact business results?	A 10% increase in retaining pivotal employees predicts a 0.7% increase in cash flow for standard companies and a 1.6% increase for financial firms.
UBS[h]	How does human capital affect shareholder value?	Companies on the best companies to work for list outperformed S&P 6.8% to 1.0%.[i]
		Based on interviews with equity analysts and thought leaders, human capital is a key factor in a company's success.
		Assessing leadership as background for human capital is problematic today.

(continued)

Table 2.2. (continued)

Study Author or Sponsor	Key Question	Key Findings
HR professional organizations: Chartered Institute of Personnel and Development (CIPD)[j]	How do human capital issues relate to firm success?	Investors are increasingly interested in human capital measures as a lead indicator of firm performance. Most investor information today comes more from personal contact and casual observation than from rigorous assessments. Human capital assessments are often lumped together with social responsibility, risk management, and governance judgments. Human capital practices around employee skills, leadership depth, and performance are often looked at in a piecemeal way and are seen as drivers of organization outcomes like customer service or innovation.
HR professional organizations: Society for Human Resource Management (SHRM)[k]	What are reporting standards for human capital issues that could be accepted by ANSI?	The result was a cost-per-hire standard that measures the efficiency of the recruiting process and a standard on the core elements of performance management.[l]
Consulting firms		Different consulting firms have linked parts of human capital to financial performance: · Great Places to Work emphasizes communication, employee goals, and employee perception of the work environment.[m] · Hay Group focuses on governance and performance management (appraisal and rewards).[n] · Watson Wyatt highlights HR practices in staffing, communication, diversity, and wellness.[o] · Mercer highlights teams and values.[p] · PWC examines the effectiveness of the HR function and employee productivity.[q] · The ROI Institute has produced some exceptional methods to test the impact of organization practices.[r]

Notes for this table can be found at the end of the notes for this chapter on page 255.

core competencies, organization systems, culture, archetypes, and resources. Investors can audit both the type of capability and the extent to which the capability is shared both inside and outside the organization.

For human capital to be accurately assessed in valuation discussions, the complex domain of processes, practices, metrics, tools, and ideas must be simplified. These micro views of leadership offer wonderful insights into components of effective leadership, but these micro views have not been combined into a macro-level look at how leadership shapes firm value. Based on human capital studies like the ones listed in this section, I have identified five additional organizational factors for a leadership capital index—one overall, and four devoted to aspects of the human capital practices that drive culture:

1. Cultural capability: To what extent has the leadership created a customer-focused culture that is shared throughout the organization? (See Chapter 8.)

2. Talent management: To what extent has the leadership invested in practices that manage the flow of talent into, through, and out of the organization? (See Chapter 9.)

3. Performance accountability: To what extent has the leadership created performance management practices (such as compensation) that reinforce the right behaviors? (See Chapter 10.)

4. Information processes: To what extent has the leadership managed information flow to gain information asymmetries? (See Chapter 11.)

5. Work processes: To what extent has the leadership created organization and work practices that deal with the increasing pace of change in today's business setting? (See Chapter 12.)

Investors can assess human capital by determining if leaders wisely invest in these organization practices. These five elements, outlined in Figure 2.3, provide a graphic roadmap for Part 3 (Chapters 8 through 12).

Table 2.3 provides an overview of the leadership capital index assessment that flows from these two domains and ten elements. Using the high-level diagnostic questions in this table, investors (and others) can assess both individual and organization domains to produce an assessment of the quality of leadership. As suggested, the individual and organization domains serve a purpose similar to the principles that Standard & Poor's uses to guide its assessments. This framework is comprehensive in that it synthesizes the range of leadership capital issues

Figure 2.3. Organization Elements

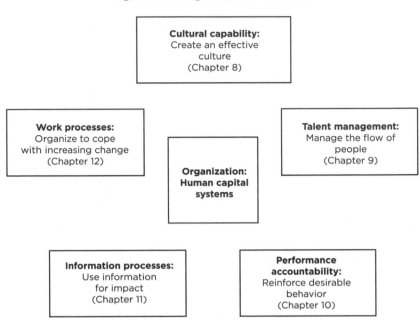

investors should attend to. It is also simple in that the two domains and ten elements both have face validity and are easily understood, and it is disciplined in that investors can examine and codify specific actions and metrics for each of the elements. In Part 2 (Chapters 3 through 7), I offer specific details and indicators for each of the individual factors, and in Part 3 (Chapters 8 through 12), I offer specific indicators for the five organization factors. However, the index in Table 2.3 enables investors to move from simplistic and intuitive opinions of leadership to more comprehensive and rigorous leadership audits.

As noted, these ten factors offer a much more robust and comprehensive way for investors to realize the market value of leadership. How would it work?

Consider the cases I described briefly early in this chapter. Leaders in the energy company could communicate to investors not only how the CEO performs on these ten elements but how potential successors are likely to perform. The company that invites investors into the organization would have visitors who were focused on the ten elements rather than asking haphazard questions and making scattered observations about leadership. The investment firm would not just look at one primary leader in an uncomfortable position; its representative could still

Table 2.3. High-Level Overview of Leadership Capital Index

Individual Domain:

(Part 2, Chapters 3 through 7)

How well does the individual leader or collection of leaders be, know, and do what matters to investors?

Factor	To what extent do leaders . . .	Rating: Low (1) to high (10)	Example metrics or indicators
1 Personal proficiency (Chapter 3)	have the required personal characteristics to be effective?		· Has successful industry experience · Has good character and health · Demonstrates learning agility · Exhibits personal presence (charisma) · Has emotional intelligence (self-awareness)
2 Strategist (Chapter 4)	have a point of view about the future and strategic positioning?		· Articulates a unique point of view about future Industry trends · Understands external business drivers (regulatory, technology, demographic shifts) · Enunciates a differentiated strategy for the firm
3 Executor (Chapter 5)	make things happen or deliver as promised?		· Gets things done · Has a proven track record of success · Is willing to hold people accountable · Meets commitments
4 People manager (Chapter 6)	build competence, commitment, and contribution of employees at all levels?		· Maintains stability of senior team · Works smoothly with people with different skills · Engages with issue of staff retention · Delivers better staff productivity than rest of industry · Has a workforce plan · Empowers others
5 Leadership brand (Chapter 7)	fit actions or behaviors with stakeholder and other expectations?		· Links firm brand to leadership behaviors (leadership competencies match firm brand) · Aligns leadership behaviors to strategy and other contingency factors · Lives the values and uses the values to guide decision making
Individual Domain Total:			Note: This score offers an overview of the individual leader or leadership team.

(continued)

Table 2.3. (continued)

Organization Domain:

(Part 3, Chapters 6 through 12)

What do leaders do to build organization capital and human capital that matters to investors?

Factor	To what extent do leaders . . .	Rating: Low (1) to high (10)	Example metrics or indicators
6 Cultural capability (Chapter 8)	create an effective culture that matches customer expectations?		· Pays attention (time, talk, and money) to defining and delivering desired culture · Connects firm brand to culture and values · Turns culture and values statement into specific, measurable behaviors · Has a clear and shared view of desired culture
7 Talent/People (Chapter 9)	manage the flow of talent into, through, and out of the organization?		· Promotes and monitors the firm's hiring success rate · Retains key talent · Invests in training and development · Maintains a succession planning process
8 Performance accountability (Chapter 10)	create a performance management process that reinforces right behaviors?		· Sets clear standards · Aligns executive compensation with performance · Spends time on performance conversations
9 Information (Chapter 11)	manage information flow to gain information asymmetries?		· Uses social media · Collects and disseminates external information · Turns big data into insights that inform decisions
10 Work (Chapter 12)	create organization and work practices that align with strategy?		· Matches organization structure to strategy · Understands and reengineers key processes for success · Has clear decision-making and governance guidelines
	Organization Domain Total:		Note: This score offers an overview of the organization or human capital systems.

take the CEO sailing but would also have a framework for rating a whole cohort of leaders against criteria of leadership readiness. Isolated, haphazard, and unstructured information can be turned into an index that helps investors have more confidence in intangibles and consequently future earnings.

Ultimately, this leadership capital index offers investors a more integrated approach to assessing leadership. For example, the Society for Human Resource Management (SHRM) and American National Standards Institute (ANSI) cost-per-hire metric may be used as a part of factor 7 (people) and become a useful component of an overall leadership capital index, even though in isolation it can't provide a comprehensive assessment of leadership quality.[7]

In addition to synthesizing this complex literature into the leadership capital index, my colleagues and I sought the insights of thought leaders in leadership and management analytics. They were asked to select the elements they felt would be the most useful information for investors. (See Table 2.4.)

It is interesting that eight of the ten received multiple votes, which implies the importance of all ten elements. It is also interesting how few votes were on the personal proficiency of the leaders, particularly since most of the investor interviews summarized in this chapter report that investors rely heavily on their personal judgment of the leaders. It is also interesting that the personal skills of strategy and talent and the organization capability of culture building are perceived as the most important factors of leadership capital.

Using the Leadership Capital Index to Improve Key Organization Processes

With the leadership capital index in use, many organization processes of interest to key stakeholders could be refined. In particular, leadership capital has a significant impact on the core processes of risk, governance, social responsibility, and reputation.

RISK

Risk has become a central topic and concept in decision making and organization action. At its basic level, risk deals with uncertainty and the ability to predict the future in the present, or the probability something will happen. It also deals with variability, or the range of potential difference in an activity. When control processes reduce uncertainty and variability, risk is reduced and organizations more predictably accomplish their goals.[8]

Table 2.4. Thought Leader Assessments of Leadership Capital Index Factors

	Individual				
	To what extent do individual leaders demonstrate the following competencies?				
	1	2	3	4	5
				Talent	Brand/
Thought leader	Personal	Strategist	Executor	manager*	different
Laurie Bassi					
Dick Beatty		X		X	
Warren Bell		X			
John Boudreau		X	X	X	
Wayne Cascio		X			X
David Creelman		X	X		
Bob Eichinger (varies by purpose)		X	X	X	
Marshall Goldsmith		X	X	X	
Lynda Gratton		X			X
Nick Holley		X	X	X	X
Mark Huselid	X			X	
David McLeod				X	X
Bob Morrison		X		X	
Ian Ziskin				X	
TOTAL	1	10	5	9	4

*Also known as Human capital developer

Organization

To what extent do leaders invest in future leaders by creating human capital processes in these areas?

6 Cultural capability	7 Talent/ People	8 Performance	9 Information	10 Work
X	X			X
X				X
		X		X
				X
	X			
		X		
X	X			X
X				
	X			
		X		
X	X			
X				
X		X		
7	5	4	0	5

Figure 2.4. Types of Risk (Based on the COSO Framework)

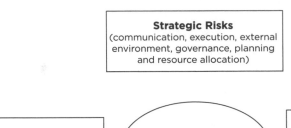

Enterprise risk assessment occurs when a governing committee identifies the major risks, then filters these risks against the criteria of uncertainty and variability to prioritize the ones that call for management attention. To guide this risk assessment, frameworks have been provided that help predict categories of risk.[9] For example, the Committee of Sponsoring Organizations of the Treadway Commission (COSO), a joint initiative of five private-sector organizations dedicated to providing thought leadership about risk management, has developed a framework with four major risk domains: strategic, operational, financial, and compliance (see Figure 2.4).[10]

Leadership capital is missing from this framework, as it is from others. Nonetheless, in a business environment of increasing complexity and change, quality of leadership becomes even more important as a source of success.[11] Leaders make decisions that affect strategic, operational, financial, and compliance risks, and leaders build control mechanisms to manage these risks. Leadership risk is the extent to which leadership throughout an organization possesses individual competences and builds organization capabilities to predictably deliver expected results. An enterprise risk assessment should consider the predictability and variability of leaders throughout an organization both to demonstrate personal competencies and to build organization capabilities. The leadership capital index provides a governing committee charged with assessing risk with a tool to determine leadership risk.

GOVERNANCE

Corporate governance deals with the control mechanisms that an organization adopts to keep self-interested managers from engaging in activities detrimental to key stakeholders.[12] These control mechanisms include managing decisions about firm strategy, enterprise risk assessment, executive compensation, acquisition of other companies, and shareholder interests. Governance clarifies who has authority to make what decisions, from the board of directors through the CEO to the senior leadership team and the frontline leaders. The topic is of wide interest, with auditors, customers, suppliers, regulators, media, analysts, creditors, and investors all monitoring governance. Investors pay a premium for a firm's assets when they perceive good governance.[13]

In the discussion of governance, leadership capital should play an increasingly central role. David Larkin, a thought leader in the study of governance, suggests that governance currently misses out on organization design, culture, the personality of the CEO, and the quality of the board. The individual competencies of the CEO and other leaders should become a predictor of good governance. Leaders who demonstrate the five factors of individual competence (personal proficiency, strategy, execution, talent, and brand) will be better able to provide governance to their organization. When leaders demonstrate the ability to develop organization capital by attending to the factors of culture, people, performance, information, and work, they will also improve governance processes. The leadership capital index allows those interested in governance to recognize and improve both individual leadership and organization capital as a source of improved governance.

SOCIAL RESPONSIBILITY

Organizations exist to serve multiple stakeholders, both internal and external. In recent years, the concept of a triple bottom line—people, profits, and planet—has become a catch phrase referring to the stakeholders an organization serves.[14] Under the "planet" umbrella, a host of corporate social responsibility initiatives can be articulated.

In 1973, the United States established the Financial Accounting Standards Board (FASB) to establish and monitor GAAP on behalf of the SEC. In 2011, the Sustainability Accounting Standards Board (SASB) was established to create and disseminate sustainability accounting standards and to disclose material sustainability issues to investors and other stakeholders.[15] SASB attempts to turn corporate social responsibility aspirations into measurable initiatives so as to inform investors about sustainability commitments. The framework for tracking sustainability highlights six areas for attention: employee, supply chain, environmental, governance, community, and customer. My colleagues and I propose that, similar to enterprise risk assessment and governance, understanding the quality of leadership would complement this framework. Leaders make decisions that influence sustainability issues in each of the six areas. Defining and determining leadership capital at the personal and organizational levels will increase the sustainability of the work on sustainability itself.

The implications are significant. Organizations that manage sustainability will become better citizens, attract better employees, and improve their customer service. Responsible investors have begun to create funds that highlight these socially responsible organizations.[16] Sustainable capitalism occurs when organizations not only profit from but also serve their people and the planet.[17] Including a leadership capital index as a component of this sustainability movement ensures that the aspirations for social responsibility are embedded in the fabric of the enterprise.

REPUTATION

Organizations seek a positive reputation in their marketplace.[18] This is more than a matter of personal satisfaction; a positive reputation leads to an estimated 5% increase in sales growth and better attraction and retention of valued employees. Investors also monitor a firm's reputation to determine how well it manages its public image. Firm reputations have directly influenced shareholder value—for example, after the Gulf oil spill of 2010, British Petroleum's stock dropped from about $62 to $27, a market loss of more than $80 billion. As of May 2015, five years later, the stock was around $42 a share, still not fully recovered.

While most discussions of reputation deal with the firm's identity, image, social media presence, branding, and public affairs, the reputations of leaders at a firm have a dramatic impact on the company's overall reputation. In private enterprises, the values and demeanor of the CEO (or the founders) generally reflect the organization's values. In public enterprises, the actions of a CEO can have a major influence on the company's reputation. Enron's downfall was not just bad business judgment; it was the reputational nosedive as leaders lost the confidence of their employees, customers, and communities. But it is not just the CEO who makes the difference. Leaders throughout an organization become identified with the organization, and their behavior shapes the organization's reputation.

The leadership capital index should give stakeholders increased confidence in the reputation of leadership. In the personal proficiency factor, investors pay attention to values and integrity, but beyond this baseline for positive reputation, the leadership index also examines the breadth of leaders' personal skills and the ability of leaders to replicate those skills through the organization factors. Leadership capital becomes a critical aspect of building a strong reputation.

Summary: Creating a Leadership Capital Index

It is axiomatic to say that leadership matters—to employees, to customers, to investors. But a large gap persists between recognizing that leadership matters and rigorously assessing leadership capital. Many thoughtful and helpful studies have been done to inform investors about how to evaluate leadership—but their advice tends to be both fragmented and narrow.

To gauge leadership capital, my colleagues and I offer an index based on two domains and ten factors. One domain assesses the competencies of pivotal leaders throughout an organization, while the other assesses the ability of leaders to institutionalize leadership. Combined, these factors constitute a leadership capital index that will help investors make more informed decisions about intangible value and long-term financial success. In addition, a leadership capital index will help those charged with managing risk, governance, social responsibility, and reputation keep up with their responsibilities. Part 2 discusses the five elements of the individual domain and Part 3 reports specific indicators of the five elements of the organization domain.

PART TWO

The Individual Elements of the Leadership Capital Index

Investors who recognize the importance of leadership pay attention to the personal characteristics of the leaders in the firms where they invest. Often they attend to one or two personal characteristics of a leader, such as the leader's personal charisma, ability to set a vision and inspire people, ability to act with integrity, and so forth. As discussed in Chapter 2, we can identify five elements of personal proficiency that characterize effective leadership. For each of these elements, I will present key dimensions and indicators that may be tracked to assess leadership.

The assessments from this part will help investors and others determine if leaders demonstrate the personal qualities of effective leadership. The logic will follow Figure 2.2 (repeated on the next page for ease of reference), with a chapter on each element.

Individual Leader Elements

Personal proficiency:
Maintain good character and
health
(Chapter 3)

**Leadership brand
proficiency:**
Act as outside
stakeholders expect
(Chapter 7)

**Individual:
Personal
leadership
proficiency**

Strategic proficiency:
Have a clear view of
future direction
(Chapter 4)

People proficiency:
Build and maintain an
effective workforce
(Chapter 6)

Execution proficiency:
Get things done
(Chapter 5)

Personal Proficiency

Investors Want Leaders with Good Character and Health

A leader is often the face of a company. In founder-led companies, the leader's personal style shapes the culture of the company—think of Alibaba, Amazon, Facebook, Marriott, Starbucks, Tata, Virgin—but it can happen later in a company's life, too—consider Ken Chenault at American Express, Alan Lafley at Procter & Gamble, and Indra Nooyi at PepsiCo. When my colleagues and I interviewed investors about what they want from leadership, the responses often focused on the personal style of the most senior leader. The top leader's charisma and personal charm do tend to boost investor confidence, but attending only to magnetism may be more superficial than substantive.

The depth of a leader's personal proficiency goes beyond dress, physical appearance, and elocution. Investors can determine a leader's style more thoroughly by assessing six elements of a leader's personal proficiency—and these assessments should be done not just with the top leader but with the whole top leadership of the organization.

The essential logic for personal proficiency comes from exceptional work that Jim Loehr and Tony Schwartz have called *creating the corporate athlete*.[1] Loehr and Schwartz found that when leaders care for themselves in four areas—physical, emotional, mental, and spiritual (or moral)—their energy, well-being, and performance will surpass that of less-attentive leaders. Using these ideas, many companies have invested in upgrading the personal proficiency of their leaders with excellent results. For example, Procter & Gamble has put more than 10,000 people through corporate athlete training. Survey results show that those who participate in the training increase energy outside of work (+36% versus those who don't attend), fitness and healthy lifestyle (+17%), personal

Figure 3.1. Framework for Assessing Leaders' Personal Proficiency

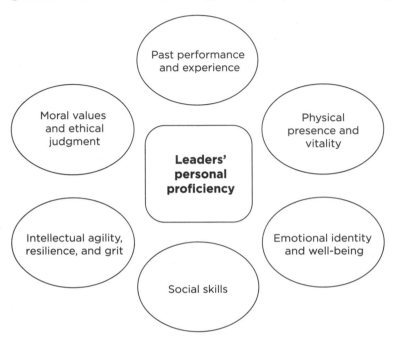

well-being (+13%), and work/life effectiveness (+13%). These personal improvements show up in increased productivity at work as well.[2]

Slightly adapting this framework gives investors a disciplined approach to evaluating the personal proficiency of the leaders in a potential investment. Figure 3.1 identifies six elements for assessing leaders in this area. While it may be that no one leader excels at all six elements, the leadership team would collectively demonstrate them to depict substance behind style.

Past Performance and Experience

Nearly every investor my colleagues and I interviewed said that the best predictor of a future leadership success is past performance and experience (a point of view not currently shared by most of the academic thought leaders whose criteria are summarized in Table 2.4; this interesting divergence may reflect a gap between practical application and theory). For the most part, investors insist on a favorable track record; they hesitate to deal with a leader without one, and it is true that past performance remains the best predictor of future performance. Leaders create patterns of how they work and those patterns show up in present and future settings. One investor tracks leaders by the organization results they produce; he looks at free cash flow versus industry average over a decade. While such a cash surplus is a useful macro indicator of performance, many factors may go into it. More specifically, investors can confirm how well leaders meet commitments they make by looking at five to ten years of performance reviews to see what goals were set and the pattern of how well these commitments were achieved. In addition to looking at historical managerial commitments, investors can observe performance predictability by tracking recent financial and personal goals.

Although past performance is invaluable as a leadership predictor, it is not foolproof. Leaders may bring the skills from their last assignment to their current assignment but find that they do not match the requirements of that assignment. In addition, effective leaders who want to improve do not want to do what they have always done; they want to learn and grow.

In our work, my colleagues and I have found that leaders who worked in a company with a strong identity and distinct culture often tried to transplant their experience when they moved to another company. Many General Electric alumni tried to transfer the GE culture to their new company—and failed.[3] In their second post-GE career move, these leaders were better able to recognize that their personal style had to match the requirements of their new organization, and they had more success.

A major investor in Brazil said that he looked for leaders who managed to deliver consistent and sustainable results in different settings. Investors can look at leaders' careers and seek a couple of indicators of past experience and success. First, in early career experiences, did the leaders demonstrate successful habits? For example, in school, did they take challenging classes or easy ones? In early career assignments, did they innovate or follow? When they describe previous career experiences, do they talk about positions, activities, or results?

Second, the investor looks for multifaceted career mosaics demonstrating that leaders learned to succeed in different settings. Career evolution can be evaluated by the stretch assignments, where leaders gain diverse experiences by moving quickly but also have time to fully appreciate and learn from each assignment. In addition, investors should assess whether the experiences enable the leaders to lead the company at hand. For example, one investor told us that he was skeptical of leaders who had worked for twenty years in a traditional hierarchical organization but then had a good idea and wanted to lead a start-up with little infrastructure and a small staff.

Possible indicators:

- *What is the free cash flow of the leader's business compared to that of competitors over time?*
- *How successful has the leader been at meeting performance commitments in previous assignments?*
- *What has the leader's career path been? Similar or different assignments? Safe assignments or risky ones?*

Physical Presence and Vitality

First impressions often linger. The way a leader looks, dresses, talks, and moves can create a strong sense of style, implying that such a person is bound to be effective on the job. But as orchestra selections have demonstrated by blind auditions, physical first impressions do not always predict long-term success.

Investors cannot do blind auditions of leaders, but they need to go beyond first impressions and develop insights on the leader's sustainable presence. Of course, leadership presence is not one-size-fits-all—leaders come in all shapes, sizes, and styles. But investors have more confidence in leaders with presence, which often starts with positive body language (eye contact, posture, elocution) but goes beyond appearance to sheer vitality.

Physical presence begins with basic health and well-being. Investors should note a leader's nutrition, exercise, and sleep habits. These habits can be tracked through a medical exam for key person insurance or for other corporate health requirements. Top CEOs and government officials (such as presidents, prime ministers, cabinet leaders) often are required to undergo annual physicals and monitoring of their health. Leaders who take care of themselves physically often have more energy for the demands of their job, reduce the risk of physical ailments that may disrupt their work, and communicate confidence by their physical vigor.

In addition, physical presence is communicated through capacity for work. Leaders who succeed have a high capacity for sustained work output, with high work endurance and stamina. People with a traditional nine-to-five work ethic may be unlikely to have the vitality for the demands of top leadership. Working hard does not mean a lack of work/life balance, but investors should have confidence in the work capacity of their prospect's leaders. This means that investors can look at work hours, checking for the personal energy and vigor required of successful leaders. Investors and others can sense leadership vitality by observing the leader's pace and work habits.

In one case, through inquiry, an investor discovered that in the targeted organization, a business crisis arose in which a team was required to work over a weekend to meet the needs of a major client. For this investor, vitality means being willing to pay the personal price when required to accomplish a task. Another simple signal of vitality has to do with global phone calls: when are these made? When convenient only to the leader or to others? One investor went so far as to say, "Is there evidence of leaders' being willing to work long weekends? You want folks who are not balanced all the time; who are a bit work crazy and obsessed with the work at hand."

Judgment of leadership presence may be personal and subjective, but it needs to be a perspective shared by many people who work with the leader to indicate that the leader has the physical well-being and vitality to meet work requirements.

Possible indicators:

- *Does the leader maintain adequate diet, exercise, and sleep habits?*
- *Does the leader have a current physical exam?*
- *Does the leader have the vitality to meet the demands of the job?*

Emotional Identity and Well-Being

Emotional intelligence has become an indicator of leadership effectiveness in many situations.[4] Emotional intelligence deals with self-awareness, identity, and stability. Investors who ascertain the emotional intelligence and well-being of key leaders will have more confidence in future performance.

Self-awareness means that leaders are able to monitor their own behavior and maintain a healthy ego. An understanding of personal work preferences helps leaders take on the right work.[5] In the following pairs, which seems more congenial?

- Strategic or tactical issues
- Ideas or things
- Large groups or small groups
- Creative or operational activities
- Nontechnical or technical questions
- Experimental or routine work

- Programs or projects
- Collaborative or individual efforts
- Interpersonal or solo work
- High-risk or low-risk situations
- Self-directed or supervised work

As leaders consciously make these personal choices, investors can also become aware of leader preferences to ensure that leaders are in the right job with the right skills.

Self-awareness also addresses the trade-off between self-interest and humility. Sometimes, egocentricity can get in the way—a leader who uses "I" messages too often and does not let others speak up can miss out on vital information. One investor described meeting with a leadership team and asking questions about future strategy. On every question, the most senior leader in the room gave a long and detailed answer. No one else spoke up. Even when the questions addressed areas in the purview of others in the room, the senior leader dominated the conversation. The investor left less confident in the leadership team as a whole and concerned that the senior leader was not aware of how his ego cast a shadow on his firm's performance.

Ego strength can also get in the way. Leaders who treat less prominent people with little respect may be allowing their positions to define their egos. It can be useful to watch the leader's interactions with wait staff, parking attendants, and others outside the office, and to find an occasion to talk to the leader's administrative assistants to get a sense of the leader's expressions of ego and style.

Investors can observe leaders' sense of humility when they have low self-focus, are open to feedback, listen intently, ask probing questions, and acknowledge weaknesses. Self-awareness also means that the leader is willing to turn to others who have complementary skills.

Emotional well-being shows up as a positive leadership trait when leaders have an identity that builds confidence in others. Another investor we spoke with likes to discover whether leaders have a clear sense of who they are and who they want to become by asking about their personal aspirations.

In one company, a senior officer was known as a "frat house member" because he wanted to be treated like one of the guys. Key investors who learned of this became concerned with the messages this identity communicated, feeling that it signaled a lack of the discipline required of senior leaders.

Finally, emotional well-being shows up in how a leader manages stress and high demand. Just as people tend to swear in their native tongue, they return to their inherent leadership style under stress. Some investors intentionally push leaders to see how they respond to conflict, differences of opinion, and high expectations. Emotionally grounded leaders tend to respond to stress by showing greater calmness, curiosity, and compassion.

Discerning emotional well-being is more art than science; more intuition than empirical data. Investors' ability to ascertain emotional well-being increases when they explicitly focus on self-awareness, identity, and stress management.

Possible indicators:

- *Does the leader have a personal identity that matches personal strengths and needs of the business?*
- *How does the leader handle emotional demands and stress?*
- *Does the leader manage ego, balancing confidence and humility? Does the leader often talk in terms of "I" messages or "we" messages?*

Social Skills

Leadership is ultimately a team sport. Leaders evolve from doing work themselves (playing the game) to supervising work done by others (coaching a team) to ensuring that work is done in their absence by the systems they establish (being a general manager for a team). To be sure of personal proficiency, investors need to know that leaders not only take care of their personal emotional well-being but can establish social connections with others. These social connections can be tracked through how well leaders build networks, engage others, and manage diversity.

BUILD NETWORKS

Are the leaders good at creating and participating in networks? Are they good at finding resources to help them do what they need to do? An early investor in Dell said that Michael Dell was a technically bright twenty-one-year-old, but his real skill was the ability to align himself with smart people who were proven industry thought leaders. His networking ability helped him both learn what it took to succeed and access resources for that success.

Effective leaders network. Investors can find out if leaders belong to social networks by asking leaders who they spend time with and who they know. A knowledge network represents who leaders learn from and their level of connection to thought leaders in their industry. Networked leaders exhibit sociability, curiosity, and energy.[6] Investors can ask the leader in question for a network report and also ask leaders in the industry about their networks to determine if the target firm's leaders are in their network. Leadership by Rolodex means that leaders have and use contacts to access information and nurture relationships.

ENGAGE OTHERS

When leaders interact with others, do the others depart feeling better or worse about themselves? Socially proficient leaders help people feel better about themselves. They share credit (Teflon) in success and accept blame (Velcro) in failure. They ask others their opinions and build on others' ideas. They are optimistic and focus on what is right more than what is wrong. They challenge the status quo without belittling the past. They recognize mistakes but learn from them rather than obsessing over them or finding someone to blame for them. They attend to personal feelings yet focus on business results. They know and care about people's personal circumstances but are equally transparent about business requirements. They offer hope for what can be done in the future and avoid dwelling on what has been done in the past.

Two research streams can help investors assess leaders' ability to engage others. Wiseman and McKeown found that the type of leaders they called "multipliers" were more likely to develop talent, challenge direction, and consult with others on decisions.[7] Investors can observe how leaders manage talent, direction, and decision-making processes. In his work on positive psychology, Martin Seligman highlights the importance of leaders' focusing on the positive.[8] He has been able to help leaders in banks, government, and the military learn to build happiness in their subordinates by training them in principles of well-being (positive emotion, engagement, relationships, meaning, and accomplishment). Specifically, his colleagues found that successful leaders had a 5:1 positive-to-negative comment ratio in their interactions with others.[9] Investors can observe and listen for this positive-to-negative ratio as leaders talk about their colleagues and work challenges. When leaders focus on the positive aspects of their personal work and the work of others, they have been found to be as much as 37% more productive.[10]

MANAGE DIVERSITY

Leaders who are socially proficient surround themselves with others who complement their skills and style. By contrast, a leader who is surrounded by a weak or sycophantic staff is apt to be weak enough to be a poor investment—someone who needs to look good by comparison probably lacks inner strength and social confidence. Investors should observe the quality of staff around the key leaders: Do they have complementary skills and backgrounds? Are they as talented as the leader, or more so? Does the leader then listen to alternative points of view before making a decision? Socially proficient leaders surround themselves with people who may not be like them or agree with them.

One investor described what happened at a strategy meeting in a large family-held company. In the pre-meeting social time, executives were congenial and courteous—very much the typical corporate atmosphere. But when the doors closed and the strategy meeting started, the senior leaders challenged the family patriarch. They posed difficult questions and offered data that contradicted his point of view and direction, and this vigorous debate was clearly a matter of business as usual for them all. Instead of bland agreement, they said in the meeting the sorts of things often shared only in small groups after a meeting ends. The investor left the meeting much encouraged by the way dissent appeared to be acceptable and even encouraged in that company. When the leader finally concluded the active debate and said, "Thanks for the input, let me share how we will move ahead . . . ," people felt heard even if their ideas were not accepted.

Possible indicators:

- *Is the leader a network builder? That is, is the leader someone who knows and is known by thought leaders in the industry?*

- *Does the leader share or take credit for success? Accept the blame or blame others for failure?*

- *Were the people around the leader chosen to make up for the leader's weaknesses or to make the leader look good by comparison?*

- *Does the leader make others feel better about themselves after an interaction? Does the leader have a 5:1 positive-to-negative comment ratio?*

Intellectual Agility, Resilience, and Grit

In one founder-led company, investors who were interested in moving to professional management conducted interviews to help pick a new president. One of the candidates had been involved in a project that laid out some avenues of future growth. He was an advocate of the analytics and findings of this project and often spoke of it to the potential investors. When asked to discuss findings of other qualified research projects for the future of the company, this candidate continually returned exclusively to his personal project and findings. He was not able to incorporate the other studies in his view of the company. While his project might have enormous viability, the investors concluded that he did not display the cognitive flexibility desirable in a new president.

In traditional assessment centers, one of the exercises is to present a business problem that candidates should solve with data that lead them to a conclusion. Then the assessors systematically present additional data to discern how well the candidate assimilates new information into an existing cognitive framework. Moving too quickly, easily losing confidence in the original diagnosis—these could be signs that someone may prove to be a vagabond leader who lacks a consistent focus. On the other hand, moving too slowly and not adapting to new information could be a sign that someone would be pigheaded on the job, unable to adapt to new information.

As it turns out, it is less important to track the leader's IQ or even EQ than to track the leader's ability to learn, be resilient, demonstrate grit, or have a growth mindset. Almost every investor my colleagues and I interviewed commented on the importance of ability to learn. Here are some of their comments:

- Find out how leaders think. Under tough questions, consider not only whether they have answers, but also how they respond to the questions. When asked awkward questions, do they face into them or hide from them?

- Most leaders know their weaknesses; they have experienced them over the years. The real question is whether they can learn to overcome them.

- Are leaders willing to face bad news and what is not going well? Are they willing to face their limitations and failures and learn from them?

- Do leaders have the ability to learn and adapt when receiving new facts?

- How do leaders think and process information? How flexible are they in addressing problems? Are they locked in? What is their cognitive flexibility?

- Do they learn? How do they handle mistakes? Do they try to hide from a mistake? Do they try to blame others or the context? Do they admit it and move on? Do they face into it and learn from it? If they fail to deliver on promises they make, what did they do?

These investor comments reinforce the research on the importance of leaders' learning to learn and being resilient. Learning agility—the ability and willingness to learn from experience and experiments, and subsequently apply that learning under new conditions—has been identified as the single best predictor of long-term leadership success.[11] Agile learners are quick thinkers who take initiative, exhibit curiosity by asking why and how, make fresh connections, acquire and use rules and principles, seek personal feedback, and think broadly about business problems.[12] Enlightened trial-and-error outperforms the planning of flawless intellects, or as David Kelly, head of IDEO product development, said, "Fail early and fail often; it is better than failing once, failing at the end, or failing big."[13]

When things go wrong, learning leaders are resilient. They face into the problem to learn from a mistake, demonstrate willingness to apologize and own up to an error, and turn insights from the past into actions for the future.

Possible indicators:

- *How does the leader handle failure? How resilient is the leader?*
- *How committed is the leader to learning? How able is the leader to accept new ideas or approaches?*

Moral Values and Ethical Judgment

In nearly every survey of effective leaders, integrity or values comes out on top. Integrity is also at the top of almost any investor leadership wish list. Integrity has a number of dimensions. Some of it is ethical behavior and doing what is right (however *right* is defined). Some of it is building trust by keeping promises and doing what you say you will do. And some of it is the ability to find meaning for yourself and create meaning for others.

FOLLOWING A CODE OF ETHICS

As one investor put it, "Leaders have to have personal integrity; once a crook, always a crook." While this all-or-nothing thinking discounts forgiveness, it presents the case for how ethics underlies nearly all decision making.

Investors need confidence that the organizations and leaders they invest in will act ethically. Nonetheless, as desirable as ethics in business are held to be, 41% of U.S. workers said they observed unethical or illegal behavior on the job.[14] Investors can receive reports on ethics of executives, but they can also monitor if leaders encourage ethical behavior in their organizations by looking for

- Written standards of ethical workplace conduct
- Training on standards
- Company resources that provide advice on ethics issues
- A process to report potential violations confidentially or anonymously

- Performance evaluations on ethical conduct
- Systems to disclose violators

In addition to building ethics into an organization culture, at a more personal level leaders act ethically when they take time to reflect on ethical danger zones and make sure that they resist ethical traps like cutting corners to deliver performance, setting unattainable goals, rationalizing behavior ("everyone is doing it"), using creative accounting, or letting up on the little things.[15] Personal ethics can't be approached as a gradient; you can't be a little bit unethical any more than you can be a little bit pregnant. One leader cannot be "more ethical" than another, but being known to be unethical quickly removes a leader from investment consideration.

BUILDING TRUST

Trustworthiness means predictably keeping promises by moderating expectations, by consistently delivering on agreements, or by exercising good judgment—which isn't always obvious or straightforward. As an example of the pitfalls, consider the cement company that had hung million-dollar paintings in the lobby. When an investor asked the leadership why a cement company would present that sort of display and if it was consistent with their company brand, industry, and purpose, they quickly sold off the paintings . . . and used the money to elaborately renovate the reception area. Both of these poor judgments reflect a lack of trust with investor capital. And they didn't understand why the investor wasn't thrilled when they explained how they had taken his feedback.

Leaders who build trust manage expectations by promising less and delivering more. The reverse is dangerous. For example, when one excellent leader promised 20% revenue growth and 15% profitability (both far beyond industry standards) and then delivered 15% revenue and 10% profitability, it was taken as falling short of expectations, when in fact the firm still outperformed industry average. Investors lost confidence in this leader because of the projections, taking them as broken promises rather than aspirations.

Leaders who build trust respond to investors in a timely way. One investor became very frustrated with a senior leader who simply would not return e-mail messages or phone calls. The investor interpreted this as a lack of respect, and it eroded the trust that the investor had in the leader, causing the investor to move money elsewhere.

Investors trust leaders who are transparent. Problems are bad, but cover-ups are worse. For example, when one organization had a major disruption on the product introduction delivery time, the leader contacted significant investors to share with them the delay and ways to resolve the problem. The investors, while not pleased, appreciated the transparency. Leaders who try to run and hide from mistakes often end up with cynical and suspicious investors.

FINDING PERSONAL MEANING

Most people seek meaning in their lives. Investors favor leaders who care deeply about something beyond themselves, who bring meaning into the workplace, and who help employees find meaning from the work they do (as discussed in Chapter 6).

When investors see leaders who operate out of a set of deeply held personal values, they are more likely to have confidence in those leaders. Leaders can become models of meaning making by using their strengths at work, by aligning their personal purpose with the organization's purpose (see Chapter 7), by encouraging positive relationships and teams at work (see Chapter 6), and by demonstrating how to learn and exhibiting a growth mindset.

Possible indicators:

- *Does the leader encourage a code of ethics to shape behavior in the company?*
- *Does the leader evoke personal trust from key stakeholders?*
- *Does the leader create a sense of meaning in the workplace?*

Conclusion

Leader charm matters; personal proficiency matters more. An investor who meets with an organization's management team should assess the personal proficiency of the whole team, not just the top leader. The insights in this chapter suggest that investors look beyond a leader's superficial style and probe more deeply into six personal proficiencies that individuals on the leadership team might possess. It is unlikely that any one leader will excel at all six, but the individuals on the team should complement one another and collectively demonstrate personal proficiency. Investors can do more than say "I like him" or "I like her" as a leader and have more rigorous confidence in personal proficiencies of leaders, as summarized in Table 3.1 on the next page. By investigating these six elements of personal proficiency, investors see beyond the face of the firm's leader.

Table 3.1. Indicators for Personal Proficiency

Leaders exhibit personal proficiency through	Possible Indicators	How to Assess
Past: experience and performance	What is the free cash flow of the leader's business compared to that of competitors over time? How successful has the leader been at meeting performance commitments in previous assignments? What has the leader's career path been? Similar or different assignments? Safe assignments or risky ones?	Look at balance sheet of leader's business over time. Review career history and performance review goals set and results delivered. Profile leader's career mosaics.
Physical: presence and vitality	Does the leader maintain adequate diet, exercise, and sleep habits? Does the leader have a current physical exam? Does the leader have the vitality to meet the demands of the job?	Look at insurance policies for leader and assess how well the leader meets requirements of these policies. Determine if leader has regular and thorough physical exams. Evaluate subjective presence at first impression and beyond.
Emotional: identity and well-being	Does the leader have a personal identity that matches personal strengths and needs of the business? How does the leader handle emotional demands and stress? Does the leader manage ego: balance of confidence and humility? Does the leader often talk in terms of "I" messages or "we" messages?	Ask others about leader's reputation and identity, or source from media. Observe leader in stressful situation. Listen for "I" versus "we" messages.

Leaders exhibit personal proficiency through	Possible Indicators	How to Assess
Social: multiplying others and working together	Is the leader a network builder? That is, is the leader someone who knows and is known by thought leaders in the industry? Does the leader share or take credit for success? Accept the blame or blame others for failure? Were the people around the leader chosen to make up for the leader's weaknesses or to make the leader look good by comparison? Does the leader make others feel better about themselves after an interaction? Does the leader have a 5:1 positive-to-negative comment ratio?	Interview industry thought leaders about the reputation of targeted firm leaders. Look at composition of team and direct reports. Observe the leader interacting with others.
Intellectual: learning agility, resilience, grit	How does the leader handle failure? How resilient is the leader? How committed is the leader to learning? How able is the leader to accept new ideas or approaches?	Find out how the leader dealt with a failure. Ask the leader about current lessons.
Moral: values and ethical judgment	Does the leader encourage a code of ethics to shape behavior within the company? Does the leader evoke personal trust from key stakeholders? Does the leader create a sense of meaning within the workplace?	Audit litigation patterns. Listen for how employees talk about leaders and their ability to engender trust. Listen for how employees describe their work.

CHAPTER 4

Strategic Proficiency

Investors Want Leaders Who Know Where They Are Going

Investors look at past performance, but what they're investing in is the future. So they look for leaders who have a capacity to create the future: leaders who focus forward rather than backward, who seem to see around corners rather than allowing themselves to be cornered in a present position, who can turn a compelling vision into committed actions, and who engage others in folding the future into the present. Figure 4.1 illustrates the six basic elements that go into the development of strategic proficiency.

These six elements echo the work of many of the most prominent thinkers and framers of strategy discussions. Although these thought leaders use different terms, they basically propose similar components for strategic proficiency. Table 4.1 synthesizes current strategic work in the field that adds up to an overall strategic approach. The remainder of the chapter reviews these elements, with indicators that investors can track to assess the leaders' strategic proficiency.

Have an Overall Strategic Approach

When investors meet with the leadership team, once they are comfortable with the personal proficiency of the team members, they often want to know if the leaders have strategic proficiency. Their inquiry begins by determining how leaders conceive strategy. They want to see a compass that gives direction—but also a map that offers a blueprint for moving forward.

One investor explained that she wants to see if and how the leaders think ahead. "Do they have a plan for the future? Where are they spending their personal time and energy? The past? Present? Or future?" For investors to determine if leaders are strategists with a point of view

Figure 4.1. Framework for Assessing Leaders' Strategic Proficiency

about the future, they need to ensure that leaders have a commitment to strategic thinking.

Strategic leaders are likely to have a blueprint that they follow for creating their future position. The specific elements of the blueprint are less important than the simple existence of an overall scheme for how to think of strategy. Figure 4.2 offers an example of such a blueprint. Investors will have more confidence in leaders' strategic proficiency if the leaders can quickly share a simple blueprint of how they translate their strategic thinking into specific planning processes.

Possible indicators:

- *Do leaders have a strategic blueprint that captures all the elements of strategic proficiency?*
- *Do they regularly apply this framework?*

Understand External Business Drivers

Strategic proficiency requires a point of view about the future of the leader's industry. This point of view comes from understanding both the general business conditions that affect the industry and the specific expectations of key stakeholders in the industry.

Table 4.1. Approaches to Strategy
Key Dimensions of Strategic Proficiency
That Create Overall Strategic Approach

Strategy Author	Understand External Drivers	Position Organization for the Future
Charan[a]	Detect patterns of external change.	Position and reposition the firm. Determine priorities.
Rumelt[b]	Define the nature of the challenge. Use your head (insight).	Focus on the right problem (kernel).
Lafley and Martin[c]	Where am I going to play to win?	How am I going to win?
Kaplan and Norton[d]		Develop strategy.
Simons[e]	Who is customer? What are strategic uncertainties?	What are priorities for key stakeholders?
Kim and Mauborgne[f]	Redefine market boundaries. Reach beyond existing demand.	Focus on big picture.
Hamel and Prahalad[g]	Determine unmet needs. Shape the future industry.	Create strategic intent: what must we do differently?
Porter[h]	Understand five forces that shape industry.	Create competitive strategy based on cost, focus, differentiation.

a. Ram Charan has presented his areas of strategic know-how in many settings. They are found in his writing: Ram Charan, *What the CEO Wants You to Know: How Your Company Really Works* (New York: Crown Business, 2001); Larry Bossidy, Ram Charan, and Charles Buck, *Execution: The Discipline of Getting Things Done* (New York: Crown Business, 2009); Ram Charan, *Global Tilt: Leading Your Business through the Great Economic Power Shift* (New York: Crown Business, 2013).

b. Richard Rumelt, *Good Strategy/Bad Strategy: The Difference and Why It Matters* (New York: Crown Business, 2011).

c. A. G. Lafley and Roger Martin, *Playing to Win: How Strategy Really Works* (Boston: Harvard Business Press, 2013).

d. Robert Kaplan and David Norton, *Strategy Maps: Converting Intangible Assets into Tangible Outcomes* (Boston: Harvard Business Press, 2004); Robert Kaplan and David Norton, *The Strategy Focused Organization: How Balanced Scorecard Companies Thrive in the New Business Environment* (Boston: Harvard Business Press, 2000); Robert Kaplan and David Norton, *Alignment: Using the Balanced Scorecard to Create Corporate Synergies* (Boston: Harvard Business Press, 2006).

Turn Aspiration to Action through Systems	Engage and Communicate with Employees	Manage the Process of Strategy Creation
Judge people. Set goals. Mold leaders.	Manage social system.	
Create proximate objective. Use design to coordinate action goals.		Overcome entropy and inertia.
What are my core competencies? How do I execute strategy?		What is winning?
Translate strategy. Plan operations. Monitor and learn.		Test and adapt strategy.
How do you measure performance?	Will your employees help each other?	What are strategic boundaries?
Get strategic sequence right. Overcome four hurdles with leadership.		Use fair process. Manage a process to build leadership profiles.
Provide employees skills to work effectively. Establish and review milestones.	Create a sense of urgency and competitor focus among all employees.	Capture the essence of winning.
Manage the value chain of supporting and primary activities.		

e. Robert Simons, *Seven Strategy Questions: A Simple Approach for Better Execution* (Boston: Harvard Business Press, 2010).

f. W. Chan Kim and Renee Mauborgne, *Blue Ocean Strategy: How to Create Uncontested Market Space and Make the Competition Irrelevant* (Boston: Harvard Business Press, 2005); W. Chan Kim and Renee Mauborgne, "Blue Ocean Leadership," *Harvard Business Review* (May 2014).

g. Gary Hamel and CK Prahalad, "Strategic Intent," *Harvard Business Review* (May–June 1989); Gary Hamel, *What Matters Now: How to Win in a World of Relentless Change, Ferocious Competition, and Unstoppable Innovation* (San Francisco: Jossey Bass, 2012).

h. Michael Porter, *Competitive Strategy: Techniques for Analyzing Industries and Competitors* (New York: Free Press, 1998); Michael Porter, *On Competition* (updated and expanded) (Boston: Harvard Business Press, 2008); Joan Margetta, *Understanding Michael Porter: The Essential Guide to Competition and Strategy* (Boston: Harvard Business Press, 2011).

Figure 4.2. A Strategic Blueprint

Where are we today?

	Strengths	Weaknesses
Internal Assessment of Capabilities		
External Assessment	Opportunities	Threats

What is our case for change?	
What are our risks for not changing?	

Where do we want to go tomorrow?

Vision: How do we position ourselves as measured by external stakeholders?

Outcomes: What happens if we are successful?

Goals	Specific Measures

Where do we want to go tomorrow?

Impact: What is the impact on key stakeholders?

Stakeholder	Specific Impact
Client	
Employee	
Investor	
Community	
Other	

How do we get there?

Keys for Transition		Choices/Actions
Relationship/ Engagement	Who to involve? When and how?	
Information	How, who, and when to communicate?	
Resources	People and people systems	
	Budget	
	Systems	
Accountability/ Adaptability	Tracking and follow up	
	Lessons learned	
	Adaptations made	
Leadership role model	Specific leader behaviors	

General business conditions provide opportunities for redefining industries and building blue ocean strategies that create a future. Investors can explore the extent to which leaders have a framework for thinking about the future. In our work on understanding future business conditions, my colleagues and I have identified six dimensions of business context, each of which might open new business opportunities. Perceiving trends in each dimension enables leaders to reshape their industry and organization. Table 4.2 summarizes this logic and gives a number of examples where leaders identified a general business trend and then created a firm that redefined the industry.

Leaders who understand general business conditions can anticipate and create new business opportunities and thus tap into the innovation premium that comes from being an industry leader.[1] Investors can audit

Table 4.2. Environmental Trends and Redefinition of Industry

Trend	Key Factors	Examples of Industry Evolution
Social	Consumer lifestyle Pace of change Urban/rural shift Emphasis on service Work/life integration Focus on wellness	Healthy foods and lifestyle (KFC, Whole Foods, Fitbit, Chipotle) Focus on services more than products (service firms like Uber, Airbnb, Yelp, Cirque du Soleil) Personalizing wellness (WebMD, Fitbit, Nike)
Technical	Computing . . . technological access, big data, information ubiquity Communication . . . social media and information access Social networking and relationship access	New distribution channels (Amazon, Netflix) New technology (Huawei, Xiaomi, Google, Instagram, Hulu, Dropbox, YouTube) New connection services (Twitter, LinkedIn, Facebook, Salesforce.com) Internet of things (Nest, Jawbone) Biotech (Gilead Sciences, Novo Nordisk)
Economic	Market conditions and trends Globalization and regionalization of markets Disintermediation of industry boundaries	Competing in new markets (Unilever's shift to third world) Bundling products and services (Apple, Comcast, Disney) Cyber security (Checkpoint) Crowdfunding (Kickstarter)
Political	Political shifts Regulatory shifts Defining role of government	Reshaping of an industry (U.S. health care) Political hot topics (terrorism and TSA)
Environmental	Concern for the planet (green movement; carbon footprint) Social responsibility Energy and water use	New forms of energy (Siemens renewable energy, Tesla Motors) Natural gas fracking (Apache Energy, Chesapeake) Philanthropy firms (Bloomberg Philanthropies, NGOs, micro financing)
Demographic	Age and cross generation Education Gender and other diversity (e.g., women in the workforce)	Focusing on the aging workforce (Marriott retirement centers) Lifetime learning (Kahn University, Phoenix University) Focusing on fitness (Curves)

the extent to which leaders have the ability to readily grasp external trends that lead to innovation.

When leaders understand general business conditions, they are also able to shift their thinking about key stakeholders. One investor asks leaders to explain how they interact with government. He found that in many industries regulation and government support was key to firm success. He was particularly interested in emerging markets when leaders moved from a corruption (bribery, hidden contracts) to a collaborative (government-industry joint problem solving) stance with government.

Another key stakeholder for investors to consider is customers. How do leaders define key customers? By looking backward or forward? By considering local or global customers? Do leaders prioritize customers? For targeted customers, do leaders understand how to move from service to partnering to anticipation? Serving customers means that leaders know who their customers are and what they want. Partnering with customers means building intimacy with customers by becoming more connected with them. Anticipating customers means seeing what customers don't yet have and foreseeing what customers would value in the future. Leaders who anticipate the needs of target customers delight them and create more value. Most of the firms in the right-hand column of Table 4.2 had leaders who recognized business trends, which enabled them to anticipate customer needs and create innovative products or services to shape an industry.

Investors can assess how well leaders anticipate general business conditions, serve key stakeholders, and derive subsequent business implications. This means that investors might track where leaders spend time and who they spend it with. Are the leaders consistently accessing information about trends in their industry? Are they spending time with lighthouse customers? Are they asking about what's next? How are they sourcing information about trends that might affect their industry?

Possible indicators:

- *Do leaders have a framework for thinking about future trends that might shape their industry?*
- *Do leaders source information about future business trends?*
- *Do leaders have an innovation premium because they turn opportunities into products or services?*
- *Do leaders move from customer service to anticipation by foreseeing what customers may want in the future?*

Create a Unique Position for the Future

Positioning an organization for the future has been captured by many terms: mission, vision, goals, objectives, intent, themes, priorities, plans, values, purpose, kernels—and the list goes on. While these words have nuances of meaning (some focus on *why*, others on *what* or *how*), they all point to differentiating the firm from competitors in the future.

Investors want to know if leaders have enunciated a viable and differentiated strategy for their organization. When my colleagues and I interviewed investors on the topic, these are some of the things they brought up:

- Do leaders avoid following the industry pack? Are they anticipating the future and are they ahead of the curve?

- Do investors have a ten-year mission or vision and a path to get there?

- Do the executives create a playbook focused on the future, not the past? Do they strategically think through the new options before others perceive them?

- Do leaders have a clear strategy for growth? This might be through product innovation, geographic expansion, or customer share, but they need to have a growth strategy that is clearly understood in the marketplace.

- Business thinkers normally focus on how to make the firm an effective entity; however, I've come around to the idea that choosing the right battlefield is the most important decision.

- I look for leaders who say things and do things that are different from the received wisdom. If leaders are following the pack, I know they are mediocre strategists; if they are unique, they may be uniquely good or uniquely bad. I want to assess the depth of the arguments; do they just have a cool vision or can they break that down level by level to show how all the pieces fit together?

These investor quotes help identify leaders who can uniquely position the firm for the future. Investors want a simple idea that captures their imagination and differentiates the firm. One successful entrepreneur described this process when he talked to investors:

> When I talk to investors, I want to give them a really simple idea. We want to show investors that there are twenty-five things we could do to make this company great, but investors generally value investment on the three priorities that we will do well. They do not want

to be sold on twenty-five things that could be done. If I convince them that we will do these three really well, they will be more likely to invest. So we have had a simple strategy of electrifying our organization around three simple strategic priorities: proof of concept (what we will do), attraction of the concept (why we will do it), and trust in our ability to pursue the concept (how we will go forward). This simple formula has helped us gain investor confidence.

If leaders cannot express their unique position in the future in less than two or three minutes, investors are apt to be skeptical about their clarity of focus. Conversely, investors find concise statements very persuasive. For example, one retail CEO shared with investors that the chain had moved from revenue growth by building new stores to increasing revenue per square foot at existing stores. This simple idea made sense to investors, who could then assess the viability of the new strategy by looking both at tangible actions to make it happen and at results to track the goal. Focusing on the essential strategy indicates an ability to prioritize, synthesize, and simplify.

One investor felt that a key to assessing a leader's strategic insight was to ignore what the strategy was and go straight for what it was not. The investor would ask leaders which businesses they were not likely to pursue. Leaders with strategic clarity are as disciplined about what they will not do as about what they will do.

Another investor evaluated leaders on specific results from strategic success for key stakeholders: customers, regulators, and communities. The investor asked leaders not only about their strategic direction but about the specific outcomes that would occur from accomplishing the strategy.

Investors are unlikely to be able to tell whether a strategy is right or not—they don't begin to spend as much time in a given firm and industry as the leader who developed it. But investors can determine if the leader can clearly state how the company will position itself to win. Investors can also ask others in the industry about competitive positioning and about their perception of the leader's strategic proficiency. Competitors respect leaders for their unique strengths, and investors who work in an industry can query many of its players to identify leaders with recognized strategic proficiency.

Finally, strategic positioning in the future should evolve as business conditions change. The retail CEO who shifted from revenue growth by building new stores to revenue growth per square foot per store showed investors that the strategy was evolving. Investors can look at letters from the CEO in annual reports over a five- to ten-year period to see if the leaders are adapting their strategy.

Possible indicators:

- *Can leaders articulate in a few words how they are positioning their organization to win in the future?*
- *Are leaders seen as thought leaders or strategic pioneers in their industry?*
- *Do leaders evolve their strategy to cope with emerging industry trends?*

Turn Aspiration into Action

Aspirations do not always show up in action—in leadership or in daily life, as almost every would-be dieter has discovered. Having a position about the future and making the future happen require different skills. Strategic positioning creates aspirations about what might happen; turning those aspirations into specific steps requires discipline. Investors can assess leaders' ability to chunk a strategy into explicit choices designed to enact it.

One investor asked leaders to identify three to five choices in the last thirty, sixty, or ninety days that drove their strategy. These choices could be about operations, customers, or organization, but they needed to be explicit in terms of what resource allocations the strategy required. Useful choices are often about systems the organization will put in place or about how to allocate resources to drive strategy. Leaders who called out such choices were more likely to make them. (The process of defining and making choices is a major part of the execution proficiency discussed in Chapter 5.)

Another investor examined minutes of executive meetings to discern what choices were defined and how they were made. Meeting minutes do not always reflect commitments, but they often indicate where the team spends collective time. In one useful but discouraging example, investors looking into an organization with a public and strategic commitment to generating new ideas for its constituents found that its executive committee minutes were about 80% focused on financial results and 20% focused on internal governance. In a six-month period, relatively little reported meeting time was spent on innovation and new ideas, which was the espoused strategic position. While individual leaders might be encouraging innovation, it was not a topic of team discussion.

Investors can ask leaders if they have a template to help them identify key choices that have to be made to turn aspiration into action. This template is likely to focus on the *how* of planning. In Figure 4.2, for example, this organization's how (bottom right corner) identifies choices around people, budget, and systems to move the strategy forward. Again, the specific items in the choice framework may be less relevant to investors than the fact that leaders have a choice framework that they actually use to turn aspirations into actions.

To assess strategic choice, investors can also monitor individual leaders' time. Some leaders advocate one thing but spend time on another—hypocrisy in action. Leaders who advocate for innovation should be spending time with R&D staff, lighthouse customers (early adopters), industry thought leaders, and new projects. Leaders who advocate for customer intimacy should be spending time with sales and marketing people, actual customers, and competitors (to see how they are differentiating themselves). One investor asked to have a leader's executive assistant (who managed his calendar) report the percentage of time devoted to strategic choice areas in the last six months, and the leader was amenable.

Possible indicators:

- *Do leaders turn strategic direction into day-to-day choices?*
- *Do leaders have a framework for what choices should be made to make strategy happen?*
- *Do leaders spend time on the key choices that move strategy forward?*

Engage and Communicate with Employees

Ultimately, real strategy is not found in documents that are presented to investors, nor is it found in organization systems that reinforce strategy. Strategy must live in the mind and heart of every employee. One organization has taken this concept so far as to use "strategy is everyone's business" as a mantra, in an effort to make strategy less an intellectual abstraction and more a personal commitment. Effective strategy becomes everyone's job.

With one mining company, investors grew more confident in the leadership's strategy when they visited a mine instead of listening to an investor call or sitting in a road show meeting with a presentation by the CEO and CFO. When they went to the mine, they were invited to don hard hats and wander (accompanied) for a couple of hours before attending the formal investor meeting. They were encouraged to meet with employees doing all sorts of work—administration, truck driving, mineral extraction, operations. They were allowed to ask any employee any question, and they were encouraged to pose some questions to employees:

- What is the price of our mineral on the spot market today?
- What is our production price in this mine?
- What are the key strategies in this mine to be effective going forward?

As these investors wandered and talked to employees, often using these questions, they learned the extent to which employees had a personal understanding of the mine's strategy and performance. When the investors reconvened, they were able to share their individual insights and were delighted that most employees knew the market price and mine price of the mineral as well as the key strategies for the future. Investors were impressed that the leaders had enough confidence to let employees interact with them. These Investors said that competitors were unwilling to let them talk directly to employees. This company had more investor confidence going forward because employees were aware of and engaged in the strategy. The strategy was not just management's but theirs.

When I proposed this idea of investor learning by wandering around to another CEO, he instantly replied, "Are you nuts?" He was very worried that investors would hear different stories from employees, including dissent.

This mining company's widespread understanding of strategy was not an accident. Management had created a clear and compelling message. The leaders wanted employees to be business literate, which meant knowing market and mine prices for their mineral. They published and talked about these numbers daily. They held town hall meetings so that employees could hear the strategy and leaders could respond to questions. They had formal and informal suggestion systems whereby employees could voice their opinions and offer their input for improvements. Transparency and consistency of messages made strategy an everyday activity.

To create broad and deep understanding, strategy needs to be formulated in simple language and then repeated over and over again. One sovereign wealth fund investor insisted on seeing strategies articulated in ways that employees could understand and repeat to others. The language of strategy needs to evolve. It starts with a simple message about where you want to take the company—a tag line. This simple message becomes a story of how this future will affect those outside the company (customers, communities, suppliers, partners, regulators) and employees inside the company. Strategy as story gains power as the story becomes personal, with intellectual and emotional messages and an antagonist who is affected by the messages. Then the collective strategic stories become a narrative with a past, present, and future. Investors should look for communications with tag lines, stories, and narratives that help employees throughout an organization understand the strategy.

Employee understanding of strategy goes up dramatically when leaders live the strategy. As Francis d'Assisi (the namesake of Pope Francis) said, "We preach the gospel and sometimes we use words." Leaders teach strategy less by what they say than by what they do. Leaders communicate more about a customer strategy by spending time with customers than by talking about spending time with customers. As noted, investors who monitor for leadership authenticity versus hypocrisy will discover what employees pay attention to.

Beyond understanding, employees own the strategy when they personalize it. One thought leader said that investors should find out if employees have a line of sight between the strategy and their personal work. When a large percentage of employees can leave work recognizing how they personally contributed that day to the overall organization's strategy, investors should be more confident about the company's future.

Employee understanding and personalizing of strategy can be tracked by investors through employee engagement surveys, senior leader strategic talks (look for unity of senior leader messages in the firm's public discourse on strategy), and communications and engagement initiatives.

Possible indicators:

- *What percentage of employees can link their daily behavior to the strategy (line of sight and personalization)?*

- *How committed are employees to the strategy?*

- *Do employees understand the strategy, and are they able to repeat its tag line, story, and narrative?*

Manage the Strategy Process

A leader involved in a strategy effort recently said, "I'll be so glad when we are finally done with our strategy." Wrong! Strategy is an iterative process of discovery. Strategy does not have an end game—it is a means of playing. It is a verb, not a noun, less a destination than a direction and as much about process as content.

When leaders manage the process of strategy, they increase investors' confidence that strategies will continually be created, uncreated, and re-created over time. The goose is more important than any golden egg it lays. Production capability is more important than the product. The innovation process is more important than the latest innovation.

Investors should explore the process used to invent strategy. As an easy test, investors can simply ask leaders to describe their strategy. Leaders who are proficient strategists will naturally respond by discussing not only the content of the strategy but also the process they used to create it. Investors should review the process for creating strategy to determine if leaders can replicate and improve the strategy. Assessing the process of creating strategy comes from four questions:

- Who is involved?
- How much dialogue and dissent is encouraged?
- How will the strategy be shared?
- How will the strategy evolve?

WHO IS INVOLVED?

Strategy may be crafted by a leader acting alone and personally seeing a future that others don't see. Or it may come from a committee or broader caucus whose members share their different points of view, after which someone integrates these ideas and creates a first draft. When leaders personally create first drafts by integrating ideas from others, they are more likely to be deeply aware of the strategy position and choices. Leaders who delegate first drafts become advisers rather than owners of the strategic thinking.

HOW MUCH DIALOGUE AND DISSENT IS ENCOURAGED?

One major investor said that he liked to see or determine dissent and constructive dialogue as part of the strategic process. Some of this dialogue goes on before the first draft, but much of it goes into the editing process. This investor said that if leaders agree too quickly on the external trends or strategic positioning, they may miss potential problems and opportunities. Disagreement without being disagreeable and tension without contention generally create more robust strategic thinking. A test of a culture of positive dissent occurs when disagreements are aired in a team setting rather than in private discussions after a team consensus. When leaders lobby in private after group discussions, investors should be worried about tolerance of dissent. Encouraging dissent when creating strategy also allows for strategies to be evaluated early in their implementation cycle.

HOW WILL THE STRATEGY BE SHARED?

Although it is true that strategic choices must sometimes remain private (as with mergers or acquisitions), more often a company is better off when the strategic positioning statements are broadly distributed in town hall meetings, websites, blogs, and newsletters. These public documents permit clear and consistent language. Verbal presentations and private conversations also become important forums for strategy dissemination. Strategic dialogue clarifies the choices and their implications. The rule of thumb for communications is 10:1; information needs to be shared ten times to gain each unit of understanding and acceptance.

HOW WILL THE STRATEGY EVOLVE?

Since strategy is an iterative process, it has to adapt and change constantly. Investors should track the ability of leaders to update their strategic position. They can look at the extent to which leaders solicit feedback from key stakeholders on what is working about a plan and what is not working. One company shared with investors this strategic mantra: *think big, test small, fail fast, and learn always.* When investors recognized that this firm's leaders were committed to constant learning, they had more confidence in their strategic proficiency. The thinking big is about positioning. The test-small provisions encourages experimentation and trial and error with strategic choices. Failing fast implies transparency and accountability about what works. Constant learning indicates curiosity and improvement.

Possible indicators:

- *What percentage of people participated in crafting the strategy?*
- *Do leaders encourage dissent and dialogue in creating and implementing the strategy?*
- *Do leaders run experiments and build in learning to improve the strategy?*

Conclusion

On investor said that when he meets with new leader or team, he asks to see the strategy. He has five criteria for reviewing the strategy he sees:

- First, simplicity: Are the leaders able to prepare a narrative about what they are doing that is simple and understandable?
- Second, confidence: Are the leaders confident that their plans make sense and are logical?
- Third, consistency: Do different members of the management team share the plans?

- Fourth, technical depth: Can the leader go into detail about the technical requirements of the business, including a sense of the strategic choices that need to be made?
- Fifth, change: Can the leader adapt to new information and manage the process of strategic iteration?

The elements of a leader's strategic proficiency capture these requests (see Table 4.3 as summary). Investors who audit a leader's strategic ability will have more insights and confidence in the future.

Table 4.3. Indicators for Strategic Proficiency

Leaders with strategic proficiency . . .	Possible Indicators	How to Assess
Have an overall strategic approach	Do leaders have a strategic blueprint that captures all the elements of strategic proficiency? Do they regularly apply this framework?	Ask for strategic documents. Monitor review process for strategy.
Understand external business drivers	Do leaders have a framework for thinking about future trends that might shape their industry? Do leaders source information about future business trends? Do leaders have an innovation premium because they turn opportunities into products or services? Do leaders move from customer service to anticipation by foreseeing what customers may want in the future?	Interview leaders on trends in the industry and why they will occur. Ask leaders for names of industry leaders to see their connection. Examine innovation premium and reputation. Which customers do leaders spend time with?
Create a unique position for the future	Can leaders articulate in a few words how they are positioning their organization to win in the future? Are leaders seen as thought leaders or strategic pioneers in the industry?	Ask leaders to articulate their future strategy. Listen for clarity. Ask others in the industry who are industry pioneers. Ask leaders to trace of evolution of strategy.

(continued)

Table 4.3. (continued)

Leaders with strategic proficiency . . .	Possible Indicators	How to Assess
	Do leaders evolve their strategy to be consistent with emerging industry trends?	
Turn aspiration into action	Do leaders turn strategic direction into day-to-day choices? Do leaders have a framework for what choices should be made to make strategy happen? Do leaders spend time on the key choices that move strategy forward?	Ask leaders to lay out key choices for implementation of strategy. How comprehensive is their framework?
Engage and communicate with employees	Determine percent of employees who link their daily behavior to the strategy (line of sight and personalization). Examine commitment of employees to strategy (from engagement survey). Do employees understand and are they able to repeat the strategy (tag line, story, narrative)?	From engagement survey, test employee commitment to strategy. Interview some random employees to test their understanding of strategy.
Manage the strategy process	Determine percent of people who participated in crafting the strategy. Do leaders encourage dissent and dialogue in creating and implementing the strategy? Do leaders run experiments and build in learning to improve the strategy?	When leaders are asked about strategy, how much do they talk about the process versus content? How many employees were involved in the strategy? Can leaders share failures and what they learned?

CHAPTER 5

Execution Proficiency

Investors Want Leaders Who Get Things Done

An investor once told me that he had almost never seen a pessimistic projection of the future. Most leaders present opportunities for growth. Fewer deliver. Leadership proficiency in execution becomes an essential part of investor confidence.

Some investor assessment of execution proficiency is found in the "past experience and performance" indicator from the personal proficiency element (described in Chapter 3), but investors want to know what is behind the pattern of meeting commitments. That insight will help them predict how well leaders will execute going forward. They also want to know if current leaders are the go-to people, the ones who can get things done when necessary. And they want to know if leaders who build strategic directions can make them happen.

Strategic and execution proficiencies go hand in hand: Strategic proficiency is the idea; execution proficiency is the reality. Strategy imagines a future; execution delivers it. Strategy makes promises; execution keeps them. Strategy envisions; execution enacts. Strategy is the script; execution is the performance. Strategy inspires; execution produces. Strategy articulates what to do; execution does it.

Investors have good reason to be skeptical of pure strategists because their vision of the future may not shape today's action. When investors can see that the leadership of a potential investment has execution proficiency, they will have more confidence in its future. Rigor in execution comes from leaders doing what they say they will do with little fanfare. Investors who peek behind the delivery of results want to discover the specific indicators of leaders who can execute consistently. (See Figure 5.1.)

As with strategy, thought leaders in the change management field have identified how individuals and organizations accomplish change,

Figure 5.1. Framework for Assessing Leaders' Execution Proficiency

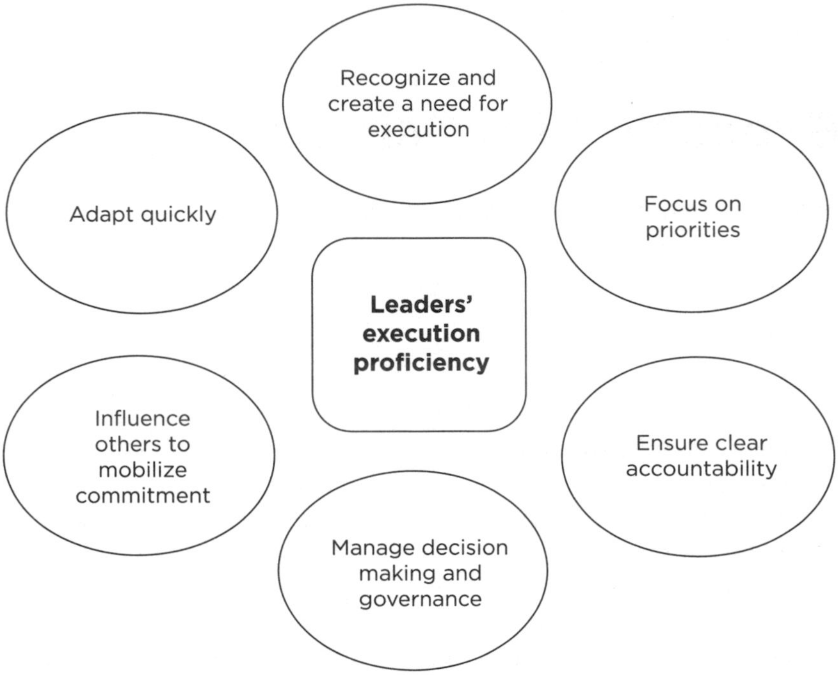

which is at the heart of execution. Some of these thought leaders' ideas are summarized in Table 5.1.

Recognize and Create a Need for Execution

The need for execution has been a topic in business circles for more than seventy years. It was worth discussing—but in no way surprising—in 1942, when the classic Dashman Company case was first prepared for aspiring managers at the Harvard Business School. (This one-page case features a purchasing VP who sends a letter to each of the company's twenty purchasing executives requesting that contracts in excess of $10,000 be cleared with him prior to signing. The branches promise to cooperate, but no notices of negotiations are received by the head office.) The lesson of this legacy case is that even good ideas without disciplined execution will not happen.

Many leaders still find it hard to get from issuing directives to making things happen. Execution requires change—and most people naturally resist change, especially when it originates outside themselves. With somewhere between 50% and 90% of daily actions done out of habit and not conscious choice, human inertia is a powerful force.[1] Leaders start execution by creating a rallying cry that intellectually and emotionally inspires others to change. For leaders to help people overcome the fly-wheel problem (getting started on change), they have to begin by building a strong business case for change.[2] In general, when leaders explain *why* something has to be done, others accept the *what,* and act on it.[3]

Investors can assess how well leaders build a case for change by asking for explanations of why the strategy exists and what benefits it will offer. As leaders explain why the strategy will be worth pursuing, investors can listen for four rationales, depicted in terms of their time horizons and change drivers in Table 5.2.

Leaders who can build a business case with all four rationales will be better able to rally and inspire others to strategy execution than those who rely on only one or two rationales.

In addition, investors can assess the process by which leaders build a business case for the strategy. Do the leaders rely on their personal relationships and goodwill, or do they also build the business case by providing data analytics about why the strategy is important and demonstrations or pilots of where the strategy has worked? As leaders share more complete reasoning behind the need for strategy, investors will have more confidence that leaders can rally support for the strategy.

Finally, in assessing leaders' ability to build a case for change, investors can determine the extent to which leaders have thought through a fault tree analysis of what can go wrong. When leaders are able to anticipate potential barriers to their strategy and address them in advance, investors will have more confidence that the business case will lead to strategy execution. Often, change efforts face three types of roadblocks:[4]

- Technical: Do we have the individual and organization resources and systems to execute this strategy?

- Political: Do we have the political support and relationships in place to execute this strategy?

- Cultural: Do we have a cultural pattern that will enable us to execute this strategy?

Although their assessments are necessarily subjective, investors can determine the extent to which leaders build a business case for strategy execution. When investors talk to and observe leaders working to build a business case, they can address the content, process, and barriers for strategy execution, not strategy alone. These leaders go beyond where they are headed to how they are going to get there.

Table 5.1. Exemplary Thought Leaders on Execution and Change Processes

Warner Burke	John Kotter	Dale Lake	Price Pritchett	Ed Lawler
Organization Change	*Leading Change*	*Change Manual*[a]	*Quantum Leap*	*Organization Agility*
Be self aware.	Establish sense of urgency.	Design a change agenda.	Give clear marching orders.	Strategizing dynamic (purpose, identity, intent)
Monitor external environment.	Create guiding coalition.	Assess the current situation.	Nail down each job.	Perceiving environmental change (sensing, communicating, interpreting)
Establish a need for change.	Develop vision or strategy.	Create dissatisfaction or need for change.	Manage resistance to change.	
Provide clear vision or direction.	Communicate change vision.	Activate change champions.	Encourage risk taking.	
Communicate the need.	Empower employees for action.	Influence stakeholders.	Create supportive work environment.	Testing responses (resources, risk, learning)
Deal with resistance.	Generate short-term wins.	Assess and overcome resistance.	Attend to transition and change.	Implementing change (autonomy, capability, performance management)
Leverage multiple actions.	Consolidate gains and produce more change.	Build team and network.	Take care of "me" issues.	
Have consistency and persistence.	Anchor new approaches in culture.	Structure for success.	Communicate over and over again.	
		Do project management.		
		Monitor progress.		
		Have continuous learning.		

a. This comes from our correspondence with Dale Lake, who is one of our change thought leaders.

b. Many were involved with the GE Change Acceleration Process. Dave Ulrich was one of the team members in creating this process.

Michael Beer	Hay Group	GE Change Acceleration Process[b]	Covey Group	Charan and Bossidy
Organization Change and Development	This Is the Hay Model for Change	Change Acceleration Process	Disciplines of Execution	Execution
Dissatisfaction	Ensure reasons for change.	Lead change.	Focus	Know people and business.
Model or purpose of change	Identify "change agents."	Create a felt need.	Empowerment	Insist on realism.
Success or outcomes	Assess stakeholders and sponsors.	Define a direction or shape a vision.	Leverage Accountability	Set clear goals.
Cost of change				Follow through.
Resistance to change	Plan project activities.	Mobilize commitment.		Reward doers.
	Communicate changes.	Make decisions.		Expand capabilities.
	Assess impact on people and structure.	Dedicate resources.		Know yourself.
		Learn, adapt, monitor.		Apply to processes including strategy, people, and operational
	Address the impacts of the change.			
	Share process change.			
	Support changes.			
	Train for new skills.			
	Measure and report on progress.			

Table 5.2. Change Rationale Matrix

		Change Driver	
		Danger	*Opportunity*
Time Horizon	**Long term**	3. Looming danger: We need to execute strategy because we don't want to be left behind as industry transforms.	4. Vision: We need to execute strategy because of new opportunities to transform an industry.
	Short term	1. Crisis: We need to execute strategy because of a looming crisis (market conditions).	2. Improvement: We need to execute strategy because of the near-term improvements we can make in process improvements.

Possible indicators:

- *Do leaders build a comprehensive rationale for how to make sure that strategies are executed?*
- *Do leaders use analytics to build a business case for disciplined execution?*
- *Do leaders anticipate resistance to strategy execution and address the problem areas in advance?*

Focus on Priorities

Leaders in complex business settings face complex choices, but it is a mistake to try to respond to complexity with complexity. Good leaders have a knack for simplifying, clarifying, synthesizing, and unifying. They prioritize and focus on what matters most. They filter and learn to listen to the right information, and they frame and identify patterns to organize complex ideas. They replace concept clutter with simple resolve, shifting from analytics with data to action with determination, framing complex phenomena into simple patterns, and sequencing change. Focused leaders know that not everything worth doing is worth doing well. Some things may require more time and others less time, depending on their priority.

Investors can audit leaders' ability to focus on priorities by asking them to walk through their prioritization process. Investors can look for how well leaders inductively expand opportunities to see new options, then see how well these leaders deductively filter opportunities into their top priorities. The inductive-deductive priority-setting cycle gives investors confidence that leaders have been thorough in their perspective but disciplined in their focus.

One investor shared his experience when he talked to the seven members of a senior management team. He asked each member to share the top three priorities for the business, but he found relatively little overlap. Each team member had a perspective on what mattered most, but as a group they had almost no shared priorities.

This is another area that benefits from an exploration of the leader's calendar. A leader who is not spending time on the stated priorities is not persuading anyone either among the workforce or among the potential investors—that these things actually matter.

Possible indicators:

- *Do leaders know how to move from creating options to determining priorities?*
- *Do team members share a common set of priorities?*
- *Do leaders spend time on the top priorities?*

Ensure Clear Accountability

Accountability is important. In the midst of a ninety-day due diligence process, for example, a company that was negotiating for an investment missed on its financial numbers two months in a row. When the investor confronted the company leadership team with this miss, they immediately started to blame business conditions and people. Market conditions had changed, they said; customers were in transition, and some key people in the company were underperforming. The investor later told me that he would have been willing to discount the value of his investment because of the missed numbers, but because of management's inability to own up to the misses, he withdrew his investment altogether.

Strategy execution requires leaders to take personal responsibility for making sure that they do what they promise. Accountability increases when leaders obtain personal commitments from others and follow up on those commitments. They don't make excuses or blame fatigue. They don't play the victim or wallow in guilt, shame, or anger. They realize that they set the standard. So they get back on their feet and lift their heads high. And their response signals everyone else to do the same. Investors can track leaders' accountability by how well they assume and assign responsibility, designate clear roles, and follow up on commitments.

ASSUME RESPONSIBILITY

Mistakes happen. In fact, if leaders don't periodically miss goals, underperform, or disappoint themselves and others, they are not taking enough risk or doing enough experiments. Execution proficient leaders should be less afraid of making mistakes than of failing to make progress. When mistakes happen, leaders who execute become personally accountable by facing into the mistake and acknowledging what went wrong and how they are learning from it. They also go public to acknowledge their mistakes and demonstrate their lessons learned.

Responsible leaders also hold others accountable. They publicly share information about performance with their team and invite others to take ownership of their actions and results. Effective leaders talk about collective performance, using terms like *joint, shared, we,* and *our.* Investors can monitor personal and shared responsibility by auditing transparency of information and by exploring how leaders and others respond when mistakes are made: blaming or problem solving? Looking backward or forward? Hiding from mistakes or admitting mistakes? Repeating similar mistakes or learning from the past? They also weave responsibility into performance conversations (see Chapter 10 on performance accountability).

DESIGNATE ROLES

To be a proficient executor, a leader needs to define clear roles. These roles are not just titles on an organization chart; they specify who does what in the execution process. Daryl Conner, building on exceptional work by Dick Beckhard and others, has identified critical roles in executing change:[5]

- *Sponsors* legitimize change and make sure it is worth doing; they deliver consequences to those accountable, and they allocate resources for the execution to happen.
- *Agents* (or champions) are primarily responsible for implementation of a change by managing their time, rhetoric, and personal energy. They devote their personal goodwill to making strategy happen.
- *Advocates* are individuals or groups who want to achieve a change but lack the authority to make it happen on their own.
- *Targets* are individuals or groups that must change for realization

to be achieved. In major change initiatives, sponsors, agents, and advocates are also targets.[6]

Investors will have more confidence in leaders who can identify key roles and individuals trained to accomplish these roles.

TRACK PROGRESS

Leaders ensure execution by tracking progress through disciplined follow-up. For example, it is nearly impossible to make personal changes (lose weight, exercise, achieve academic success, and so forth) without tracking progress. Leadership follow-up may be made through formal systems (such as those discussed in Chapter 10 on performance accountability), but it may also be a leadership style and skill

Without a commitment to tracking progress and following up, people do not feel accountable and are unlikely to execute. Leaders track progress by monitoring how well people do on commitments. Follow-up tracking needs to be timely and consistent, focusing less on the person and more on the problem or goal. Tracking progress enables leaders to focus on the future and what can improve rather than on the past and what has gone wrong.

One investor often asks, "How well does the leader track the progress of people meeting or missing their performance goals?" Sometimes the honest answer is "Not very well." Leaders who track progress are better able to execute against goals because they follow up. A lack of follow-up discipline discourages the investor.

Tracking progress and following up come from a set of behaviors and mindset of leaders. Investors can audit this mindset by being aware of it and looking for signals.

Possible indicators:

- *Do leaders have clear indicators about what they expect from others?*
- *Do leaders follow up on what people promise they will deliver?*
- *Do leaders have candid and timely conversations when employees miss goals?*

Manage Decision Making and Governance

Decisions matter.[7] Leaders who choose rather than slide into choices are more proficient executors. Decision-making and governance processes underlie not just what results are delivered, but how. Organization charts clarify roles and what is expected from a person in an assigned job; decision protocols clarify rights and who will make what decisions. Execution increases with clarity about both roles (who does what) and rights (who makes decisions).

Investors can audit how leaders manage both the content and the process of decision making. The content has to do with the clarity of leaders as they specify choices they need to make to execute. In so doing, leaders turn big projects into specific choices. These choices might be around operations, finance, organization, or customers. By being clear about choices, leaders turn aspiration into action (as discussed in Chapter 4). For example, one investor probes deeply into the leader's decision-making approach to firing people. He is nervous about investing in leaders who clean house with massive terminations because that shows of lack of differentiation between good talent and poor talent; however, a CEO who is not firing anyone at all is probably not holding people accountable for execution.

Leaders should also attend to the process of decision making, which can be captured in a decision protocol asking these five questions:

- What is the decision to be made? Leaders should approach each choice with two or three specific options about what could be done.

- Who will make the decision? Leaders need to be clear about who will make the final decision. A number of accountability templates can be used in this process; RAPID (Recommend, Agree, Perform, Input, Decide) is one example. A decision grid helps determine decision rights and accountabilities.

- When will the decision be made? Leaders who set decision deadlines generally meet them.

- How will the decision be made? Leaders determine a process for defining the rigor required of a decision, collecting information to make the decision, and managing who is involved in the process and how the decision will be shared.

- How will the decision be tracked and followed up? Leaders measure results and encourage improvements in decision making.

Investors can monitor the extent to which leaders appreciate and use a governance grid like that displayed in Table 5.3. By making both choices and processes explicit, leaders can ensure continuous improvement in how they govern.

One investor told me that he likes to identify two to four major decisions the leader has made in the last month or two, then go more deeply into the process used for making those decisions. Leaders who think not

Table 5.3. Decision-Making Governance Grid

		Decision Process or Protocol				
		What is the decision to be made?	Who will ultimately make it?	When will it be made?	How will it be made?	How will it be tracked and followed up?
Decision Domain and Choices	Operations/ technology					
	Financial					
	Organization/ people					
	Customer interface					
	Other					

only about the choices they make but also about the ways they go about making those choices build governance systems that give investors more confidence.

Another investor first looks at the organization chart to see formal roles and titles, then asks leaders to discuss the governance process and profile who makes what decisions. Leaders who are able to articulate governance processes are more likely to execute what they intend.

Possible indicators:

- *Do leaders manage the content of decisions by breaking big projects into specific choices?*
- *Do leaders have a decision protocol for who is involved and how they go about getting decisions done?*
- *Do leaders appropriately involve people in decision making?*

Influence Others to Mobilize Commitment

In our research on making change happen, we found that mobilizing commitment is the most critical step in a change process.[8] Executors who

Figure 5.2. Model of Influence Based on the Values of Others

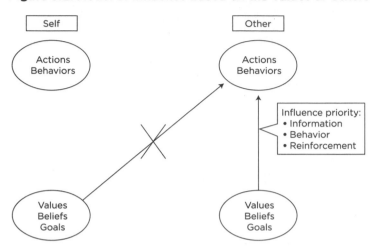

mobilize commitment influence others to get things done; they shift the process of getting things done from themselves to others. Leaders who execute don't have to do the work themselves, but they must ensure that the work gets done. To transfer ownership for projects or decisions to others, they master the skills of influence.[9]

Leaders influence by focusing on what's in it for the people involved. These leaders recognize that influence comes by helping others see the connection (or disconnection) of their wants or values and behaviors or actions. One investor said:

> The outstanding leader creates meaning and purpose for people in the organization and ensures the values required to deliver that purpose are ever present. They ensure that the behaviors within the organization and the behaviors of employees when interacting with external stakeholders are consistent with the values that deliver that purpose.

These leaders influence less by imposing their values on others and more by helping others see that their own values may be accomplished by changing their behaviors (see Figure 5.2). They use information, behavior, and reinforcement to influence others.

INFORMATION

Leaders who execute through influence help others see what's in it for them to engage in a project or initiative. They avoid talking about how they themselves will benefit by the choices, instead focusing on how the choices will help others. Investors can observe how much leaders focus on the value to others by seeing how much they help others succeed. An investor who helps private firms go public often monitors how much of the public equity is shared with others as opposed to being retained by the individual leader. Leaders who share more equity are likely to influence others to be more committed. In day-to-day actions, investors can detect the extent to which leaders think about the impact of their actions on others, not just themselves.

BEHAVIOR

Leaders influence others by encouraging them to publicly behave as if they are committed to a project or organizational goal. When someone behaves as if they are committed, they will become more committed. Instead of the leader presenting a case for change, the leader influences others by having them present the case for change. To retain the most talented employees, wise leaders allow these most talented employees to present the firm's strategy to groups inside and outside the company, and they ask these pivotal employees to refer others to join the firm. The key to referral hiring is not just who is hired, but who gives the referral. Here again, investors can observe how much leaders share the spotlight and stage with others so that others become more committed.

REINFORCEMENT

Leaders who execute mobilize others by reinforcing their positive behavior. Sometimes this reinforcement comes through formal talent management or compensation processes (as discussed in Chapter 9), but it often comes through informal recognition and praise. One investor noticed that leaders in a target organization were frequently expressing employee appreciation through notes, words, and celebrations. The employees' behavior reflected the leaders' positive energy.

Possible indicators:

- *Do leaders see how strategies, choices, and projects will benefit others?*
- *Do leaders transfer personal ownership for success to others?*
- *Do leaders influence others through information, behavior, or reinforcement so that others get what they most want?*

Adapt Quickly

Leaders who are successful at execution adapt quickly; they do iterative learning. Execution of priorities, accountabilities, or decisions generally does not occur as planned—it has to be adapted.[10] In our work, my colleagues and I have found that leaders who sustained change were able to "meliorate." Leaders meliorate when they improve by learning from mistakes and failures and demonstrate resilience. Quick adaptation requires that leaders master the principles of learning: to experiment frequently, to reflect constantly, to become resilient, to face failure, to rejoice in success, and to improvise as needed. This means leaders act without final plans, but with good directions.

Leaders who execute can draw lessons from the past to solve current problems. In his classic Stanford commencement speech, Steve Jobs talked about learning calligraphy in college with no hope of a practical application, but then he used this insight in the typography of the first Mac. Strong executors define failure as opportunity and continue to learn: Abraham Lincoln lost far more elections than he won; Henry Ford declared bankruptcy before perfecting his production techniques; Walt Disney's first studio ("Laugh-O-Gram") went bankrupt; Milton Hershey failed in his early candy-making ventures.[11]

Leaders who adapt quickly are not afraid to take risks. Michael Jordan did not succeed just by winning, but by adapting: "I've missed more than 9000 shots in my career. I've lost almost 300 games. 26 times, I've been trusted to take the game winning shot and missed. I've failed over and over and over again in my life. And that is why I succeed."[12] Despite setbacks, leaders who execute don't dwell on the moment or feel sorry for themselves. They learn and move on.

One investor likes to ask how leaders respond to a setback and to see the insights they carry forward and the speed with which they rebound. Investors want to see if leaders are able to change more or less quickly than their competitors, to be ahead of or behind the industry cycle, and to become the fastest learners in their industry rather than the first movers.

Possible indicators:

- *Are leaders willing to try something even if not fully finalized?*
- *Do leaders learn from failures and incorporate insights into the next project?*
- *Do leaders focus on speed and moving quickly?*

Conclusion

A key investor said about this proficiency: "I would seek out people who have worked closely with the leader in the past and ask: 'Can this person execute?' This information is not the kind of thing that could end up in an annual report, but it's relatively easy detective work for a big investor." When my colleagues and I asked investors whether they would rather have leaders with 100% strategic proficiency and 50% execution proficiency or 50% strategy and 100% execution, they nearly all chose the 100% execution. Better to be able to get things done, even if not the perfect things in the beginning. Executors are the go-to people who build investor trust in what *will* (not what *can*) be done. Table 5.4 summarizes the indicators and possible follow-up measures.

Table 5.4. Indicators for Execution Proficiency

Leaders with execution proficiency . . .	Possible Indicators	How to Assess
Recognize and create a need for execution	Do leaders build a comprehensive rationale for how to make sure that strategies are executed?	Survey employee commitment to strategic change. Look for both overall score and variance around the score.
	Do leaders use analytics to build a business case for disciplined execution?	Interview leaders on their business case and determine thoroughness of their business case.
	Do leaders anticipate resistance to strategy execution and address the problem areas in advance?	
Focus on priorities	Do leaders know how to move from creating options to determining priorities?	Ask leaders how they go about setting priorities. Alternatively, ask them to divide points against choices.
	Do team members share a common set of priorities?	Interview team members about top priorities to see if there is a consensus.
	Do leaders spend time on the top priorities?	Examine leaders' calendars to see where they spend their time.
Ensure accountability	Do leaders have clear indicators about what they expect from others?	Ask leaders to report what they are personally accountable to do and deliver. Compare results from others.
	Do leaders follow up on what people promise they will deliver?	Who has the leader fired and why? Ask subordinates when they last had a follow-up session on goals.

(continued)

Table 5.4. (continued)

Leaders with execution proficiency . . .	*Possible Indicators*	*How to Assess*
Manage decision making and governance	Do leaders manage the content of decisions by breaking big projects into specific choices?	Ask leaders to share how they go about making decisions; see if they follow a protocol.
	Do leaders have a decision protocol for who is involved and how they go about getting decisions made?	Ask leaders how they have broken big projects into specific choices.
	Do leaders appropriately involve people in decision making?	Ask leaders the key decisions to be made and see if they have choices in each category.
		See if the leader follows the guidelines in the protocol in making decisions.

CHAPTER 6

People Proficiency

Investors Want Leaders Who Take Care of Their People

Organizations don't think or act; people do. When investors spot leaders who help people think and act in the right way, they gain insight on future organization performance.

By definition, leadership requires accomplishing tasks through others. Leaders matter because they guide followers who take direction or establish organization systems that institutionalize decisions. Some make the case for less focus on individual leaders and more on collective leadership able to ensure that people have both competence to do the right work and commitment to do it well.[1] But both individual leaders and collective leadership need to be proficient at managing people. Assessing leaders' ability to get the most out of their people is more art than science, but investors can look at some leadership traits that signal an ability to do so.

Most have firsthand experience of how leaders either inspire or hinder exceptional human performance. The risk of relying only on firsthand experience with leaders, however, is that it is too easy to assume that personal experience is sufficient to assess a leader's people proficiency. Social scientists have worked for decades to identify the traits of leaders who get the most out of their people, an achievement that goes by many names: motivation, job satisfaction, employee morale, engagement, involvement, social capital, well-being, and so forth.[2] While using different names and concepts, the essence of this work is that leaders with people proficiency make conscious choices to get the most out of employees, which leads to employees with higher personal well-being and productivity as well as to improved organizational performance and national competitiveness.[3]

The research on people in work organizations also tends to find a lack of employee engagement. This shows up in lower scores on engagement surveys (anywhere from 40% to 60% of workforce feeling unengaged) in the last decade and a higher percentage of employees who are seriously considering leaving their employer.[4] Some have proposed that leaders are now getting an average of about 60% to 70% of their people's actual capability.[5]

In addition to extensive academic and consulting firm studies on managing people, dozens of companies have done internal studies to show how leaders influence human potential. One of the most thorough of these internal studies is Google's Project Oxygen, which serves as an exemplar to confirm what companies are doing to guide how leaders can build people proficiency.

During Project Oxygen, Google uncovered eight basic tenets that its good managers followed:

1. *Be a coach.* Give specific and constructive feedback on performance, with a balance between the good and the bad. And have regular individual meetings with those you manage, identifying how employees can progress based on their strengths.

2. *Empowerment and being there.* Avoid micromanaging but be available for advice. Provide freedom and stretch assignments to help your group tackle big stuff.

3. *Be interested in your employees.* Show you care about people's success and well-being. Know what their whole lives consist of, not just their work lives. Focus on integrating new team members well.

4. *Be the grown-up.* Demonstrate what it means to be productive and results-oriented.

5. *Listen and communicate.* Listen to your team members and share information with them. Hold team meetings, and be clear about messages and the goals of the team. Don't hide the ball. Encourage open dialogue and listen to your employees' concerns and issues.

6. *Career development.* Help your people develop their careers.

7. *Strategy.* You have a clear vision and strategy for your team, and you keep the team focused on goals and strategy. The team is involved in setting the vision, the evolution of the vision, and the progression toward it.

8. *Technical chops.* With solid technical skills, you understand the specific challenges employees face and can advise based on knowledge. You are willing to pitch in.

Figure 6.1. Framework for Assessing Leaders' People Proficiency

Leaders have a direct impact on human performance at work as they interact with people, and they also have an indirect impact through the systems they create (the talent process discussed in Chapter 9). Some leaders are more natural people managers, but all leaders can learn people management skills—and investors can assess how well leaders exhibit these skills. Investors can observe, interview, and track the extent to which leaders demonstrate the six indicators of people proficiency sketched in Figure 6.1.

Have a Positive People Management Philosophy and Behavior Pattern

Beliefs drive attitudes, which then shape behavior. For over sixty years, leaders' philosophy about people has been tracked as an indicator of their positive beliefs, attitudes, and behaviors. Douglas McGregor labeled leaders' positive assumptions about people Theory Y and pointed out that when leaders turned these positive assumptions into actions, employees were more self-directed and able to realize their potential.[6] Theory Y assumptions evolved into ideas about *servant leadership,* wherein leaders manage people by serving them.[7] They also morphed into *authentic leadership,* wherein leaders act out of their values to lead their people.[8]

More recently, leadership authenticity work has shifted toward *positive leadership,* which draws on principles from positive psychology to define how leaders improve their management of their people through positive emotions.[9] In this work, leaders turn their own attitudes and beliefs into positive actions toward their employees. These actions might include showing compassion, expressing gratitude, being enthusiastic, finding higher meaning from work, focusing on strengths and what is right more than what is wrong (as with the 5:1 positive-to-negative ratio discussed in Chapter 3), showing forgiveness, and encouraging virtue.[10]

When leaders have Theory Y assumptions, servant leadership attitude, authentic style, and positive actions, they become people proficient and get the most out of their employees. They improve their own outlook as they pursue their happiness, while simultaneously focusing on others as they work to improve the well-being of the people who work with and for them. They become talent magnets and magnifiers who look for talent everywhere, who use people to their fullest potential, and who build on people's strengths to strengthen others.

When investors visit with leaders, they can interview them about their assumptions and explore specific ways in which they handle people issues. They can also interview employees, look at employee surveys, or go to social media sites (such as Glassdoor.com) to find out if employees perceive leaders as positive. They can also observe leaders as they interact with employees in formal and informal settings and listen for the ways that leaders describe employees in private and in public. They can also look at the way leaders have responded in personal or business crises. Over time, leaders' philosophy about people will emerge. When investors perceive a positive philosophy reinforced by actions, they can have more confidence in how effectively leaders get the most out of their people.

Possible indicators:

- *What is the ratio of positive to negative comments when the leaders talk about others? (Look for 5:1.)*
- *Do the leaders serve as talent magnets who attract and retain people who work for them?*
- *Do leaders generally have a positive (reinforcing, abundant) or a negative (belittling, deficit-creating) style?*

Know and Trust People

To be personally proficient, leaders need their people to trust them (as discussed in Chapter 3); to be people proficient, leaders need to trust their people. When leaders trust their people, they believe that employees have both competence (knowledge, skills, and ability) and commitment (willingness to work hard) to deliver results. Trust between leaders and employees significantly reduces the costs of controlling employee behavior—no need to observe employees or enforce rules to make sure employees do the right work. Trust enables change to occur more quickly because employees will accept leaders' directives. Trust also enables employees to develop their potential and feel more commitment to work.[11]

In interviews, investors talked about the importance of trusting the leaders, but also of detecting trust between leaders and employees. Here are some investor comments about trust-related issues:

- I want to see how leaders sincerely care about their employees. I want to see if they have the employees' interests in mind. How widely will they share the profits of the firm? How do they respond in a crisis?

- I believe employees will treat each other and customers the way they are treated. The old saying "Do unto others as you would have them do unto you" has relevance today. Leaders who treat others with respect see it amplified throughout the organization. Leaders have to be the example of respect and character that others follow.

- I see if leaders have checked their ego at the door. I want leaders to be confident and assured, but not arrogant and demeaning.

- I think leaders build trust one step at a time with consistency more than major acts. Trust comes from a pattern, not from a single event.

Trust is an underlying element of leaders' people proficiency, and investors care about it. One investor looks for signs of how well leaders know key people two or three levels below them. He believes that this personal touch at multiple levels demonstrates that leaders care and are aware of what is going on. He pointed to an example where two talented employees were about to leave the firm because of frustrations inside and opportunities outside. The leader, realizing this risk, was able to personally connect with these employees to keep them in the company—which the investor read as a sign of high people proficiency.

Investors pay attention not only to the existing level of trust but also to how leaders build trust so it can be sustained over time. Many have worked to identify the behaviors or approaches to building trust at work, at home, and in a marriage.[12] We have synthesized much of this work into six behaviors investors should look for in leaders:

- *Promote others.* Trusted leaders know others' dreams, hopes, and interests—and want people to see them become real.

- *Nurture fondness.* Trusted leaders see what is good in others and help them build on their strengths. They are appreciative and grateful and encourage people to express warmth to each other.

- *Be open.* Trusted leaders talk candidly about relationships; they share feelings and thoughts.

- *Connect with each other.* Trusted leaders spend time with employees; they encourage employees to turn to them and toward each other when things are difficult, to share successes, and to find and build on common values and interests.

- *Be willing to yield.* Trusted leaders listen and accept others' influence, and they know when to compromise.

- *Be reliable and dependable.* Trusted leaders are persistent and consistent; they have a long-term view, and they do what they say they will do.

Investors who are aware of these trust behaviors can keep an eye out to see if leaders consistently deliver them. Leaders who create trusting relationships will get more out of their people.

Possible indicators:

- *How long have key support staff or other key colleagues stayed with the leaders (average tenure)?*

- *Do the leaders know and have relationships with individuals two or three levels below them in the organization? Do they mingle easily with them?*

- *Do leaders behave in ways that engender trust?*

Attend to Their Personal Succession

The ultimate test of good parenting is how well children deal with the challenges they inevitably face. Good parents do many things to prepare their children for their future.[13] Likewise, leaders' long-term success comes from how they manage their personal succession. Weak leaders often surround themselves with weaker subordinates who, by contrast, make the leader feel and look better in the short term. But in the long term these weak leaders debilitate their organizations; when they leave, their replacements can't pick up the load. Strong leaders surround themselves with people who complement or exceed their skills. When they leave, these confident leaders can be assured that the organization will be viable for the future.

Succession planning includes building formal workforce planning systems (reviewed in Chapter 9) but also focuses on leaders' personal proficiency in being a succession leader. Succession leaders are aware of talented employees who may be best matched with roles for the future. Succession leaders know best what their replacements will need to know and do, recognizing things that have been out of reach. With these future challenges in mind, succession leaders establish criteria for their positions and identify selected candidates who might best meet these criteria. Succession leaders then give these potential candidates opportunities to shine, empowering them to solve problems and demonstrate their abilities. In particular, current leaders want to know if candidates can learn and grow (see the intellectual element of personal proficiency discussed in Chapter 3). Succession leaders participate in the selection of the next incumbent and then work to transfer leadership equity forward by shifting relationships with key stakeholders to the new leader. And at the transition, succession leaders have the wisdom and ability to let go and allow the new leader to lead.

Investors can monitor each phase of this personal succession process. When they meet with leaders, they can ask: Does the current leader . . .

- Recognize the importance of managing succession?
- Choose stronger or weaker subordinates?
- Consider the future requirements of the position when setting criteria for a successor?
- Identify high-potential candidates who might meet future criteria?
- Give those candidates projects and opportunities to demonstrate their skills?
- Help select the best candidate for the future position?
- Transfer leadership equity to the selected candidate?
- Let go and allow the new leader to lead?

By posing these questions and observing leaders' succession behaviors, investors can determine how well leaders attend to the next generation. When investors validate a leader's ability to find a successor qualified for future requirements, they can have more confidence in future earnings and organization success.

This succession process is particularly demanding for family-owned

Table 6.1. Leadership Shift from Command and Control to Coach and Communicate

An Effective Leader Will Say . . .		
Command and Control	→	*Coach and Communicate*
What I want you to do now is . . .	→	What do you think you should do?
You should have done . . .	→	Looking back, how would you do it differently?
That won't work; it will upset clients because . . .	→	What do you think the effect on clients will be if we do that?
You need to get this done!	→	How can I help you make this happen?
You must change!	→	How can I help you change?

or small to medium-sized enterprises where current leaders often have their personal identity tied to their role in the organization. For example, an investor deliberating a large investment in a leading firm in a growth industry visited with the current chairman and CEO, a man in his early seventies. The investor asked about leadership succession, and the CEO described how he had prepared his son to replace him. When the investor asked further questions, he observed that the current CEO was not willing to relinquish control and planned to remain chairman, with a strong voice about the company's future. The investor discounted leadership because he felt that the current leader could not let go and allow the next generation to take over. One investor said that in his experience about only 5% of entrepreneurs were able to make the shift and become professional managers.

Possible indicators:

- *How willing is the current leader to address succession issues?*
- *Do the current leaders work to define the future requirements for each position?*
- *Do the current leaders nurture possible candidates to prepare them for future responsibilities?*

Table 6.2. Coaching and Mentoring Complementarity

Time Frame	Coaching: Short Term	Mentoring: Long Term
Outcomes	Personal improvement on the job through behavior change or delivering results	Personal insights about career choices and organizational settings
Key Success Factor	Identification of specific behaviors that lead to results	Relationship based on shared values
Contribution	Problem solving	Personal advice
Metaphors	Sports	Parenting and teaching
Intervention	Directive intervention to correct weaknesses	Consensual intervention to nurture the person
Focus	Performance improvement	Individual growth
Conversations	About roles, responsibilities, and expectations	About wide-ranging areas of concern and hope

Coach and Mentor Others

As with many professions, business coaching began in dribs and drabs, with individuals here and there being and using coaches. In the last twenty years, as use of business coaches has mushroomed, the range of coaching expectations and services has exploded. *Coaching* has become a management buzzword.[14] Traditional command-and-control leadership styles have been replaced with a coach-and-communicate style, in which leaders focus on questions more than directives, manage a process and not just an outcome, and work to engage and not just enlist their employees. This evolution is captured in Table 6.1.

When leaders lead by coaching, good things follow. Coaching has two general outcomes: changing employee behavior and delivering desired results.[15] When leaders coach, employees accept more personal accountability for results; they learn and grow, and they are more productive.[16]

Coaching is not just an event where a leader sits down with an employee to review goals, lay out performance improvement, and discuss desired behavioral change. Coaching needs to become a mindset coupled with daily actions about how leaders interact with their people.

Mentoring complements coaching. Both coaches and mentors encourage reflection to help individuals grow and change based on trusting relationships between two parties. So how are they different? Table 6.2

highlights some differences that may help coaching and mentoring work to better complement each other.

Mentoring matters because, today as always, the wisdom of elders can help the next generation navigate personal and professional choices and help them succeed more quickly. With the pending exit of baby boomers from the workforce, the organizational baton is inevitably going to be handed on—and without mentoring and other development investments, the new leadership cohort will find itself needing to learn some difficult lessons in real time on the job.[17]

Investors who want to assess leaders' people proficiency should determine the extent to which they are both coaches and mentors.

Possible indicators:

- *Can the leaders each name two or three people they are intentionally coaching or mentoring? What specific activities have they worked on in the last thirty, sixty, ninety days?*
- *Do the leaders believe more in the command-and-control or the coach-and-communicate style?*
- *Do the leaders ask more questions or give more directives?*

Excel at Communication

Coach and *communicate* go hand in hand. In one company, it became a standing joke that the answer to every "How do we improve [our strategy, financial performance, customer service, supply chain, and whatever]?" question was "Communicate better." But "What is better communication?" is more than a *Jeopardy* answer to any management challenge. It is a leadership skill that builds people proficiency.

Good communication is the same in good or bad times. A healthy diet is a healthy diet whether you are heavy or skinny. Tough times put communication under a microscope, making it more critical rather than less. Here are some generic tips for effective communication that may help investors assess leaders' people proficiency.

- *Focus on why, not what or how.* When employees understand why something is happening, they are more likely to accept what has to be done. Employees need to be educated, not just informed.
- *Touch the heart as well as the mind.* Communicating tough decisions should not just be about what is rational, logical, and right—it needs to include how things feel. When leaders communicate with both feeling and logic, employees will know not only what to do

but also how it feels to do what is asked. Communication is not just stating intellectual facts, but also being sensitive to the emotional feelings associated with a message.

- *Listen and empathize.* Leaders share the general human tendency to see the world through their own eyes, but they need to rise above this. When they communicate, it is important that they pay attention to not only what is said but also how it is said—and how others receive what is said. Since value is defined by the receiver, the sender needs to be very aware of how others are receiving the messages.

- *Communicate completely.* Language works to share messages, but language isn't enough on its own. You also need to employ graphics, direct experiences, and personal examples. No single communication mechanism works all the time. In addition, complete communication means sharing good news and bad, without hiding from or overemphasizing either.

- *Keep the message simple and redundant.* In increasingly complex organizational settings dealing with an onslaught of information, it is important to focus on the key points. Essentialism matters. Good communicators see patterns, look for themes, and highlight things the audience will remember and act upon.

Investors can monitor the quality of leaders' communication both with firsthand experience as they observe and interact with leaders and also with access to leaders' communication patterns as derived from social media, surveys, and archived information (videos, annual reports, public speeches). Effective communication entails being able to hold substantive conversations that give employees and investors confidence that the leader knows what to do and how to do it; style (extroverted or introverted, showy or reserved, assertive or passive, confident or humble) is secondary, as any style can be used effectively.

Possible indicators:

- *Do the leaders connect personally and adapt their message to their audience?*

- *Do the leaders capture their audience's attention and inspire people to take action?*

- *Do the leaders have credibility as communicators because of their content and process of communicating?*

Understand and Use Teams

Examples of the value of teamwork come from multiple settings. In the Academy Awards, about 20% of the time the movie that receives Best Picture also features a performance that receives the Best Actor or Actress award. In contrast, 70% of the time the Best Director is the director of the movie that wins Best Picture. Individual talent matters less than the leader who brings the talent into an effective ensemble cast or team. In the NBA, the team with the top scorer wins the NBA championship only about 15% of the time (and only 5% for teams that didn't include Michael Jordan). And when Michael Jordan led the league in scoring and his team did not win the NBA championship (four times), he averaged 34.55 points per game. In the six years that he led the league in scoring and won the championship, he averaged 30.5 points per game.[18] Teamwork wins. Individuals may be champions, but teamwork builds championships.

Like movies and basketball, business today requires teamwork. In a world where knowledge (as measured by information on the Internet) doubles every four years, where the pace of change has increasingly increased, and where global complexity changes the rules of competition, no isolated individual has the ability to respond effectively. An increasing amount of work is being accomplished through all sorts of teams—formal work groups, matrix structures, task forces, joint ventures or partnerships, staff groups, committee assignments, project teams, communities of practice, clusters, networks, you name it. Some have said that teamwork is the true and sustainable source of competitive advantage today.[19] The "war for talent" needs to be supplemented with a focus on victory through organization. To have sustainable organizations in a world of change and complexity, individual abilities must be combined into organization capabilities. People proficiency requires teamwork.

Many have documented characteristics of high-performing teams.[20] My colleagues and I have distilled this work into four general processes:

- *Purpose:* People have a clear mutual understanding of why they are meeting, what they need to accomplish, and how they define success.

- *Governance:* People have ways to handle who is on the team, what skills members bring and what roles they play, how decisions are made, how time is managed, and how information is shared.

- *Relationships:* People care for one another and manage conflict constructively so they can work together smoothly.

Table 6.3. High-Performing Team Audit

	Score
Purpose: Are We Focused?	*(1 to 5)*

1. The team goal outweighs my personal goals.

2. I understand my team's purpose and the results we're expected to achieve.

3. I understand the tasks we need to finish to get the results expected of us.

4. I understand why our team is important and necessary.

5. I am excited about the goals of the team and feel like I want to give my all so we can succeed.

Governance: Are We Clear?

6. I understand my role.

7. I understand the role of each member of my team.

8. I understand what's expected of me on the team.

9. I understand what will happen if expectations are/aren't met.

10. We have a clear plan that includes time lines, specifications, and budgets.

11. I know what decisions I can make and who I need to involve or consult.

12. We have a clear decision about how decisions are made.

(continued)

- *Learning:* People continually assimilate information and improve on how they are doing.

Leaders who lead through teams make the whole group more than the sum of the individual participants. They empower others to act, creating a unit that is greater than the individual leader. Managed well, teams can develop sustained financial performance and individual well-being.

One investor tries to observe leaders working with their teams to see how they set a shared direction, involve others, listen, manage differences, and encourage continuous learning. This investor believes that the microcosm of a leader and team sets a tone for the rest of the organization, how other leaders manage their teams, and how the organization approaches work.

Another investor uses a team audit to determine how well teams work. This audit of twenty simple questions asks team members their views on the four processes listed in this section. (See Table 6.3.)

Table 6.3. (continued)

Relationships: Are We Connected?	Score (1 to 5)
13. When things get tough, I feel comfortable approaching other team members for help.	
14. We care for each other as team members.	
15. Disagreement is voiced in our meetings rather than in our hallways.	
16. We have a process for managing disagreements that allows disputes to be resolved productively.	

Learning: Are We Adaptive?	
17. We discuss key learnings from completed projects and milestones.	
18. We try new models and approaches to problems.	
19. We attend trainings and take learning assessments as a team.	
20. We acknowledge and learn from our failures.	

Howard Schultz, the founder and CEO of Starbucks, said, "To become a great leader, you must develop a great team or, one might say, a well-oiled machine."[21] Investors can look for signs of smooth lubrication in the firms they are considering.

Possible indicators:

- *Do the leaders appreciate the multiplication factor and importance of teamwork?*
- *Do the leaders consistently and appropriately use teams to accomplish work?*
- *Do the leaders audit team processes to make sure each team is working well?*

Conclusion

Much of the quality of leadership comes from people proficiency—and has done so from the birth of human society. These days we have a huge range of technological options for connecting with one another, yet the challenges of getting along have not diminished. In fact, the anonymity of e-mail, tweets, web-based bulletin boards, and blogs often reduces the personal touch so central to meaningful relationships. Globalization and equal hiring initiatives mean more and more of us work with people of different cultures, backgrounds, orientations, races, and life stages. This increased complexity increases the amount of work required to manage people to bring products to fruition or provide the range of services expected, but also increases innovation, responsiveness to markets, and ability to be flexible. Table 6.4 summarizes the possible indicators investors can use to audit the six skills for people proficiency. As investors audit these skills, they will develop more confidence in the current leadership of the organization—and its next generation.

Table 6.4. Indicators for People Proficiency

Leaders with people proficiency ...	Possible Indicators	How to Assess
Have a positive people philosophy and behavior	What is the ratio of positive to negative comments when the leaders talk about others? (Look for 5:1.) Do the leaders serve as talent magnets who attract and retain people who work for them? Do leaders generally have a positive (reinforcing, abundant) or a negative (belittling, deficit-creating) style?	Interview leaders and their associates about how they treat people; look specifically at critical incidents. Look at employee surveys, social media sites, and reputations.
Know and trust people	How long have key support staff or other key colleagues stayed with the leaders (average tenure)? Do the leaders know and have relationships with individuals two or three levels below them in the organization? Do they mingle easily with them? Do leaders behave in ways that engender trust?	Look at time-in-position records for key roles to see if those who report to leaders are retained. Observe the leaders in social settings (lunchrooms, town hall meetings). Interview subordinates about how they perceive the leader.

(continued)

Table 6.4. (continued)

Leaders with people proficiency . . .	Possible Indicators	How to Assess
Attend to their personal succession	How willing is the current leader to address succession issues?	See if leaders can name succession candidates and discuss strengths and weaknesses of each.
	Do the current leaders work to define the future requirements for each position?	Interview leaders to determine knowledge of succession process.
	Do the current leaders nurture possible candidates to prepare them for future responsibilities?	
Coach and mentor others	Can the leaders each name two or three people they are intentionally coaching or mentoring? What specific activities have they worked on in the last thirty, sixty, ninety days?	Ask leaders who they are coaching and interview those they name.
	Do the leaders believe more in the command-and-control or the coach-and-communicate style?	Look at leaders' 360-degree feedback for questions related to coaching style.
	Do the leaders ask more questions or give more directives?	
Excel at communication	Do the leaders connect personally and adapt their message to their audience?	Observe leaders in communication forums.
	Do the leaders capture their audience's attention and inspire people to take action?	Find out how leaders communicate in person, online, in videos, or by other means.
	Do the leaders have credibility as communicators because of their content and process of communicating?	Interview or survey employees for leaders' ability to communicate.
Understand and use teams	Do the leaders appreciate the multiplication factor and importance of teamwork?	Observe leaders directing their own team.
	Do the leaders consistently and appropriately use teams to accomplish work?	Review reports of whatever team audits leaders might have done.
	Do the leaders audit team processes to make sure each team is working well?	

CHAPTER 7

Leadership Brand Proficiency

Investors Want Leaders Who Fit the Requirements of the Situation

Adapting behavior to situations should come naturally. It's the rule in all sorts of activities, after all. We don't wear boots to a beach or go barefoot on a mountain hike; we don't boo and hiss in church or behave with sober reverence at sporting events; we don't eat fast food with cutlery or haute cuisine with our fingers. Effortless as all this is, leadership is another matter. Because it is all too easy to fall into a pattern in which one form of leadership always takes precedence, investors can gain a substantial advantage by assessing whether leaders have the proficiency to fit their skills to their particular business situation.

Leaders bring their own biases to their role. Research on the nature-nurture debate has shown that leaders' predispositions account for about half of how they behave, while the other half can be learned.[1] The importance of innate leader behavior (nature) implies that leaders are more successful when their natural skills match the requirements of their position, which implies recruiting and placement of leaders into the right job. The importance of learned leader behavior (nurture) suggests that leaders consciously adapt to their circumstances, which suggests the value of helping leaders develop and grow into their position. Matching the leader to the situation requires that investors recognize the business setting in which leaders operate and find a fit between the leaders and this setting.

Situational or contingency models of leadership have captured a number of variables that investors might consider in assessing leaders' fit for the situation. These five stand out:

Figure 7.1. Framework for Assessing Leaders' Brand Proficiency

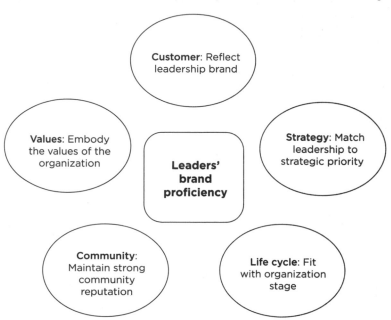

- *Customer:* Do leaders' personal behaviors represent the brand that the firm is trying to create with customers?
- *Strategy:* Do leaders have the knowledge and skills to deliver the unique strategy of their organization?
- *Life cycle:* Do leaders have the skills to manage an organization of the size and age of the one in question?
- *Community:* Do leaders have the ability to manage the community setting in which the organization operates?
- *Values:* Do leaders' personal values reflect the organization's values statements?

Not all leaders will be excellent in all situations. For example, someone who is superb at customer service may not be as good at managing cost; someone who is gifted at creating a business may not be as talented at the sort of management required to run the business over time; someone who has worked for decades in one country setting may not adapt successfully to the community norms in another country. The contingencies in this chapter enable investors to assess the fit between leaders and their situation.

Customer Fit

Leadership expectations generally show up in competency models. In 1954, former Colonel John Flanagan published research on requirements for successful military pilots based on how they responded to critical incidents.[2] This early work preceded the competency movement of the 1970s and 1980s, in which Dave McClelland and his colleagues worked to identify key competencies of successful leaders.[3] Since then, leadership competencies have become the recipe for defining effective leadership. Competency models have evolved to become more firm-specific and less generic, to focus on the future instead of the past, to be developed by line managers—not just human resource professionals or consultants—and to be tailored to the specific leader role and not overall leadership. But even with this evolution, most competency models continue a version of the critical incident technique whereby desired competencies are determined by how leaders behave on key tasks.

Investors want to define not just how leaders behave but also the impact of that behavior on key firm outcomes. In our focus on results-based leaders, my colleagues and I encouraged leaders to develop competencies "so that . . ." The "so that . . ." query shifted the focus of leadership from attributes (such as *good communicator*) to the outcome of the communication (*so that customers understand our unique value*).[4] In our research on top companies for leaders, more than 75% of 450 global companies had a leadership competency model.[5] But only about 20% of these companies based their leadership competencies on the expectations of customers. We found that those we deem top companies for leadership create competency models that include customer expectations, and they are two to three times more likely than other companies to include customer perspectives in their development curriculum. We have advocated for an outside-in view for defining leadership, talent, and capability and for designing HR practices.[6] For example, we would define the leading athletes for a sports team as the ones who cause paying fans to attend the games.[7] An outside-in view of competencies creates a link between customer expectations and leader behavior.

Great companies build trust by managing expectations with customers. Customer expectations show up in firm tag lines, product or marketing initiatives, advertising, and social media communications. These external identity messages are often woven around a firm brand, or what the firm wants to be known for by targeted customers.[8] A brand began as a way for people to mark their products (roving animals with literal brands, watermarks on documents, trademarks on merchandise and

Figure 7.2. Evolution of Brand Logic from Outside to Inside

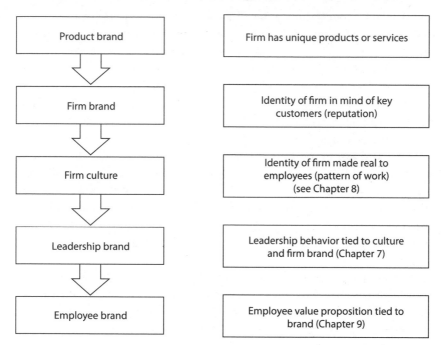

packaging), but the concept has broadened to refer to promises, expectations, and identities. We believe that the logic of brand has evolved from products that customers purchase to employee connections to their firm, as shown in Figure 7.2. Customers use products and experience firm brand; then employees inside the firm experience the firm culture through leadership behaviors and the employee value proposition.[9]

Investors assessing leadership-customer fit can assess the overlap between a firm's brand and its leadership brand. This leadership-customer assessment starts by examining the messages the firm is sending to customers (through marketing, advertising, social media, and other tools) to discern the external promises and expectations embedded there—that is, its brand. Investors can then compare this brand to the target firm's leadership competency model.

The overlap will capture the extent to which leaders inside the firm are expected to act in accord with promises made to customers. As a rule of thumb, the firm brand and leadership behaviors implied by the competency model should overlap at least 65% to 75%, or the firm risks making customer promises that leaders are not required to keep.

Table 7.1. Branded Leadership

Firm	Firm Identity: This Firm Is Known for . . .	Leadership Identity and Competencies: Leaders at This Firm Are Known for Their Ability to . . .
Walmart	Everyday low prices	Manage costs efficiently; get things done on time
Lexus	Relentless pursuit of perfection	Manage quality processes (lean manufacturing and design, Six Sigma); do continuous improvement
P&G	Managing brands	Define and grow brands in the marketplace; know customer trends; ensure product innovation
McKinsey	Analytical, smart strategists	Ensure leaders think strategically with very high analytical skills; organize people into teams to solve client problems
Apple	Innovation and design	Create new products and services outside the industry norms; learn to experiment
Amazon	Deliver anything anywhere	Manage logistics in a disciplined way; constantly look for cost efficiencies; focus on customer service
Facebook	Helping you connect and share with the people in your life	Work together though collaboration to get work done; encourage personal relationships
Infosys	Powered by intellect, driven by values	Solve technical problems with analytical tools; demonstrate ability to live a strong moral code

In addition, investors can then compare the overlap of the firm brand with the content of senior leadership training programs and the performance management standards for senior leaders. Again, when training programs and performance standards match customer expectations, investors can have more confidence that leaders' behaviors will consistently deliver on promises to customers.

Far too often, however, it turns out that firm brand statements were crafted by customer-focused professionals (marketing, sales, public affairs), while leadership competency models and programs were drafted by internally focused HR professionals. Where such work has been separate, investors need to be particularly concerned to see whether leaders focus on the issues customers care most about.

Following this logic, investors would work to make sure that firm identity and leadership identity overlap. Table 7.1 gives some examples of what this looks like in practice.

When investors determine that customer promises become leadership behaviors, they can have higher confidence in leadership.

Possible indicators:

- *How much overlap is there between firm brand as promised to customers and the leadership competency model used for the organization?*

- *How much overlap is there between firm brand as promised to customers and investments in leadership training and performance standards?*

- *Are customer promises and leadership behaviors created jointly or separately?*

Strategic Fit

In one of our executive programs, my colleagues and I asked participants to post their leadership competency models. We then took off the company names and played "match the company to the competency model." Most could not begin to match other companies' models to their names, and a few were even iffy on their own. The problem was that the models were too bland; they were generic statements of what any effective leader should know and do anywhere, and thus useless to investors.

Investors do not want generic results or competencies. To get differentiated results, they should expect differentiated leadership competencies. The competency model should reflect the ways that leaders will position themselves to win in their own marketplace. Leaders should give investors confidence that they have the precise competencies to deliver on their firm's strategy.

Organizations find unique ways to position themselves to win through the strategies they create. A company's strategy can be defined on two dimensions: first, the focus of growth, which describes how the company will increase revenue; second, differentiation, which explains why customers buy from the company and not from its competitors. Growth strategies can be sorted into five categories:

- *Product or service innovation:* Finding more customers (Kellogg's, Lego)

- *Customer share:* Meeting a larger share of customer needs (Nike, Disney)

- *Technology:* Creating more applications or solutions (3M, Qualcomm)

- *Production:* Reducing unit costs (Ryanair, Southwest Airlines)

Table 7.2. Strategic Options Matrix

		Differentiation: Why Do Customers Buy from Us?				
		Low Price	Quality	Speed	Service	Innovation
	Product or Service	1	2	3	4	5
Growth:	Customer Share	6	7	8	9	10
What Is Our	Technology	11	12	13	14	15
Strategy for						
Growth?	Production	16	17	18	19	20
	Distribution	21	22	23	24	25

Note: Numbers in the cells are simply assigned for identification of combinations.

- *Distribution:* Putting more things through a channel (Tesco, Amazon)

Customer buying criteria can also be classified into five categories:

- *Low price:* Buy based on the lowest price (EasyJet, Walmart)
- *Quality:* Buy based on superior performance (Rolex, Audi)
- *Speed:* Buy based on operational or delivery speed or responsiveness (Samsung, Amazon)
- *Service:* Buy based on customer service (American Express, Four Seasons)
- *Innovation:* Buy based on meeting needs in new ways (Intel, Apple)

These two dimensions may be combined to create a strategic options matrix that lays out choices for investors, as shown in Table 7.2.

Investors should assess the extent to which a strategic consensus exists among leadership teams. We have assessed strategic consensus either by asking members of the leadership team to select the top three to five cells for an organization's strategy or by dividing 100 points across the strategic options matrix. Investors should see a high level of leadership agreement on the strategic focus.

With this strategic consensus, investors can determine if leaders have the skills required for the different cells in the strategic options matrix. For example, leaders in the low price, production cell (Cell 16) would be expected to have more experience and spend more time managing costs than innovating. Investors can examine the extent to which leadership development activities such as competency models, hiring, training, promotions, and performance reviews match with the skills required for the strategic option.

Again, no leader will be equally effective in every situation. When investors determine that leaders have the specific mix of skills for the target organization's strategy, the firm's value is enhanced in their eyes.

Possible indicators:

- *Does the leadership have a consensus about the strategic priorities in the strategic options matrix?*
- *Do leadership investment activities align with the requirements of the strategic option?*

Life Cycle Fit

Just as most people can appreciate strategic fit, life cycle fit applies at a personal level. As they pass from infancy to childhood to adolescence to young adulthood to maturity and beyond, people face different challenges, opportunities, and requirements.[10] Likewise, organizations go through evolutionary stages, from the nub of an idea to a professionally managed enterprise. A number of authors have described anywhere from four to ten stages of organizational evolution and the subsequent leadership challenges associated with each stage.[11] Perhaps the best illustration comes from the classic work by Paul Hersey and Ken Blanchard, who advocate for situational leadership depending on the maturity of the team.[12] They suggest four levels of team maturity, each requiring a different leadership skill set. New teams require *telling* leaders, who set direction; moderately mature teams require *selling*, then *participating* leaders who increasingly involve members in team business; and mature organizations require *delegating* leaders, who allow others to do the work. The effectiveness of each type of leadership depends on the maturity of the organization.

In our investor focus groups, we ran into an investor who felt that the life cycle of the organization dramatically affected how he assessed leadership. He mapped his life cycle–leadership fit process using the logic in Table 7.3. When he considered investing in a firm, he would assess which of the six evolution stages was the best match; then he would determine the implications for organization and leadership. He wanted to make sure that the leaders had the skills suited to that evolutionary stage.

Life cycle–leadership fit is especially helpful for angel investors, venture capitalists, or start-up private equity funds. In these settings, investors should be aware of the critical importance of leaders' having entrepreneurial talents that enable them to create innovative products and services. Investors should also be aware that as these companies evolve, many entrepreneurial leaders will not have the bandwidth to bring the organization through maturity challenges. Knowing when and how to change leadership becomes almost as important as spotting the right leadership in the first place.

Possible indicators:

- *Are leaders aware of the unique challenges of their organization stage?*
- *Do leaders have the ability to evolve their leadership from one organization stage to the next?*
- *Are leaders consciously moving their organization through the current stage and into the next?*

Community Fit

At a personal level, most of us appreciate traveling outside our home country—but we at least privately admit to feeling somewhat uneasy because of the local customs and less confident of our ability to react to new situations. Similarly, leaders' ability to lead is affected by their ability to adapt to the communities where they live and work. Hofstede and his colleagues have done exceptional work describing how country norms differ along five dimensions:[13]

- *Power distance:* Social inequality, including the relationship with authority.
- *Individualism-collectivism:* The relationship between the individual and the group.
- *Masculinity-femininity:* The social (emotional) implications of having been born as a boy or a girl.
- *Uncertainty avoidance:* Ways of dealing with uncertainty, relating to the control of aggression and the expression of emotions.
- *Time:* Ways of thinking about long- versus short-term orientation.

Robert House of the Wharton School of Business did a complementary study called Global Leadership and Organizational Behavior Effectiveness (GLOBE). He and his colleagues looked at cultural differences for sixty-two countries and leadership dimensions for twenty-four countries.[14] Countries differ on these cultural dimensions. Effective leaders are not only sensitive to country differences but adapt their behavior accordingly.

Table 7.3. Organizational Evolution: Stages and Leadership

	Organization Evolution Stage		
Issue	*Stage 1* *Idea*	*Stage 2* *Loose federation*	*Stage 3* *Proof of concept*
Definition	An individual has an idea.	The idea is shared by others.	The idea turns into products or services.
Task	Invest concept	Share and shape concept	Market concept
Challenges	Passion, creativity · Do I care about this idea (willing to pay a price)? · Why does this matter to me?	Share passion with others · Who else appreciates what interests me? · How broadly shared is our concern? · Who has what skills to move this forward?	Offer products/services · How do we market our ideas to early adopters?
Funding	Personal money	Seed money	Angel investor
Leader metaphor	Player	Connector	Marketer
Structure	Informal, no need	Team	Process orientation
Key leader skills	Ability to articulate vision to others; ability to commercialize ideas into clients and money; salesmanship	Adapt and build on ideas of others; identify and hire initial talent to commercialize ideas	Ensure product/service can be delivered efficiently; enough consistency in approach to scale

Organization Evolution Stage

Stage 4	Stage 5	Stage 6
Early formal processes	Mature	Professional/sustainable
The ideas turn into processes and disciplines.	The concepts outlive the founders.	Organization creates its own identity over time.
Reproduce concept	Market expansion; viable product	Dominate or define a niche
Create formal processes · *Customers:* Who are our customers? What do they want? How do we deliver to them? · *Financing:* How do we fund it? · *People:* What roles do we need? Who plays them? · *Systems:* What systems do we need?	Organization outlives founders · Who will replace the founder? · What skills will we need?	Organization survives over time · What is the organization identity (DNA, culture) we hope to establish over time?
Early round	Mezzanine financing	Public markets
Designer	Professional manager	Concierge
Functions and roles begin	Product lines, customer oriented	Multidivisional organization
Systems thinking; ability to learn from mistakes and continue to adapt; build more formal organization design	Willingness and time to groom a successor; relationship equity transferred to key stakeholders	Pay attention to next generation of leaders; rigorously invest in innovation "S" curve to stay relevant

In our study of Asian leadership, my colleagues and I asked a targeted roundtable of Asian executives and global thought leaders to weight the relative impact of country distinctiveness on leadership requirements.[15] While "attention to customer" received more points (out of 100), "country awareness" received between 15% and 20% of the relevant votes.[16] Country flavoring exists. Just as the same basic food groups are consumed everywhere, but the food is flavored differently in different countries, the basic leadership roles must adapt to a country context.

In addition to country, the community context for leaders today resides in social media. A number of the investors examined leaders' social media presence. This meant accessing Facebook, YouTube, Dailymotion, Pinterest, and the like to find out what leaders were posting about themselves. While these investors acknowledge the distinction between private conduct and public scrutiny, they reasoned that senior leaders were increasingly public figures and that their personal social media sites were likely to be accessed by those interested in the firm.

Other investors are also starting to use social media as a way to evaluate the social reputation of leaders. For example, Glassdoor.com offers anonymous ratings of leaders and company cultures. While the data may be biased or skewed, investors have found it to be a useful signal about how the leaders may be perceived. Social media analytics (using the cloud and big data) can also serve as tools for tracking positive or negative content analysis about leaders.

Another community factor comes from the leaders' connection to trade associations. One investor looks at how much a target firm's leaders are invested in industry trade associations. He felt that increased participation in trade associations indicated thought leadership and a greater chance to shape industry standards. In addition, investors can look at how leaders participate in community events by volunteering, serving, or contributing to the community where they live.

One thoughtful investor explored how leaders thought about their community and who they served as a company. He found that most leaders had a high level of interest in and awareness of how their actions would impact customers, suppliers, regulators, and regulatory agencies. But he was most interested in how leaders perceived the impact of their actions on their progeny. He found that the most effective community leaders were committed to making wise decisions and investments so that their grandchildren would be able to live and work in a better community. He felt that these forward-thinking and community-focused leaders were more likely to build strength for the future.

The community contingencies of country, industry associations, social media, and progeny give investors a view of the adaptability, presence, and breadth of leaders.

Possible indicators:

- *Do leaders adapt their styles to work in different country cultures?*
- *What ratings of the leader appear in social media such as Glassdoor.com?*
- *Do leaders work to become part of a broader community network?*

Values Fit

As human beings, we are drawn to people who share our values. When leaders embody the values of their organization, they are more likely to be followed by employees and endorsed by investors. In our book *Why of Work*, we found that when leaders play the role of meaning makers, they help others find their personal value from working with the company—which in turn makes money for the company.[17]

Investors value values.[18] As discussed in Chapter 3 on personal proficiency, leaders' values guide behavior, ensure continuity, and build trust. But even more, investors can assess the congruence between leaders' personal values and the organizations' espoused values. In the last twenty years, almost every organization has published some version of a values statement that declares its core beliefs, ideals, and code of conduct. These creeds espouse a philosophy, but until they show up in leadership behaviors, they are not viable. When leaders do not live the values, the statement is hypocrisy. When a firm claims to value innovation but the leader discourages risk taking; when a firm claims to value openness and transparency but the leader hoards information; when the firm claims to value collaboration but the leader acts autonomously—investors rightly discount leadership. One investor told us that he wishes he could watch a leader in dozens of separate situations to see how the leader demonstrated or repudiated the firm's values.

Investors can also assess the value of values by seeing how well leaders build meaning and purpose into work settings.[19] Purpose-driven organizations outperform organizations with no purpose.[20] When employees believe that their organization has a strong sense of purpose, which comes from a distinct brand and shared values that outsiders can observe, then these organizations have stronger financial performance.[21] Purpose enables employees to be meaningfully engaged; it drives growth and inspires innovation. When leaders help employees find meaning, they also help make money.

Investors auditing values fit should see if the leaders' personal values match the espoused values of the organization. They can see how often the leaders talk about values, how their calendar reflects their personal values and those of the organization, and how they make decisions based on values. One investor had a simple test about leaders' commitment to values; he simply asked the leaders he interviewed to share the firm's values (could they repeat them from memory?), then to share a personal experience of a time they demonstrated the values in their personal behavior or a business decision in the last month. He found that most leaders could pass this value test, but some struggled, which gave him pause on that investment.

Values questions often show up on employee engagement surveys, either directly or indirectly, and they become embodied in the physical layout of the leaders' work space. For example, closed office doors communicate information concealment, colors convey attitude, and personalization of office space signals autonomy. (Physical setting is further discussed in Chapter 12.)

Possible indicators:

- *What percentage of the leadership team can repeat the values of the company (what the company stands for) without help?*
- *What percentage of the leadership team can point to a specific incident or decision affected by values in the last thirty days?*
- *How do employees rate the extent to which leaders are "meaning makers" as they fulfill their role?*

Conclusion

What individual proficiencies make leaders effective? It depends. But investors who want to fully assess the quality of leadership to mitigate their investment risk can go behind the superficial "it depends" to identify specific contingencies that should influence leadership behavior. Table 7.4 sets out the potential indicators I've identified for this area and sketches approaches for assessing them. Some of leadership fit means matching leaders' predispositions to key positions (nature) and some means helping leaders develop their skills as required by the position (nurture).

Table 7.4. Indicators for Differentiated Leaders

Leaders adapt according to	Possible Indicators	How to Assess
Customers: Reflect leadership brand	How much overlap is there between firm brand as promised to customers and the leadership competency model used for the organization?	Examine firm brand and compare with leadership competencies, senior leader training content, and performance standards.
	How much overlap is there between firm brand as promised to customers and investments in leadership training and performance standards?	Audit who creates the firm brand and leadership competence and development tools.
	Are customer promises and leadership behaviors created jointly or separately?	
Strategy: Match to strategic priority	Does the leadership have a consensus about the strategic priorities in the strategic options matrix?	Interview or survey key executives about strategic options.
	Do leadership investment activities align with the requirements of the strategic option?	Examine the leadership competency model and investment activities for their content.
Life cycle: Fit with organization stage	Are leaders aware of the unique challenges of their organization stage?	Interview leaders about the unique challenges of their organization in this evolutionary stage.
	Do leaders have the ability to evolve their leadership from one organization stage to the next?	Identify competitors in this stage and compare leaders.
	Are leaders consciously moving their organization through the current stage and into the next?	Assess leaders' ability to grow to next stage.
Community: Maintain strong community reputation	Do leaders adapt their styles to work in different country cultures?	Do content analysis (big data analytics) of leaders and firms.
	What ratings of the leader appear in social media such as Glassdoor.com?	Examine the community involvement of leaders and their social network presence.
	Do leaders work to become part of a broader community network?	

(continued)

Table 7.4. (continued)

Leaders adapt according to	*Possible Indicators*	*How to Assess*
Values: Embody the values of the organization	What percentage of the leadership team can repeat the values of the company (what the company stands for) without help? What percentage of the leadership team can point to a specific incident or decision affected by values in the last thirty days? How do employees rate the extent to which leaders are "meaning makers" as they fulfill their role?	Interview members of the leadership team and keep track of how many can repeat the company values statement and can describe an incident where their action was affected by values. Review employee surveys or social media commentary on leaders' ability to make work meaningful and to personally act consistently with firm values.

PART THREE

The Organization Elements of the Leadership Capital Index

While it is tempting and common for investors to look primarily at the personal characteristics of leaders discussed in Part 2, investors can also look at organization or human capital processes in the organization. These organization processes define the organization and how it operates. As discussed in Chapter 2, we can identify five elements of organization that characterize effective leadership. For each of these elements, I will present key dimensions and indicators that may be tracked to assess leadership.

The assessments from this part will help investors and others determine if leaders have the ability to build these organization processes that create effective leadership. The logic will follow the figure on the next page, with a chapter on each element.

Organization Elements

Cultural capability:
Create an effective
culture
(Chapter 8)

Work processes:
Organize to cope
with increasing change
(Chapter 12)

**Organization:
Human capital
systems**

Talent management:
Manage the flow of
people
(Chapter 9)

Information processes:
Use information
for impact
(Chapter 11)

**Performance
accountability:**
Reinforce desirable
behavior
(Chapter 10)

CHAPTER 8

Cultural Capability

Investors Want Organizations with Effective Cultures

As Peter Drucker is credited with saying, "Culture eats strategy for lunch."[1] It is easier to craft a new strategy than to renew a culture—and hard as personal habits are to change, organization cultures are worse. My colleagues and I recently worked with a company that had competed through product innovation for decades but wanted to evolve its strategy to customer intimacy. Leaders could articulate this pivot, talk about why it mattered, define desired outcomes in financial and customer terms, and recommend the actions to make it happen. But when they started doing so, nothing seemed to change; they ran into deep-rooted work patterns and assumptions that were difficult to uncover and more difficult to adjust.

Personal experience affirms the impact of culture. When you visit a restaurant, hotel, store, or other establishment, you encounter an ambiance that shapes your shopping experience. This feeling is not just a response to the product or service—it is a matter of how it feels to do business with the organization. The Nordstrom sense of service increases revenue per customer visit; the Disney theme parks' commitment to family entertainment makes them one of the top tourist destinations; the Apple Stores' technology-enabled service helps them maintain double the sales per square foot of the rest of its industry; and so forth. As consumers, all of us can quickly sense a culture, and it impacts our reaction to a company.

Research has confirmed that culture helps companies deliver their financial goals, shape customer experiences, deliver consistent team performance, and increase employee productivity.[2] The evidence for operational patterns' impact on business success is compelling.[3]

- From 1997 to 2013, the stock return of Fortune 100 Best Companies to Work For (a surrogate for culture) averaged 11.8%, compared with 6.4% for Russell 3000 index companies and 6% for those on the S&P 500 index.

- A study of a hundred German companies in ten industries found that companies rated higher on employee focus earned a greater total shareholder return than those that did not.

- A study of 129 Korean firms found that those rated higher on organizational commitment to their employees earned a higher return on assets.

- Companies that emphasize share of heart (a consumer behavior corollary to "share of market") through emotional, experiential, and social value (called "firms of endearment," another surrogate for culture) have experienced a total shareholder return between 1995 and 2012 of 636% (annualized 40%) versus 204% (annualized 7%) for the average S&P 500.[4]

- It is not a surprise that nearly 60% of 1,440 respondents to a 2011 McKinsey survey of senior business leaders say that building organizational capabilities is a top-three priority for their companies.

Clearly, culture issues affect firm performance. While consumers experience culture and organization scholars validate its impact, it has been very difficult to describe just how leaders define and shape a culture—and thus even more difficult for investors to audit a culture. In our interviews, a number of investors essentially said that culture matters, but it is so difficult to define and measure that they look past it and assess talent, performance, information, and work process instead (the topics discussed in Chapters 9 through 12).

One of the challenges investors face in assessing culture is finding a simple but robust logic for defining and recognizing it. The possibilities are rich to the point of embarrassment, as the following list of the related concepts, terms, and prescriptions makes all too clear (or unclear, as the case may be):

- *Resources.*[5] Organizations consist of a set of resources that they have to manage to differentiate themselves and compete in the marketplace. These resources may be called strategic or dynamic capabilities and often emphasize things like an organization's ability to learn or collaborate.

- *Core competencies.*[6] Organizations may be represented by core competencies—things they do well. These core competencies often deal with application of functional expertise: marketing, R&D, supply chain management, distribution channels, and so forth.

- *Health.*[7] McKinsey has summarized many management practices into nine dimensions of organizational health. It has found that healthy companies generate three times the total shareholder return of unhealthy companies.

- *Climate.*[8] Employees have a general feel for the climate of an organization—the net effect of organizational practices like innovation, communication, senior management, and so forth—that feeds back into their performance on the job.

- *Processes.*[9] Organizations can be dissected into core processes (for example, new product to commercialization, order to remittance, onboarding people) that could be reengineered to build organization success. Processes can also be defined as the integrated flow of management practices (such as talent, performance management, information, work).[10]

- *Values.*[11] Organizations have both written and unwritten value statements that represent beliefs and assumptions and that shape expected behaviors. These values (sometimes called orthodoxies or norms) show up in rituals, rites, and stories. In one effort, organization cultures can be clustered into four types based on competing values: adhocracy, market, hierarchy, and clan.[12]

- *Mindset.*[13] Organizations create shared mindsets about what they should focus on to succeed. These become automatic thoughts, schema, or unwritten rules that shape how people think and act.

- *Organization types.* Dan Denison and his colleagues have identified four types of organization cultures (mission, adaptability, involvement, consistency), each of which represents a pattern of management practices.[14]

- *Systems.* Organizations are defined as complex systems and parts that come together to create a collective organization. Organization diagnosis often comes from doing system audits of organization practices (for example, 7-s, STAR, congruence model, high-performance work systems).[15]

No wonder investors shy away from assessing culture! The concept clearly matters, but it seems impossible to articulate or define with any

**Figure 8.1. Framework for Assessing Organization's
Culture Capability Processes**

precision. However, it is interesting to note that even the Chartered Institute of Auditors (a group traditionally focused only on "hard" facts and figures) has prepared recent documentation to help auditors monitor culture.[16]

Figure 8.1 synthesizes the cultural quandary into six elements of culture capability that investors can audit to give a premium or discount based on culture. First, leaders need to have a sense that organization capabilities matter. As stated by Peter Drucker, as shown by research, and as experienced, capabilities matter.

Second, become clear about which capabilities matter most. I use the word capabilities to capture the diverse thinking in the above conceptions of culture. Organization capabilities represent what the organization is known for, what it is good at doing, and how it allocates resources to win in its market. Organizations should be defined less by their structure and more by their ability to establish the capabilities required to win—that is, to serve customers in ways that competitors can not readily copy. Organization capabilities might include ability to respond to or serve customers, drive efficiency, manage change, collaborate both inside and outside, innovate on products and business model, access information, and establish the right culture. Investors can do capability audits to determine if the organization has prioritized the right capabilities to win.

Third, culture represents the pattern of how people think and act in the organization. While organizations can have many capabilities, culture is likely the key for future success. The right culture takes what the organization should be known for by key customers and uses this external identity to shape internal thought and action. Investors can audit the extent to which an organization has the right culture.

Fourth, management actions can be identified and implemented to create and sustain the desired culture. My colleagues and I have classified these actions into intellectual, behavioral, and process agendas. Intellectual agendas ensure that managers create a shared culture inside and outside the organization, behavioral agendas show the extent to which all employees behave consistently with the desired culture; and process agendas institutionalize the culture through management practices.

The capability, culture, and management action dimensions in this organization logic parallel psychologists' understanding of individuals. Individuals have personalities (parallel to organization capabilities) that have been categorized into the "Big 5": openness, conscientiousness, extraversion, agreeableness, and neuroticism. These five personality traits capture domains that can be observed and measured. Individuals then have habits (organization culture or patterns) that determine how they approach life. Psychologists say that 50% to 80% of what people do comes from habits or routines. These habits show up in how people think (cultural intellectual agenda), act (cultural behavioral agenda), and manage emotions or sentiments that signal and sustain behaviors (cultural process agenda). Psychologists who diagnose individuals look at each of the three levels (personality, habit, action); likewise investors who assess culture can look at three levels (capability, culture, and management action) by examining the six elements of cultural capability noted in Table 8.1. The first three stages culminate in the definition of the culture an organization needs, followed by three agendas for implementing that culture.

Definition Stage One: Recognize Need to Build Capability

As noted in the chapters on individual proficiencies, leaders devote their time to things that matter most to them—generally issues that affect business goals. Business leaders who see cultural capability as a part of their business success will spend more time on it than those who don't. This gives investors a means to assess how seriously leaders regard cultural capability as a key to their business results.

Table 8.1. Making Sense of Organization Capability, Culture, Management Action

Key Question and Focus	Previous Research	Audits That Can Be Done	Analogue with Individual
Stage 1: Recognize need for capability			
How does capability logic redefine definition of organization? What do capabilities matter to success	Different conceptions of culture	Assess management's commitment to working on improving organization.	Why is attending to personality important to one's well-being?
Stage 2: Capability			
What is the organization good at doing and what should it be known for?	Resources and strategic capabilities Core competencies Competitive differentiators	Capability audit: What do we have to be known for and good at to win? This should be tightly linked to strategy. Measure the extent to which priorities are shared about capabilities required to win.	What is my personality? We each have a personality that can be dissected into five core personality traits based on what comes naturally to us.
Stage 3: Culture			
How do we shape the right patterns that will enable us to win? How the organization works: Event, pattern, identity	Competing values Organization types Organization health	Cultural audit: Do we have the right patterns for thinking and behaving? Measure the clarity and accuracy of the culture.	What habits affect my lifestyle and identity? We each have habits or routines that determine who we are.

Stage 4: Management actions

One way investors can assess the effect of overall capability on business success is to examine a publicly traded firm's price/earnings (PE, or price/book) ratio compared to competitors' over the course of a decade. The average PE ratio indicates whether investors are giving a firm a premium or discount for its earnings compared to competitors. For example, Table 8.2 shows the PE ratio of competitive firms in the computer devices business. The table shows that over the last decade, Apple

Key Question and Focus	Previous Research	Audits That Can Be Done	Analogue with Individual
Management action 1: Intellectual agenda			
Create a clear message about the desired culture to share inside and outside.	Shared mindset Values	Unity audit: Do we have a shared culture? Do we make our assumptions implicit? Measure unity of culture and clarity of assumptions.	What are my thought patterns (schema)?
Management action 2: Behavioral agenda			
Turn culture identity into employee actions.	Climate	Behavioral audit: Do employee behaviors link to the culture? Measure behavior alignment and change.	What are my daily actions (calendar test)?
Management action 3: Process agenda			
Create, shape, and reinforce culture through management practices.	Systems · 7s · STAR · High-performing work system Organization processes	Process or system audit: Do we have processes that reinforce and embed the culture? Measure process alignment and change.	How do my emotions shape my experience and sustain my desired routines?

has a PE ratio well above that of its industry (25.5 to 14.2). So Apple has received a 65% premium for every dollar it has earned compared to its competitors. (25–14=9; 9÷14=65%)

Investors can readily access this information to determine the overall premium or discount (IBM in this case) that markets place on a firm's earnings. This PE comparison represents an overall evaluation of how investors value a firm's intangibles, of which cultural capability plays a

Table 8.2. Price/Earnings Ratio of Firms in Computer Devices Industry

	2004	2005	2006	2007	2008	2009	2010	2011	2012	2013	TTM[a]	Ten-Year Avg.	Market Cap (2014)
Apple	50.5	38.8	30.8	43.5	15.8	20.5	18	11.5	12.1	13.9	16.5	25.5	$612.3b
IBM	20.0	16.8	16.0	15.1	9.4	13.1	12.7	14.1	13.3	12.5	12.1	14.3	191.3
Samsung	—	—	—	—	11.8	12.6	6.1	7.5	4.9	5.2	5.0	8	146.4
HP	18.3	34.7	18.9	18.9	11.2	16.4	11.4	7.8	—	10.7	13.4	16.5	71.1
Lenovo	13.8	22.8	—	26.9	4.7	—	22.4	16.9	18.3	17.2	19.6	17.9	11.8
Average (of these companies excluding Apple):											12.5	14.2	105.2

Data sourced from financials.morningstar.com on August 28, 2014

[a]TTM = trailing twelve months

All negative P/E ratios are shown as "—"

key part (as discussed in Chapter 1). In addition, investors can see how leaders respond to this information—which can be quite revealing.

My colleagues and I have prepared this information for hundreds of senior leadership teams. We have had reactions at both extremes. One senior leadership team did not want to share the data at all because it showed a PE discount and was seen as "sharing bad news" with the executives. Another group of senior leaders openly presented the data, shared it widely within the company, and talked about how to make improvements. Leaders who embrace this kind of data are clearly more valuable to investors—and in the long run likely to lead more valuable companies—than leaders who hide from it.

Investors can also examine the extent to which culture is formally woven into business strategy frameworks and discussions. For example, in his original "STAR" model for organization diagnosis, Jay Galbraith focused on five organization systems that needed to be aligned (strategy, structure, processes, rewards, and people). He and his colleagues have since added a sixth element to their STAR model: *organization design criteria.*[17] This is another way of talking about capabilities required for success and cultural patterns that will integrate the other five systems.

Investors can also see the extent to which leaders refer to culture (however defined) as part of their leadership agenda. Such references might appear in an annual report letter to shareholders, or in investor calls, town hall meetings to employees, public forums, or publications about the company. Here are some noteworthy examples of CEO statements on culture:

> Last week in my email to you I synthesized our strategic direction as a productivity and platform company. Having a clear focus is the start of the journey, not the end. The more difficult steps are creating the organization and culture to bring our ambitions to life.
>
> —Satya Nadella, CEO, Microsoft

> For eighty-five years, we've said, "Take care of our associates, and they'll take care of our guests." This core value of putting people first underpins our commitment to diversity, but we also believe that it drives our profitability. Hospitality is by definition a diverse industry.
>
> —Arne Sorenson, Marriott Company

> An organization's ability to learn, and translate that learning into action rapidly, is the ultimate competitive advantage. . . . Culture drives great results.
>
> —Jack Welch, General Electric

> Google is run by its culture and not by me   Google is probably the best example of a network-based organization. Very flat, very nonhierarchical, very much informal in culture and ideas—ideas come from everywhere. . . . Part of the job of being a CEO in a company like Google is to have an environment where people are constantly throwing you their best ideas as opposed to being afraid to talk to you.
>
> —Eric Schmidt, Google

> Culture is not the most important thing, it's the only thing.
>
> —Jim Sinegal, Costco

While the executives in targeted firms may not be this articulate, investors can ascertain how much they appreciate culture as part of their success. In addition, investors can monitor how candid leaders are about what part of the culture is not working as well as about what is working.

Finally, investors can assess how much the organization analyzes and works to update its culture. One investor was impressed that an organization periodically hired external advisers who analyzed the culture to determine if it was aligned to the customers and strategy of the company.

Possible indicators:

- *How has the market valued the company's intangible assets over time?*
- *Do leaders talk about culture as part of the success of the company?*
- *Are cultural assessments woven into formal decision-making and planning processes?*

Definition Stage Two: Set Capability Priorities

Investors should know the extent to which leaders attend to the prioritization and creation of capabilities. As discussed earlier, capabilities represent what the organization is known for and good at doing. They represent the ways that people and resources are brought together to accomplish work, forming the identity and personality of the organization by defining what it is good at doing and, in the end, what it *is*. They are stable over time and difficult for competitors to copy—unlike access to capital markets, product strategy, or technology. Because capabilities are not easy to measure, managers often pay far less attention to them than to tangible investments like plant and equipment—but they will give investors confidence in future earnings.[18]

Investors should monitor how well leaders have prioritized their capabilities by doing a capabilities audit. A capability audit generally includes six steps (outlined in Table 8.3). For example, a large financial institution recognized that they had been trailing their competitors in price/earnings ratios for a long time, and their leaders wanted to do a capability audit with the steps in Table 8.3.

1. Select unit: they chose retail banking as the first organization unit.
2. Create content: they identified a number of possible capabilities they could build to help retail be more effective (using ideas from Table 8.4).
3. Collect data: they collected data on the organization's desired capability and health from senior leaders, employees, and customers.
4. Synthesize data: they analyzed the data to set priorities on which capabilities they should focus on—in this case customer service, agility/change, and simplicity.
5. Create action plan: they implemented a series of action plans to build these capabilities into their culture including management communications, employee actions, and revised HR systems.
6. Follow up: they monitored their progress through surveys, observations, and other tracking mechanisms.

Table 8.3. Organization Capability Audit

Step	Question	Outcome
1. Select organization unit for audit.	What organization unit should be the target of the capability audit?	Define organization unit where the capability audit will occur (corporation, business unit, region, plant).
2. Create content of the audit.	What are the key capabilities that an organization might consider? (See Table 8.4 for thirteen possible choices.)	Prepare a list of possible capabilities that an organization might possess; tailor the generic capabilities to the organization.
3. Collect data through survey or interviews.	How do different groups (leadership team, employees, customers, suppliers, partners) prioritize these capabilities?	Involve multiple stakeholders to determine which capabilities should be priorities.
4. Synthesize data to see priorities.	What are the top two to four capabilities for this organization?	Look for patterns In data to Identify the top two to four priorities most likely to help the organization succeed.
5. Create capability action plan.	How can the organization implement the chosen capabilities throughout the organization?	Prepare action plan for each capability with definition, decisions to implement, and actions to move forward.
6. Follow up and monitor progress.	How can the chosen capabilities be institutionalized?	Track progress of capability implementation and improve as required.

As a result, this bank's market value increased.

Leaders who have done such audits can then focus on a few key capabilities to embed in the organization. When a firm exceeds industry average on these prioritized capabilities, it is likely to create sustainable success.

Possible indicators:

- *Does the firm have a regular process for doing capability audits?*
- *Does the firm prioritize key capabilities?*
- *Does the firm have a capabilities implementation plan?*

Table 8.4. Capability Audit of Generic Capabilities

How effectively do we currently perform on each of the following thirteen capabilities?	How Effective Now: 1 = low; 5 = high					Two or three most critical
	1	2	3	4	5	
1. **Talent:** We are good at managing things like intellectual capital, know-how, competencies, skills, commitment, workforce.	O	O	O	O	O	
2. **Leadership:** We are good at building leadership depth through the company, with things like bench strength, quality of management, leadership brand.	O	O	O	O	O	
3. **Culture:** We are good at managing or changing our culture, firm identity, firm equity, firm brand, shared agenda, shared mindset.	O	O	O	O	O	
4. **Speed:** We are good at doing things fast, with agility, adaptation, flexibility, cycle time, responsiveness.	O	O	O	O	O	
5. **Learning:** We are good at knowledge management, sharing best practices.	O	O	O	O	O	
6. **Collaboration:** We are good at teamwork, working across boundaries, doing merger integration, or sharing information.	O	O	O	O	O	
7. **Innovation:** We are good at administrative, product, channel or strategic innovation.	O	O	O	O	O	
8. **Accountability:** We are good at holding people accountable with clear performance expectations, and we can execute and implement what we promise.	O	O	O	O	O	
9. **Strategic Clarity:** We are good at creating a shared agenda, setting strategic priorities, and having a shared point of view.	O	O	O	O	O	
10. **Efficiency:** We are good at reducing costs through redesign, reengineering, or restructuring.	O	O	O	O	O	

How effectively do we currently perform on each of the following thirteen capabilities?	How Effective Now: 1 = low; 5 = high					Two or three most critical
	1	2	3	4	5	
11. **Customer Service:** We are good at customer relationships with a customer-focused organization and customer intimacy.	O	O	O	O	O	
12. **Social Responsibility:** We are good at being sustainable by managing our carbon footprint, philanthropy, and values.	O	O	O	O	O	
13. **Risk:** We are good at managing risk by attending to disruption, predictability, and variance.	O	O	O	O	O	

Definition Stage Three: Equate Culture with Identity in Customers' Minds

In many capability audits, culture—item 3 in Table 8.4—shows up as a critical (and currently deficient) capability for a company's success. And even when it is seen as effective or not critical or both, the process of implementing any of the other capabilities requires a cultural shift. So culture has multiple applications, and any strategic shift will require a corresponding cultural shift. For example, in the case at the beginning of the chapter, the company was pivoting from a product to a customer strategy, and it did not work until the leadership induced a change in the culture—that is, the patterns of how people thought and acted. Investors can monitor the extent to which executives define the right culture.

Investors can also determine if leaders think of the right culture as an event (an all-employee meeting, training program, communication message) or a pattern (how people think and behave as defined by values statements or cultural typologies) or an identity (what we want to be known for by our best customers). By focusing culture on an organization's external identity, the leadership can give events and patterns a clear focus. When an organization's external identity both drives and reflects its internal culture, investors can have more confidence that it will be both effective and sustained.

The extent to which a firm's desired culture has been linked to external customer expectations is also a trackable quantity following the brand logic in Figure 7.2. A firm's brand (its identity in the minds of key customers) can shape the firm's culture (its identity made real to employees). Investors can compare the promises the firm's brand makes to customers with its value statements and other articulations of culture (such as employee value proposition, cultural speeches, or cultural presentations). Tying culture to the external brand creates what I like to call a *value of values* and makes sure that cultural typologies are tailored to unique customer requirements. The overlap between external promises and internal values and behaviors leads to investor confidence in creating the right culture.

One investor complained to me that leaders are sloppy when describing their culture with abstract and generic terms. When leaders derive it from their company's brand, however, the culture becomes more focused, measurable, and important to success. Terms used to define a firm's brand should show up in cultural statements.

Another investor was concerned about how often to change the culture and how to determine the future direction of the culture. When culture is defined through customer identity, these questions are more readily answered. The culture should be changed as often as customer expectations change. For example, in a retail bank, customers were changing their buying expectations and patterns through technology. The bank had to respond to these customer changes with internal culture changes focused on access, ease of use, and speed of decision making. Organization cultures should change when customers change—and in the direction of the customer change.

Possible indicators:

- *Does the firm have the right culture for future success?*
- *Does the internal culture reflect external customer expectations or brand promises?*

Intellectual Agenda: Clear and Shared Cultural Message

A culture statement must have a clear, simple message—not too complex, too transient, or too elegant. Repeated redundantly throughout the organization, it can set the intellectual, top-down agenda for senior management, resonate with employees, and capture the intellectual basis for the new culture. Investors can track some of the characteristics of such a message that help make sure it will have impact:

- Simplicity
- Openness
- Clarity
- Redundancy
- Business relevance

SIMPLICITY

In one firm trying to transform, the senior team worked for many months to create a document that had six elements of a mission, seven strategies, five operating principles, seven superordinate goals, six values, and a vision. They fondly believed that the fact they could put it on one page made it simple. Not so. Few in the firm could remember the twenty-plus items that crowded the page. Simple means memorable.

Another firm working on innovation captured the logic in four terms: think big, act small, fail fast, and learn rapidly. Using this simple mantra (in addition to other disciplines), they were able to increase the percentage of revenue from new products. Investors should ask to see simple, memorable, customer-focused rallying phrases that define a desired culture.

REDUNDANCY

Researchers on communication have found that people don't fully grasp a message until they have heard it ten times.[19] When simple and similar cultural messages are shared through multiple media (video, speeches, forums, town hall meetings, phone calls, and so on), they are both better understood and likelier to have real impact. In particular, it is critical for leaders to share the messages in private, resisting the temptation to back off from the implications of a desired culture in face-to-face conversations.

OPENNESS

The desired culture can't be a secret; you have to go public with it. To employees, going public means sharing the desired culture in written, personal, and verbal communications. To customers, going public means making promises to them about how the firm will interact with them in the future. Going public also means sharing ideas with investors and encouraging investors to see beyond the financials—to have confidence in the processes used to generate the financials.

BUSINESS RELEVANCE

Culture deals with how work is accomplished. It becomes an adjective and not a noun. The "nouns" are the outcomes or results of work. *Culture* as an adjective talks about how that work will be accomplished. If culture becomes the end or goal ("we want a culture change"), attention is misdirected. By having the goal of culture rooted in investor and customer value, culture is an enabler, not the end game. For example, we want a culture of agility, innovation, or customer service *so that* customers buy more from us and investors have more confidence in us. Culture as a means should be linked to desired business results—the end.

CLARITY

Culture tends to be murky and hard to study because it is rooted in unspoken assumptions that employees don't consciously recognize. David Foster Wallace offered a wonderful metaphor for surfacing assumptions:[20]

> There are these two young fish swimming along, and they happen to meet an older fish swimming the other way, who nods at them and says, "Morning, boys, how's the water?" And the two young fish swim on for a bit, and then eventually one of them looks over at the other and goes, "What the hell is water?"

Often long-term employees don't recognize the water, or culture, they work in. Investors can observe whether leaders work to surface implicit assumptions, often called orthodoxies, by listening to new employees who may observe what others live, by purposefully exploring patterns of behavior that get in the way of accomplishing work, or by creating a candid forum for dialogue. (I picked up the concept of industry or organization orthodoxies from personal discussions with C. K. Prahalad and Gordon Hewitt.)

Investors can test for a shared culture by doing what my colleagues and I have called the *unity of identity* test. Each member of a leadership team answers the question, "What are the top three things we want to be known for by our best customers in the future?" These responses are then categorized. For example, a team of twelve leaders will produce thirty-six answers. Sorting them into like categories may result in nine that address "efficiency," seven that address "reliability," six that address "customer focused" and fourteen scattered over other categories. Add the total number of responses in the top three categories (twenty-two in this example) and divide by total responses (thirty-six) for a rough measure of shared mindset (61% in this case). Our rule of thumb is that this score should be 80% to indicate a unity of identity. This is a very quick and easy test of any leadership team or group of employees. Cultural insights can also be derived from employee surveys that pose climate, value, or cultural questions. The variance in employee responses may be as useful as the mean scores on these tests to determine if there is unity about the cultural message.

Possible indicators:

- *Does the firm have a "unity of identity" about its cultural message?*
- *Does the firm have redundant communications to share the cultural message?*

- *Do employees and customers recognize and resonate with the cultural message?*

Behavioral Agenda: Employee Actions Align with Culture

A great leader once said, "We teach people correct principles and let them govern themselves." A culture transformation occurs if and only if it changes behavior throughout the firm. This is the bottom-up, behavioral agenda for managing culture. Words, phrases, concepts that resonate without changing behavior create cynicism. Generally, employees who experience day-to-day business problems know what to do to turn cultural concepts into actions. Developing mechanisms to engage employees and to enable them to figure out what behaviors to change creates enduring culture. Investors should look for evidence that the intellectual agenda of culture translates into specific employee behaviors.

It makes a difference if leaders impose behaviors or allow employees to determine which behaviors go with the desired culture. When a top leader demands that the team practice participative management, it keeps them from taking personal ownership for the culture—and the innate hypocrisy will filter out through the organization. By contrast, when people are involved in an activity, they are more likely to feel ownership. Owners almost always feel far more intensity than agents. In the Work-Out program (the 1990s cultural change at General Electric), for example, the leadership team articulated the desired culture of speed, simplicity, and self-confidence, then engaged tens of thousands of employees in determining how they could turn these corporate aspirations into their personal actions.[21]

Investors also monitor the extent to which local managers encourage employee behaviors. An obvious and well-tested experience in union relations is to avoid having corporate leadership attend a local unit meeting to try to convince employees to be nonunion. Union relations improve with local, not corporate management. Local managers build long-term relationships and embody the values of the corporate leaders. When local leaders behave differently, employees believe in the new culture.

Finally, investors can look for small behavioral changes that add up to larger culture capability. In tipping-point logic, changing a lot of little things may not have much impact in each instance, but then when a few more little things are added, overall patterns begin to change fast. Crime in New York City began to fall rapidly after a lot of relatively petty crimes were attended to (graffiti tagging, windshield washing, panhandling, and the like). A tipping point occurs when a lot of small changes culminate in large systematic change.

When employees behave as if they are committed to the desired culture, they will more likely become committed. As investors observe a culture permeating a targeted organization, they can observe employee behaviors that are consistent with the desired culture.

Possible indicators:

- *Do employees personally define how their own behaviors reflect the desired culture?*
- *Does the desired culture show up in day-to-day employee activities?*
- *Do employees take personal ownership of the culture (refer to "my culture" as opposed to "management's culture")?*

Process Agenda: Management Processes Align with Culture

A real cultural capability is thoroughly embedded in the organization's systems and processes. My colleagues and I call this the *side-to-side* or *process* agenda for culture change. Established ways of doing things endure beyond any one leader or any single event, so a desired cultural identity should be part of decisions that affect all organization practices, including financial processes (budgeting, auditing), strategic processes (segmenting customers, innovating and delivering products and services), operational processes (manufacturing, managing supply chain, sharing information), and human capital processes (managing talent, information, and work).

One thoughtful investor said that she would look for existing survey questions about the alignment of process and culture or ask questions of her own, looking for answers like these:

- At XYZ Company, people are rewarded (through compensation and promotions) for exhibiting behaviors that are consistent with our values and culture.
- The material we teach in our training programs is consistent with our desired culture.
- My work environment supports me in delivering excellent customer service (or whatever the objective is that the leaders are attempting to achieve through their culture initiatives).
- At XYZ Company we work hard to improve the processes that are critical to achieving our key business goals.

Investors can see how the culture shows up in decision making, information, problem solving, and people practices. For example, a customer-centric culture would include customer participation in making decisions, sharing of customer information, problem solving with benefits to the customer as the desired outcome, and hiring, training, and paying people able to serve customers especially well.

In more boundaryless organizations, each of these processes can be increasingly shared with customers. Customers can co-fund new ventures, co-create strategy, share in information, and participate in human capital processes. One investor assessed the extent to which customers were involved in these management processes. For example, did customers help create training programs, co-facilitate the delivery of the programs, and attend the programs? When investors are assured that management processes deliver customer value, they can regard cultural capability as increasing the value of the organization.

Possible indicators:

- *Do management practices in financial allocation, strategic planning, operational performance, and human capital reflect and reinforce the culture?*
- *Do customers sense that the management practices will meet their needs?*

Conclusion

Culture matters. If investors can become more clear about what it is and how to track it, they can discern a major element of what leaders create that builds confidence in future value. Culture is likely to be one of the capabilities an organization requires to win. Investors' confidence in cultural capability increases when it is clearly articulated, linked to customer expectations, and translated inside the organization. One metaphor we have used to embed culture is getting rid of mosquitoes. Government agencies need to have a mosquito abatement program (intellectual agenda), people need to slap the mosquitoes that land on them (behavioral agenda), and the pools and puddles where mosquitoes breed need to be managed or dried out (process agenda).

The definition and assessment of six elements of cultural capability (Table 8.5) should help investors make more thoughtful decisions about the organizations (not just the people) they invest in. These assessments can also help internal auditors who are becoming concerned about culture, senior leaders who are owners of the culture, HR professionals who often architect culture change process, and cultural consultants who counsel on the culture capability process. As these multiple stakeholders attend to cultural capability, they can assess the organization's chance of outlasting the individual leaders.

Table 8.5. Indicators for Capability or Culture

Indicators	Possible Indicators	How to Assess
Definition Stage One: Leaders recognize need to build capability.	How has the market valued the company's intangible assets over time? Do leaders talk about culture as part of the success of the company? Are cultural assessments woven into formal decision-making and planning processes?	Look at price/earnings (or price/book) ratio of firm compared to competitors over a ten-year period. Examine how often culture is mentioned in letters to shareholders, annual report, public leadership forums, and planning processes.
Definition Stage Two: Leaders set capability priorities.	Does the firm have a regular process for doing capability audits? Does the firm prioritize key capabilities? Does the firm have a capabilities implementation plan?	Determine if the firm prioritizes capabilities where it wants to exceed industry average. Examine the capabilities implementation plan.
Definition Stage Three: Leaders equate culture with identity in customers' minds.	Does the firm have the right culture for future success? Does the internal culture reflect external customer expectations or brand promises?	Measure the overlap between firm brand and internal culture and values.

Indicators	Possible Indicators	How to Assess
Intellectual Agenda: Leaders have a clear and shared cultural message.	Does the firm have a "unity of identity" about its cultural message? Does the firm have redundant communications to share the cultural message? Do employees and customers recognize and resonate with the cultural message?	Create a unity score among executive team of the top three things the firm wants to be known for by customers in the future. Examine communication processes to see if similar messages are shared in multiple ways.
Behavioral agenda: Employee actions align with culture.	Do employees personally define how their own behaviors reflect the desired culture? Does the desired culture show up in day-to-day employee activities? Do employees take personal ownership of the culture (referring to "my culture," not "management's culture")?	Ask cross-section and cross-level groups of employees what they think the culture is. Ask employees how much their personal behavior reflects the culture. Listen to how employees talk about the culture.
Process agenda: Management processes align with culture.	Do management practices in financial allocation, strategic planning, operational performance, and human capital reflect and reinforce the culture?	Examine management practices to see if they encourage and sustain the chosen culture. Determine the extent to which targeted customers participate in human capital practices.

CHAPTER 9

Talent Management Processes

Investors Want Organizations That Manage the Flow of People

We know *it* matters. Some go to war for it. Professional sports teams draft for it. Actors and musicians audition to show they have it. CEOs consider it the ultimate solution and try to manage it. Agents contract for it. Some are innately endowed with it; others strive diligently to earn it. All try to grow it. *Talent*.

Talent matters, but talent management processes matter more, because those processes are what ensure a continuous flow of future employees and the skills they possess, not just reliance on the current talent. McKinsey's 2000 study, *The War for Talent*—now a classic—highlighted the importance of investing in an organization's talent management processes for positive outcomes for multiple stakeholders.[1] When organizations have an effective talent management process:

- Employees are more productive.
- Customers receive better service.
- Strategies are fulfilled and the right cultural capabilities are established (as discussed in Chapter 8).
- Community reputations are increasingly positive.

The cumulative effect of these talent outcomes is that investors who stay alert for them will be more effective over time. In our 2009 research on Asian talent and again in 2013, my colleagues and I found a strong and positive correlation between overall business performance and quality of talent management processes. This finding held true in Singapore, India, and China, and across all industries.

Talent management processes are hard to assess because of the multitude of programs and investments intended to attract, upgrade, and retain talent. Investors need to avoid the allure (and pitfall) of looking

Figure 9.1. Framework for Organization's Talent Management Processes

Overall commitment to talent management

Out: Removing poor performers

In: Acquiring the right talent

Organization's talent management processes

Out: Managing retention

Through: Developing current talent

Through: Building commitment

Through: Preparing future successors

at one talent process (say, hiring or engaging or training or succession planning) and missing the importance of the overall talent management system. When my colleagues and I interviewed investors, they almost uniformly agreed that people matter and that talent management processes should affect their valuation of the firm. One thoughtful investor said he asks the following questions about talent management:

- Does this company attract good people?
- Would I want to hire anyone from this company?
- Does this company keep people?
- Does the company engage people?

While this investor understood the importance of talent and posed good questions, he did not have an integrated way to think about the talent management process. He was not alone; few investors have an overall talent management process approach. Others have built on the idea that investors should pay attention to people, but they often focused more on the reporting standards for measuring people than on an index.[2]

Under the umbrella of commitment to workforce development, talent processes can be indexed by synthesizing choices about the flow of talent into the organization (bringing new talent onto the roles), through the organization (developing current talent, building commitment, preparing future successors), and out of the organization (managing retention of key performers and removal of poor performers).[3] Figure 9.1 sketches the elements of this overall talent process.

Overall Commitment to Talent Management

Investors can track an organization's overall commitment to talent by looking at its place in top leaders' conversations, public presentations, and calendars (the time each spends on talent issues). When leaders devote real attention (time, energy, and money) to talent, good things happen to the organization—as shown by the studies cited in Chapter 2 that found a link between human capital investments and financial return. For example, consider the strong correlation between improved financial performance and top-quartile performance in these four talent management areas:[4]

- Strategic workforce planning, which involves identifying the skills critical to company operations and how these needs match up against the existing workforce.

- Staffing services, including recruitment, staffing, and exit management, along with workforce development services such as training and career planning.

- Overall organization effectiveness, including labor and employee relations and performance management.

- Organization design and measurement.

The top-quartile firms in that study generated EBITDA of 16.2% versus 14.1% for typical companies. This gap netted a typical Fortune 500 company (based on $19 billion in revenue) an additional $399 million annually in improved EBITDA (a measure of a firm's cash flow, standing for earnings before interest, taxes, depreciation, and amortization). In brief, companies can improve earnings substantially by improving their talent management function. Because talent investments drive financial outcomes, leaders should spend time, energy, and money on talent management. Investors can track this commitment through interviews, content analysis of public speeches, reviews of meeting minutes, and calendar tests.

In addition, investors can track an organization's overall commitment to talent by examining productivity measured as output per unit of input. Changes in gross domestic product (GDP) per capita indicate overall labor force productivity and indicate country wealth.[5] In our interviews, investors described a number of output-input measures that they use to track overall organization commitment to talent:[6]

- Revenue per full-time employee
- Total labor cost (payroll, contingent and contract worker pay, benefits) as a percentage of revenue
- Total labor cost as a percentage of operating expense
- Benefits cost to revenue expense percent (total benefits cost as a percentage of revenue)
- Benefits cost to operating expense percent (total benefits cost as a percentage of operating cost)

These labor productivity measures should be compared to competitor firms and industry averages over time.

Another indicator of overall commitment to talent is the extent to which the target organization has codified and applied the service-profit chain.[7] The service-profit chain connects employee attitude (satisfaction, commitment, or engagement) to customer attitude (loyalty, satisfaction) to financial results (profitability, revenue growth). Firms that understand and track this chain have created a strong business case for talent management. Many firms keep employee, customer, and financial data in separate streams, but firms committed to talent management show the relationships among these stakeholders.

Finally, investors can look at social media to determine a firm's reputation for talent management. Various groups do public rankings of company people-management reputations. The Great Place to Work Institute ranks companies and produces *Fortune*'s 100 Best Companies to Work For. *Fortune*'s Most Admired Companies list measures quality of management and people management subdimensions of overall high-ranking companies. Aon Hewitt and *Fortune* produce the Top Companies for Leadership; Hay Group produces Best Companies for Leaders. These ratings differ from one another to some extent, but they all offer investors public insights on a firm's commitment to talent. For a less public view, Glassdoor.com and other social media sites provide forums where employees can anonymously comment on and rate the culture and talent of their organization. These ratings can give investors a peek inside a company and its commitment to talent management.

Possible indicators:

- *Do leaders allocate attention (time, energy, money) to talent management activities?*
- *How does the firm benchmark with competitors on labor productivity?*
- *Does the firm link employee, customer, and financial data?*

- *What is the firm's reputation both in overall rankings and in specific employee responses?*

In: Acquiring the Right Talent

Talent management begins by bringing the right people into the organization. One company calls each professional hire a $9 million decision—the estimated total cost of an employee from recruiting to retirement. Even if few people spend their entire career with one company, acquiring the right talent becomes key to investor confidence. Research shows that nearly 70% of businesses have suffered from a bad hire in a twelve-month period.[8]

Five practices improve talent flow into an organization. Investors can audit the extent to which a company performs on each of these practices to improve talent acquisition:

- *Standards.* Standards delineate the cultural and technical behaviors companies seek in new hires. These behavioral standards reflect expectations from business strategies. In general, companies should hire for cultural fit, which is something people bring to the job, rather than technical competence, which can be developed through training.

- *Sourcing.* Sourcing identifies the pool from which future employees will be drawn: schools, employment agencies, social media (such as LinkedIn), search firms, and referrals. One investor monitors whether the company has a high flow of qualified résumés coming in. He asks for sourcing analytics, which report the qualified applicants per vacancy (which indicates company reputation), and for specifics about where people are hired (which indicates rigor of hiring process).

- *Screening.* Through interviews and other assessments, companies screen candidates to identify the ones who best fit with the organization. Investors can assess the quality of screening by monitoring the number of people involved in interviews and the rigor of the interviews.[9] For example, at Nemours Children's Hospital in Florida, patient care candidates are interviewed by families of patients, who ask about specific experiences of delivering care. Involving families in interviews and training them to ask behavioral questions increases the quality of hires.[10]

- *Securing.* Companies create employee value propositions that the top talent will find compelling. An employee value proposition explicitly states what the employee gets from contributing to the firm. Investors can ask to see presentations or documents on the employee value proposition—or look at social media, to see what the company is doing to communicate with Gen Y job candidates. Investors can also monitor the percentage of offers accepted as a measure of the quality of the offer.

- *Steering.* Once talent is in the door, companies orient new people to help them understand the company strategy and their specific role in implementing that strategy. Orienting new employees includes the logistics and policies of working at the company, but also the culture of working at the company—its history and an overview of the strategies, values, and customs of the workplace. Investors can monitor these on-boarding strategies to assess the company's strength at reducing the time-to-productivity of new hires.

As investors audit these talent acquisition practices, they can bolster their confidence that the company has attracted and held the right talent.

Possible Indicators:

- *Does the company have a rigorous talent acquisition process?*
- *Does the company have a reputation for attracting top talent (e.g., a strong employee value proposition)?*
- *What is time-to-productivity for new employees?*

Through: Developing Current Talent

Some companies buy new talent; others build existing talent. Companies are more likely to buy than build at earlier life stages (see Table 7.3) and when facing major strategic shifts. When choosing to build existing talent, companies invest in training and development activities—which require both the resources to support those activities and a commitment to use training as a way to accomplish strategy.

Investors can monitor a company's overall commitment to developing current talent by assessing the training budget per employee, the percentage of employee time spent in training or development activities, or the amount of time top managers spend in employee development activities.[11] In particular, investors should pay attention to the development of high-potential employees, who often represent 5% to 15% of the overall workforce.[12] These top performers often receive disproportionate development investments and represent future leadership capability.

Investors can also track the extent to which companies deploy innovative development activities. Development activities can be clustered into development on the job, development through training, and experiences outside of work.[13] Collectively, my colleagues and I found in our Top Companies for Leadership Research that high-potential employees would spend 5% to 15% of their time in development activities. We found in our Talent Accelerator study that development was one of the top three (out of thirteen) talent management practices that affected business results.[14]

DEVELOPMENT ON THE JOB

Most learning comes from experience. Sometimes work experiences are informal and depend on an individual leader's personal proficiency for learning (as discussed in Chapter 3), but investors can also assess the extent to which companies intentionally invest in on-the-job development experiences. A number of ways to develop employees on the job have been identified:[15]

- Coaching, either receiving or providing
- Learning from role models—mentors, bosses, peers
- Accepting stretch or challenging assignments, generally with a sponsor
- Managing career development intentionally by rotating jobs and having career plan conversations
- Being assigned to a project team either inside or outside the company
- Participating in an executive exchange, often in a loaned leadership role
- Shadowing a leader either informally or formally in an assistant role

Investors can explore the extent to which organizations formally offer these development experiences and look at the percentage of high-potential future leaders with personal development plans that include a mix of these development experiences.

DEVELOPMENT THROUGH INNOVATIVE TRAINING

The amount spent on leadership training has gone up about 14% a year the last few years—to about $15.5 billion, out of more than $150 billion spent on total employee learning.[16] As noted, investors can audit a target organization's overall budget for training as an indicator of commitment. Investors can also audit the quality of training to see if the firm addresses key training innovations:

- *Who is trained:* Individuals, to master skills for new positions; teams, to implement business agenda; external stakeholders, to build relationships.

- *What is taught:* Moving from generic theory and research to best practices to action learning to learning solutions whereby participants solve current business challenges.

- *Who teaches:* Experts who bring innovative insights, line managers who bring discipline to act, customers who encourage action on the right things.

- *Where training occurs:* Learning to use a mix of external vendors such as universities and faculty and internal learning at a training center or on the job.

- *How learning occurs:* Using a mix of training tools including presentations, case studies, facilitated discussions, technology-enabled, and blended learning.

- *How to ensure follow-up:* Focusing on application and implementation of ideas taught through coaching, leadership sustainability, and behavior change reviews (360-degree feedback).

- *How to measure results:* Using analytics to determine impact of training based on who attends, what is taught, who teaches, and how it is taught.

Investors who audit these training processes will find out whether or not the firm is committed to building talent.

DEVELOPMENT THROUGH EXPERIENCES OFF THE JOB

Increasingly, the boundaries blur between work and non-work, making it more and more feasible for employees to learn from experiences outside their formal work setting as well as inside. Investors can monitor the extent to which the firm helps high-potential employees learn from experiences outside the firm such as these:

- Representing the firm to external groups. Key employees can serve as ambassadors of the company to universities, community agencies, government regulators, trade associations, or service organizations.

- Presenting insights in public forums like workshops, seminars, or trade groups.

- Visiting best practice sites on areas targeted for improvement.

- Coaching not-for-profits, being part of teams to serve the

community, or managing firm charity—all ways of using
philanthropy as a way to build leadership and team-building skills.

- Committing to personal learning through reading and life
experience and having time to reflect on how life experiences
influence leadership behavior.

Possible indicators:

- *What is the training and development budget per employee? As a ratio to sales?*

- *How well does the company encourage employees to develop from experience?*

- *How innovative is the company in training programs at work and development outside work?*

Through: Preparing Future Successors

Depending on demographics, most companies have to replace half of
their top managers about every five years. Many of the investors we interviewed suggested that a target firm's succession process for leadership
positions was a key indicator of confidence in overall talent management. Investors can audit both the outcome of the succession process
and the process itself. My colleagues and I found in our research on
talent management that managing promotions (placing high-potentials
in key jobs) and leadership (building a process for shaping a leadership
brand) were the two most critical of the thirteen talent practices identified as driving business performance.[17]

Many succession outcomes can be tracked. One investor tested
whether the target firm was a source of leadership talent in its industry.
Leader feeder firms often have a depth of talent that others admire.
Another investor assessed a backup ratio—the number of employees
regarded as being fully prepared for key positions. In some leading
firms, this ratio was 2:1 or even 2.5:1, but with streamlining, this ratio
has often fallen into the 0.5:1 to 0.7:1 range. Another investor focused
on the percentage of key positions staffed from inside rather than
outside. He felt that internal succession indicated a positive talent
pipeline.

Preparing future successors comes from confidence in a rigorous succession planning process. This process often begins with clarity about
expectations for key positions. One of the most common mistakes of
succession planning is starting by focusing on the people rather than
the requirements of the position. Inviting a leader to "tell me about your
succession" often reveals assumptions about how the leader thinks about

the process. Too often the first response is about which individual could move into which job. Better succession planning starts by identifying key positions (those that create wealth for the company), then defining the expectations or criteria for those jobs in the future.[18] One thoughtful investor said that the best leaders focused on the future by looking over the horizon and seeing what the company would require for success after they are gone.

With criteria identified, succession focuses on which individuals best match those criteria. Often these high-potential individuals (usually about 5% to 15% of the workforce) have been identified early in their careers and given many opportunities for personal learning and growth. Ideally a company has a regular annual process of anticipating future key positions and reviewing how key people can be prepared for those positions. Succession works best when line managers personally commit to supervising the process, rather than delegating it to HR professionals or outside advisers.

Ultimately, the outcomes and processes of succession give investors confidence in future leadership—which is more important to the long-term success of the investment than current leaders are.

Possible indicators:

- *Does the firm have a strong talent pipeline?*
- *Does the firm have a regular annual process for anticipating future key positions and reviewing how key people can be prepared for those positions (for example, through a rigorous succession planning process)?*
- *Do leaders take primary responsibility for succession, or do they leave it to staff groups?*

Through: Building Commitment

Developing current talent and preparing successors ensures competence, but real talent management comes from a simple formula: competence * commitment * contribution.[19] Commitment and contribution characterize employee engagement. Investors should pay attention not only to competence but also to engagement of employees. Engagement has been shown to be a key predictor of organization success. Organizations with high levels of engagement (65% or greater) outperform the total stock market index, posting total shareholder returns 22% above average. On the other hand, companies with low engagement (45% or less) had a total shareholder return that was 28% below the average.[20] Organizations with disengaged employees experience 50% higher turnover rates among their workers and productivity rates nearly 50% lower.[21] In another study of fifty global companies, Towers Perrin found that companies with high engagement had 19% improvement in operating income, 14% increase in net income, and 28% increase in earnings per share—compared to corresponding declines of 33%, 4%, and 11% in companies with low engagement.[22]

Despite the obvious rewards of employee engagement, these days most researchers find that employee engagement scores are falling rather than rising.[23] Investors can track overall engagement indicators of productivity, retention of key employees, and engagement surveys. Surveys have shifted from measuring satisfaction ("Do you like your boss?") to engagement ("Does your boss give you the tools to do your job?") to more active questions ("Did you do your best to work with your boss?"). Regardless of the concepts measured, investors can review the history of these engagement measures and see trends in the data. Investors can also monitor the extent to which engagement scores are shared, translated to specific leadership actions, and used for other talent management practices such as promotions, pay, and training.

In addition, it is useful to track the extent to which a company has an articulated employee value proposition that lays out clear expectations of what employees give and get on the job. When employees contribute more to the firm, they get value back that is meaningful to them. Wendy Ulrich (a prominent psychologist) and I have summarized seven dimensions of meaningful work in our book *The Why of Work*:[24]

- *Identity:* Shaping an identity at work based on one's strengths.
- *Purpose:* Sensing that the organization's purpose aligns with the employee's own purpose.
- *Relationships:* Working with colleagues who share values and work as teams.
- *Work environment:* Creating a positive work culture.
- *Work itself:* Doing work that suits one's personal predispositions.
- *Learning and growth:* Making personal improvements from work.
- *Fun:* Finding a sense of personal joy or fun from work.

When employees experience these seven factors, they find more meaning in their work. Investors can assess the extent to which these factors are woven into the employee value proposition.

Finally, when investors or their surrogates visit a targeted company, they can get a feel for the engagement of employees. Researchers tend to rely more on historical, survey, or interview data that leads to data analytics, but even the most scholarly among us also know that instinct through experience and observation can also confirm engagement. In one case, an investor group walked with management through a plant and noticed that the demeanor of the employees and the interactions among them were lackadaisical. In addition, the employees were not talking to their managers and were in fact avoiding eye contact with them. When investors asked questions, none of the employees talked about their work in enthusiastic terms. These observations led to a strong impression of a sluggish workforce unlikely to rally behind management's new projects.

Possible indicators:

- *Does the company regularly track and use employee engagement indicators?*
- *How does the company define engagement? Satisfaction, loyalty, commitment, personal responsibility?*
- *Does the company have an employee value proposition?*

Out: Managing Retention

A leader lamented that his firm spent enormous amounts of money, energy, and time bringing good people in and developing them; then, too often, these talented employees would leave. If they couldn't keep the best employees, it was not worth investing to find and develop them. In fact, some firms have chosen to buy rather than build talent because of the high risk and expense of retaining the top talent. In addition to the direct costs, turnover has negative consequences in work disruption, quality problems, customer dissatisfaction, management distraction, and loss of experience and knowledge.[25]

Investors can monitor turnover of pivotal positions and compare the targeted firm with competitors. Winning the war for talent comes from retaining the top talent. One investor asks about "regrettable losses" of key people who have left the firm in the last year or two. He wants to see if management can face and learn from such losses, because they may signal underlying cultural challenges.

Investors can also examine what the company does to retain the best. One investor described awarding a "people premium" to a firm where the leader figured out who the best talent was through interviews and assessments and word of mouth, and then "put a wrapper around" this talent so they would not leave. Retention of key employees was an indicator of a stable talent management process. The leader in question knew who the key people were and was consciously working to retain them. Retaining talent often comes from measures such as these:[26]

- Equity compensation, whereby high-potential employees reap long-term benefits for staying (performance shares, options, retention bonuses).

- Career opportunities, whereby top employees have varied and interesting chances for development on the job.

- Personal mentoring, whereby key employees are coached by business leaders who continually ask them what it would take to keep them at the company.

- Professional visibility, whereby employees demonstrate their commitment to the organization by making presentations about it to external stakeholders.

- Rehiring, wherein some top employees may leave but then return to the original firm. Rebound hiring often results in longer-term retention.

Watson Wyatt, a consulting firm, found that about 50% of firms did not have any regular talent retention strategy.[27] Nonetheless, firms with a robust retention strategy tend to be better investments than those that make do without one.

Possible indicators:

- *What is the voluntary turnover rate by major job categories and by pivotal employees?*
- *How many regrettable losses are there? Is there a pattern?*
- *Does the company have a thorough talent retention strategy?*

Out: Removing Poor Performers

Encouraging top performers sometimes involves dealing with low performers. If poor-performing employees suffer no consequences, the high and average performers may be demotivated and not see the benefit of hard work. Poor performance can have lots of reasons: mismatch of skills and requirements of position, personal distractions, lack of commitment to work hard, disbelief in the goals or purposes of the company, or low incentive to be diligent. When poor performance is an event, leaders can often coach and help employees improve. But when poor performance is a pattern, organizations need systems to recognize and remove the people concerned.

Sometimes removing poor performers is constrained by regulatory policy, social norms, or a labor contract. But even when action is difficult, most employees know who the poor performers are, and leaders lose credibility if they fail to act in accord with this collective knowledge.[28] Some companies have experimented with formal employee performance distribution systems (20% excellent, 70% average, and 10% poor) that include a provision for formally removing the bottom 10%. Although this rigid approach can help shake up a culture and allow leaders to justify removing poor performers, it is generally not something investors should encourage for the long term.

Investors should be alert to the importance of dealing with poor performers. One investor my colleagues and I spoke with was quite adamant that leaders should have a zero-tolerance policy for employees who foster destructive behavior. The process of performance management is discussed in more detail in Chapter 10, but in the context of talent management, investors should pay attention to several aspects of the way the company handles poor performers:[29]

- *Listen*. It is important to find out why the poor performer is performing poorly. Sometimes a recent poor performer may have a reasonable and improvable circumstance for the performance decline. Other times, the poor performer may simply not be aware of the performance decline.

- *Reassign*. Sometimes expectations don't match skills. Employees may be asked to do work that is not within their zone of capability. In this case, it might help to reassign an employee to a more suitable position.

- *Boldness*. Leaders need to have the managerial courage to move or remove people. In debriefing leaders on managing transformation, almost all leaders say, "I wish we had moved faster and more boldly." With further exploration, this generally refers to dealing with people. Leaders generally have early indicators that an employee may not meet future skill requirements, but they try and retry to coach, nurture, and develop the employee to fulfill the job duties. Good leaders move quickly.

- *Fairness*. Maintain a due process that requires tough-minded performance but is fair to those involved. In one company, any employee with more than ten years' tenure could not be fired without review by two levels of management above the employee. Fairness also includes treating the employee who is being terminated with respect throughout the process.

- *Choice.* It is generally more effective when the leaders give poor performers a choice to improve. By having a candid and positive conversation about what constitutes good performance, the poor performer can make a conscious choice to meet performance standards. In this way, the leader is not removing the poor performer—the poor performer is making the choice to depart by failing to act.

Investors can monitor the extent to which organizations appropriately handle poor performers. Correctly applied, involuntary terminations signal a commitment to a performance culture. Managing good talent sometimes requires removing poor talent.

Possible indicators:

- *Are leaders willing to have difficult conversations with poor performers (within regulatory and contract constraints)?*
- *Do leaders act boldly and decisively with poor performers?*

Conclusion

Recent years have seen a push for improved talent analytics.[30] These analytics should enable investors to track not only the general outcomes of talent management processes but also the specific actions that led to the results. While investors can look at high-level talent indicators (such as productivity per employee), it is the details about the practices that move people in, through, and out of the organization that really allow them to assess the quality of talent management processes in the organization. Talent is not just a vague aspiration, but a series of specific leadership choices. Often we say that we are known by the company we keep; companies are known by the talent they bring in. They are also know by what they do with that talent once inside the company. Table 9.1 summarizes the components and indicators that investors can audit for grading talent management processes.

Table 9.1. Indicators for Talent Management Practices

Indicators	Possible Indicators	How to Assess
Overall commitment to talent management	Do leaders allocate attention (time, energy, money) to talent management activities? How does the firm benchmark with competitors on labor productivity? Does the firm link employee, customer, and financial data? What is the firm's reputation both in overall rankings and in specific employee responses?	Interview leadership about their commitment to talent. Track labor productivity scores by industry. Monitor predictive analytics of employee, customer, and financial data. Monitor reputation of talent management rankings.
In: Acquire new talent to bring into the organization.	Does the company have a rigorous talent acquisition process? Does the company have a reputation for top attracting talent (e.g., a strong employee value proposition)? What is time-to-productivity for new employees?	Examine the talent acquisition process to see if the company follows the planned steps. Track the number of qualified applicants per advertised position. Look for other indications of the company's reputation as a place to work. Find out how long it takes, on average, before new employees are fully productive.
Through: Develop current talent.	What is the training and development budget per employee? As a ratio to sales? How well does the company encourage employees to develop through experience? How innovative is the company in training programs at work and development outside of work?	Monitor training budget. Examine percentage of key employees who have an individual development plan and review content of plans. Audit development on the job, training, and off-work initiatives.

(continued)

Table 9.1. (continued)

Indicators	Possible Indicators	How to Assess
Through: Prepare future successors.	Does the firm have a strong talent pipeline? Does the firm have a regular annual process for anticipating future key positions and reviewing how key people can be prepared for those positions (e.g., a rigorous succession planning process)? Do leaders take primary responsibility for succession, or do they leave it to staff groups?	Track backup ratio for key leadership positions. Note what percentage of key leadership positions are filled from inside and from outside, and whether this is according to plan or a matter of happenstance.
Through: Build commitment.	Does the company regularly track and use employee engagement indicators? How does the company define engagement? Satisfaction, loyalty, commitment, personal responsibility? Does the company have and use an employee value proposition?	Review the engagement process, survey scores, and use of information. Review the formal employee value proposition and determine if there is an accepted framework for engagement.
Out: Manage retention of key talent.	What is the voluntary turnover rate by major job categories and by pivotal employees? How many regrettable losses are there? Is there a pattern? Does the company have a thorough talent retention strategy?	Examine voluntary turnover by job category and level. Interview to identify regrettable losses and causes. Review depth of retention strategies.
Out: Remove poor performers.	Are leaders willing to have difficult conversations with poor performers (within regulatory and contract constraints)?	Identify past poor performers and ask leaders how they have dealt with them. Interview poor performers who have left and ask how they feel they were treated. Interview current employees to determine how poor performers are treated—for example, can they slide along without improving their performance?

CHAPTER 10

Performance Accountability Processes

Investors Want Organizations That Reinforce Desirable Performance and Behavior

"We've done away with performance appraisal," a senior leader recently told me, "because it causes so many problems." She explained that instead of performance appraisal, her firm trained managers to help employees set goals, then to have conversations with those employees about their goals to make sure they were on target. In a somewhat similar situation, a business school recently decided to avoid grades and the tension they created, going instead to a high pass, pass, and low pass system.

Despite the problems with formal appraisals that have led these leaders (and many others) to attempt to abandon them, it is still clear that people must be held accountable to improve their performance. This is true in all parts of life, not just on the job. After all, few wash their rental cars before returning them, but many fill up with gas—dust carries no penalty, but gas from rental car agencies costs three or four times the service station charge. In bowling, if you can't see the pins knocked over or keep track of the score, you have no incentive to improve or even to keep bowling. And in thirty years of teaching, I have never seen a student audit and complete a course. Students who want to audit a course may pledge a commitment to learning, with a desire to sit in on lectures, but without grades and assignments, they don't put in the work of learning.

Research has shown that firms with performance evaluation systems have higher shareholder financial returns than firms without them (total shareholder return of 7.9% versus 0%; return on equity 10.2% versus 4.1%).[1] Indeed, performance management and variable pay are HR practices' most significant impact on financial performance.[2] And performance management is also the biggest predictor of hospital success.[3]

While performance management discipline increases employee pro-

Table 10.1. Variance in Performance

Quarter	Firm A	Firm B
1	3	9
2	15	12
3	18	8
4	6	13
5	12	10
6	4	11
7	18	9
8	4	8
Average	10	10
STANDARD DEVIATION	6.5	1.85

ductivity and financial results, most studies suggest that current performance appraisal systems do not perform well.[4] An SHRM survey found that 90% of HR professionals are dissatisfied with appraisal systems and only 55% felt that the annual performance reviews are an accurate appraisal for employees' work.[5] The Corporate Executive Board (CEB) found that only 14% of organizations are actually happy with their performance management system, and 23% say performance management reflects employee contributions.[6] The Institute for Corporate Productivity found that 8% of HR executives feel performance management made a contribution to business.[7] Finally, World at Work/Sibson found that 60% of HR executives give their own performance-management systems a grade of C or below.[8]

Through examining all the dimensions of a performance appraisal process, investors can learn more about how firms embed a commitment to performance accountability.[9] Performance accountability increases investor confidence by reducing risk in two ways. First, accountability manages expectations so that results are more predictable. A top investor relations officer said that one of the key factors in communicating with investors was to show that the firm delivered as promised. This means promising less so that expectations are realistic about what can

Figure 10.1. Framework for Assessing Organization's Performance Accountability Processes

be delivered. This also means sharing information when expectations change. Predictability reduces risk and increases confidence.

Second, performance accountability reduces variance, which improves the value of an investment. Consider the two firms in Table 10.1: both have average earnings of 10 over eight quarters, but Firm A has a high standard deviation (risk or variance) and Firm B has a low standard deviation—6.5 versus 1.85. Investors prefer Firm B, with its lower variances, because they don't want surprises or uncertainty.

Performance accountability emphasizes the level of confidence investors have in the target organization's likelihood of keeping promises at both the individual and business level. At the individual level, accountability often shows up in how high and low performers are treated. One investor asks business leaders how they deal with poor performers. The investor said, "Organizations waste money on those employees who aren't working on the things that make the company money." This investor wants to know that the executives are willing and able to confront poor performance. When executives lack the courage to handle poor performers, they enable slackers. At the organization level, investors want to have confidence that the organization has established accountability practices. These practices are laid out in Figure 10.1 and can be audited to give investors insights into an organization's performance accountability process.

Overall Commitment to Accountability

Performance becomes a habit when it is consistent. Consistency requires accountability. For organizations, accountability may occur for customers, investors, and people.

Customer accountability deals with brand promises. Companies often make promises to customers; accountability indicates the extent to which firms live up to those promises. High-end restaurants receive far more complaints than cheap diners because people expect more from high-end restaurants. Here are some examples of customer promises that shape expectations:

- *Federal Express:* Deliver on time every time.
- *GEICO:* 15 minutes or less can save you 15% or more on car insurance.
- *Nationwide Insurance:* Nationwide is on your side.
- *Gillette Fusion ProGlide:* Against the grain closeness, comfortably.
- *Cadillac:* The promise of luxury.
- *Mercedes Benz:* Engineering, quality, performance, consumer service.
- *McDonald's:* Fast service, consistent food taste and quality, consistent pricing.
- *Microsoft:* Where do you want to go today?
- *Google:* Access to the world's information in one click.
- *Patagonia:* We provide for environmentally responsible adventure.
- *Ritz Carlton:* Ladies and gentlemen serving ladies and gentlemen.

These promises become tag lines, advertising slogans, or rallying cries that build customer expectations. Investors can track the extent to which these promises are kept through company customer surveys, net promoter scores, or external reputation reviews (such as rankings in media listings, or generating word clouds from comments in social media).

Financial accountability deals with how well firms meet financial expectations. Most firms offer guidance to the investment community, forecasting growth and earnings based on their plans. This guidance builds a consensus about expected financial performance. A number of investors track the variances from this guidance over time, and this variance from guidance indicates the financial risk of the enterprise.

People accountability deals with how well an organization manages employee performance. This process involves the robust conversations, clear standards, links between standards and consequences, targeted rewards, and follow-up discussed in the remainder of this chapter. It can develop spontaneously from the relationship between leaders and employees, but it is desirable to develop processes to institutionalize this accountability. People accountability inside a company often defines a broader commitment to customer and financial accountability outside the company.

The sum of customer, financial, and people accountabilities represents an overall commitment to performance accountability—and a commitment to performance accountability gives investors confidence in a firm's ability to reduce risk.

Possible indicators:

- *How well does the organization live up to its brand promises?*
- *How much variance is there in financial performance from guidance?*
- *How well does the organization hold people accountable for meeting or missing goals?*

Positive Accountability Conversation

When we ask people about organization processes for performance accountability, most quickly focus on the performance appraisal process of setting standards, evaluating and differentiating people against standards (called *rack them and yank them* or *stack them and rack them*), allocating rewards against performance, and doing follow-up. While these steps in appraisal are important and can be audited, they cause a lot of frustration because they tend to be bureaucratic, disconnected from business results, focused on what is wrong instead of what is right, and slow to adapt to changing business conditions. In one study, only 3% (of 1,065 companies) reported that their overall performance management system delivers exceptional value.[10]

For example, over the course of fifteen years, one leading company implemented a host of best practice performance appraisal systems, including management by objectives, behavioral anchored rating scales, key performance indicators, ranking employees, and a 9-box grid. None of these initiatives improved performance. Upon reflection, the leadership concluded that the key to effective performance accountability was less the specific performance appraisal practice and more the ability to have a candid, thorough, positive, and specific performance conversation with employees. They worked to help leaders have a mindset of—and skills for—positive conversations in which employees would leave a dialogue feeling better about themselves. They also trained leaders to have a three-step affirming performance conversation:

- "Help me understand . . .": This lead-in frames the leader as a coach who wants to help rather than a superior who wants to control.

- "The data . . .": This discussion introduces specific data about an employee's performance and behavior. Focusing on data allows the leader to help people know where they stand on specific behaviors and outcomes without judging the personality or style of the individual.

- "So that we can make improvements . . .": This focuses on the future and what can be done better rather than on the past and what has gone wrong.

These affirmative conversations are not just a calendared event; they work best as an ongoing process in which leaders interact regularly with employees. With these productive conversation techniques in use, almost any performance system can work effectively. The most important thing that managers can do to improve performance accountability is to have candid dialogue between leaders and employees.[11] By having these conversations, leaders model how to be transparent about accountability issues without being burdened with complex processes.

These positive conversations help people gain what is called a growth mindset, concentrating on what can be improved.[12] By focusing on the future, they encourage resilience and perseverance. They address the behavior problem without judging the person, and thus validate people and their potential. When leaders focus on helping people learn from both successes and failures rather than critiquing, they can offer career opportunities that match skills and commitments. The locus of control for improvement shifts from the leader to the employee. The resulting conversation is not about the forms, tools, or processes but about creating a positive relationship between leader and employee.

Investors can assess the extent to which executives build accountability through positive conversations by looking at the percentage of employees who have had a positive performance conversation with their boss in the past twelve months. Investors can also assess the extent to which leaders are prepared to have positive accountability conversations. Further, employee surveys can indicate the quality of those discussions and whether they focus on leaders as coaches more than commanders. One company tracked the percentage of each leader's employees who reported having a positive formal conversation in the past year. This conversation measure was a major indicator for leaders' evaluation.

Possible indicators:

- *What percentage of employees have had a positive accountability conversation within the last year?*
- *How well are leaders trained to have ongoing positive conversations?*
- *How do employees feel about the accountability conversations?*

Clear Standards That Differentiate Performance

Through positive conversations, managers and employees build an affirming relationship. But performance accountability requires that this conversation include a clear set of expectations about what the employee should deliver and how to differentiate high-performing from low-performing employees. A productive discussion on standards is less about filling out forms and more about building understanding of what is expected. Without standards that differentiate employees, accountability languishes. Investors can look at what standards are set for employees and how they are set to see if they encourage accountability.

WHAT STANDARDS ARE SET

Employees need to know what is expected of them so that they know if and when they have done a good job. This starts by creating a line of sight from the strategic direction of their organization to the personal action of the employee. Employee accountability goes up when expectations are within the employee's control. While all employees should be concerned about the firm's overall financial performance and stock price, they need to focus on behaviors and outcomes within their own control; otherwise, they become motivated observers but not doers. Balancing behavior with outcomes (at the individual, team, or organization level) helps employees deliver the right outcomes in the right ways.

Employees should know their priorities so as to focus their attention properly. Investors can ask employees whether they know what they can personally do for business success or feel that their behavior will lead to important organization outcomes, and whether they have an agreement with their boss and teammates about their priorities. One investor merely asks leaders or targeted employees to share what they are focused on for the next time period (quarter, year, or two years). To begin, the investor wants to know if employees can quickly articulate what is expected of them in a rigorous way. Then the investor wants to confirm that these personal expectations tie to business results, that employees feel personally committed to them, and that employees recognize how their personal actions achieve the standards. Without clear standards, employees do not know what is expected of them; they may be engaged or motivated, but it is not clear if they are engaged in the right work. Engagement without expectations may well prove to be misdirected energy.

HOW STANDARDS ARE SET

The process for setting expectations is as important as the standards set, or more so. When imposed, standards become obligations performed out of duty—which tends to evoke minimum effort, lacking in flexibility or personal engagement. When employees actively participate in defining what is expected, they are much more likely to be committed to those standards. Productivity increases when employees are (or feel as if they are) self-employed and in control of what is expected of them.[13] In addition, if situations change, employees who have set their own standards can more readily adapt them to changing conditions without waiting to be told.

Investors should ask employees how much they participated in setting expectations for themselves. Through participation in defining expectations, employees take personal ownership for delivering results. When employees show investors their standards, investors can ask the extent to which the employee participated in defining the standards and the degree of personal commitment to the standard.

One major investor probed clear standards by asking key employees some targeted questions:

- To what extent do you feel personally accountable to promote your business's strategic vision?
- Do you have and set clear key performance indicators that tell you what you contribute to your business's success?
- How well do you and your team create a solid return on invested capital that is consistent with expectations?
- To what extent do you and your team have a solid track record of achieving results?

The investor had much more confidence in the organization when responses to these questions were positive because people knew and accepted what was expected of them.

Possible indicators:

- *What percentage of employees see how their personal work fits with the overall organization strategy?*
- *What percentage of employees have clear expectations for what defines effective performance?*
- *What percentage of employees participate in defining their expectations and standards for effective performance?*

Standards Linked to Consequences

Even if employees have a positive conversation with their boss and know what they should to do be effective, accountability requires consequences. Lack of consequences can show up in many settings. For example, one company had an average salary increase of 3%, with a range of 2.5% to 3.5%. It is unlikely that employee performance varied by just 1%, so the low range of salary increase minimized rewards for high performers and actually encouraged low performers.

Another organization leader missed reaching goals and received a letter from senior leaders acknowledging the miss, but suffered no further consequences. It was not a surprise that this leader missed goals again.

One newly appointed CEO from outside the company asked his top executives to report how well they did on meeting their goals (green, yellow, red). In a team setting, he shared their reporting—almost all goals were said to be in the green (fully met)—then asked the obvious question: "If all of you are meeting your goals, how come we lost a billion bucks last year?" Either the goals were wrong or misleading, or they were not really met, or they were not tied to organizational outcomes. In each of these cases, linking standards to consequences communicates a message about accountability.[14]

Differentiated performance requires differentiated consequences. Consequences can be positive or negative, financial and nonfinancial (see Table 10.2). Companies with high performance accountability use all four cells, depending on how well employees meet standards. Positive financial results have the benefit of being precise, measurable, and comparable across positions and people.

Some organizations publish salary increases as a way to signal employee performance in the past year. By observing who received the

Table 10.2. Types of Reinforcers and Consequences

		Type of Consequences	
		Financial	Nonfinancial[a]
Types of Reinforcers	Positive	· Salary increase · Bonus · Equity	· Recognition · Work itself · Work and career opportunity
	Negative	· Lack of salary increase · Loss of bonus · No equity	· Reprimand · Negative review · Absence of work and career opportunity · Limited work choice

[a]There are wonderful lists of nonfinancial rewards: Bob Nelson, *1501 Ways to Reward Employees* (New York: Workman Publishing Company, 2012); Bob Nelson and Barton Morris, *1001 Ways to Energize Employees* (New York: Workman Publishing Company, 1997).

largest increases, employees can see the financial relevance of good performance. However, nonfinancial reinforcers sometimes matter even more. Recognition, interesting work, and unique opportunities send even louder and often more public signals of how well an employee has performed. These consequences are often visible as employees and organizations compare how they do relative to peers.

To build accountability, performance needs to be directly tied to consequences. Annual performance reviews rarely do much to ensure consequences; they happen up to a year after actual performance of the work, which is usually too distant to have much impact. Immediacy of consequences sends timely signals about what matters most.

Our colleague Steve Kerr has created a rewards diagnostic that investors can use to track how well an organization links standards to consequences (see Table 10.3).[15] In this diagnostic, the rows represent the standards or expectations in terms of the behavior (in this case a desire to improve innovation) required to make it happen. Then leaders can divide 10 points across three columns of possible consequences if someone engages in the behavior (positive, negative, unpredictable) so that the row totals 10 points. This diagnostic helps leaders and investors see the extent to which the desired behaviors align with the consequences. In many firms, most of the 10 points are in the "unpredictable" column,

Table 10.3. Reward Diagnostic

Measures and Behaviors (in this case, innovation)	Consequences			
	Positive reward or approval	Negative punishment or disapproval	Unpredictable, don't know, can't detect	Total (10 points)
Coming up with or trying new ideas				= 10
Exceeding authority to get job done				= 10
Presenting boss with unpopular view				= 10
Setting easy goals then making them				= 10
Violating chain of command if necessary				= 10
(Other Items can be added as needed)				

Source: Adapted from Steve Kerr.

where it is not clear whether a positive or negative consequence follows the desired behavior. These organizations lack performance accountability because standards are not tied to consequences.

This exercise will help investors know the extent to which standards translate to behaviors that link to consequences.

Possible indicators:

- *What percentage of executive compensation payouts are linked to the top five performance commitments?*
- *To what extent are bonuses and incentives tied to the interests of shareholders?*

Reward Systems That Drive Behavior

People generally do what they are rewarded for doing. As noted in Table 10.2, rewards can include financial or nonfinancial benefits, or a mix of the two. Both employees and investors look at rewards for information about what matters most. Investors should look carefully at the supplemental pay disclosure and at the executive summary of the compensation philosophy and practices to make sure that executive incentives line up with investor intentions.

FOCUS

The criteria for incentives send clear signals about what matters most. Investors should monitor the extent to which pay is linked to strategy, whether it be growth through innovation, customer share, or geographic expansion, or cost control through productivity, capital expenditures, or process improvements. Investors should be able to discern the strategy by reading the compensation disclosure, and the strategy should be reflected in the focus of reward systems. For example, one investor found that firms he was investing in were competing by managing costs, so he looked at total compensation costs per employee compared to competitors as a compensation ratio that reflected commitment to efficiency. Another investor saw that his targeted firm would grow through innovation, so he examined the bonuses and incentives of leadership to see if they were aligned with innovation initiatives that would differentiate the firm. He measured the firm's vitality index—the percentage of revenues (or profits) from products created in the past four years—and compared his target firm with competitors to guide his confidence in the firm's accountability for innovation.

DURATION AND RISK

Incentives can be tied to the short term (annual salary or bonus with lower risk) or to the longer term (stock options, stock appreciation rights, restricted stock, and performance shares with higher risk). Recent studies of U.S. executives show the following allocation of incentives:[16]

- Base: 18%   - Stock: 23%
- Bonus: 43%   - Options: 10%

Investors should make sure that executive risk incentives match investor expectations. To implement this kind of match, almost all firms with long-term incentive plans have begun including total shareholder return (TSR) as a factor. Aligning investor and leader risks also includes investors' assessing the extent to which key leaders have a sizeable portion of their personal net worth in the firm's equity. Another investor looks closely at employee trading in the firm's stock, which is public information. When internal leaders are buying or selling stock, the investor claims it is a signal about their confidence in their firm's future.

SHAREDNESS

The extent to which incentives are shared within the organization sends a signal about equity (differentiated pay) versus equality (similar pay). One investor compares the CEO's pay to the average income of first-line managers. Another looks at the percentage of profit distributed and the gap between top executives and middle managers. Still another investor looks at the gap between the top leader's total compensation and that of the top four executives. In each of these cases, investors want to know the extent to which companies share the financial gains of the company broadly throughout the organization. A broader distribution of economic gain builds employee engagement, retains top employees, and aligns employee interests with investors. The pay disparity between top leader and average employee pay has become an increasingly visible and sensitive issue. In the United States, recent statistics report a gap of 350% between CEO pay and average worker salary.[17] Investors should be aware of this income disparity, which may signal an inequity culture where workers are likely to feel disengaged.

Possible indicators:

- *To what extent do executive incentives reflect business strategy?*
- *To what extent do executives have their personal net worth tied to investor objectives (for example, with stock options)?*
- *To what extent do employees throughout an organization share in the gains of the organization?*
- *How much gap is there between CEO (senior leader) pay and the pay of employees throughout the company?*

Performance Follow-Up

Performance accountability begins and ends with positive accountable conversations. As discussed earlier, investors can monitor how well leaders have positive conversations to set expectations, link behavior and outcomes, and manage rewards. For sustainable accountability, however, investors should also know the extent to which leaders follow up on expectations. In one company, investors discovered that if a leader overspent his financial budget, he would receive a harassing letter that essentially said, "You missed your budget." No other consequences occurred. Leaders, and investors, soon recognized that there was little or no performance follow-up.

Without follow-up, goals—no matter how they are set—are rarely

Table 10.4. Good Practices in Follow-Up for Performance

Current Practice	Emerging Practice
Have a performance conversation only at one point in time.	Have performance conversations in real time (ongoing) as well as around events (annual celebration, promotion, salary).
Focus on ability ("You are smart") that creates a fixed mindset.	Focus on effort ("You work hard") to create a growth mindset. Praise efforts as well as results.
Look back to emphasize performance: ("You are good at . . .")	Look forward to see opportunity and create learning ("What did you learn that you can apply in the future?").
Emphasize what is wrong.	Emphasize what is right (keep a 5:1 positive-to-negative ratio).
Leader behavior is to command and control, being distant from the change process.	Coach and communicate by modeling change and personal improvement.
Focus on action.	Focus on sustainability of action.
Talk and tell what has happened and should happen.	Listen and engage in affirmative conversation on what could happen next.
Prepare by going through paperwork process.	Prepare by thinking about how to help the individual person.

accomplished. Often good intentions do not lead to sustainable actions.[18] In large-scale studies, even moderate follow-up has been shown to help people sustain change.[19] Table 10.4 summarizes good practices in follow up for accountability. Investors should see if top leaders engage in these practices. My colleagues and I have found that without follow-up, about 20% of new ideas are implemented, but with follow-up, people may sustain 60% to 70% of what they intend.

When investors monitor how leaders follow up, they ensure greater performance accountability.

Possible indicators:

- *To what extent do leaders, in their follow-up, focus more on what is right than on what is wrong?*
- *To what extent do leaders help employees learn from mistakes rather than punish them?*
- *To what extent do leaders have timely performance conversations when things need improvement?*

Conclusion

For good reasons, most people do not like bureaucratic appraisal processes that monitor performance, belittle participants, and focus on what is wrong. But performance accountability matters. Without personal and public accountability, people don't improve, and organizations do not meet expectations. Investors need to know that employees have a sense of personal accountability for delivering results. This means focusing much less on performance appraisal as a bureaucratic annual process—and much more on performance accountability, which means that leaders hold positive conversations with employees, mutually establish expectations, link expectations to consequences, implement accountable reward systems, and follow up on performance. When investors explore these processes through the indicators in Table 10.5, they will have more confidence in the organization's ability to reduce risk.

Table 10.5. Indicators for Performance Accountability Practices

Indicators	Possible Indicators	How to Assess
Overall commitment to performance accountability	How well does the organization live up to its brand promises?	Examine public perceptions of brand promises and net promoter scores.
	How much variance is there in financial performance against guidance?	Track variance in guidance versus results over time compared to competitors.
	How well does the organization hold people accountable for meeting or missing goals?	Find out what happens to low performers.

(continued)

Table 10.5. (continued)

Indicators	Possible Indicators	How to Assess
Positive accountability conversation	What percentage of employees have had a positive accountability conversation within the last year? How well are leaders trained to have ongoing positive conversations? How do employees feel about the accountability conversations?	Survey employees to determine if they have positive conversations about performance, and how often. Interview leaders about how they do performance conversations to see if they are positive or negative.
Clear standards that differentiate performance	What percentage of employees see how their personal work fits with the overall organization strategy? What percentage of employees have clear expectations for what defines effective performance? What percentage of employees participate in defining their expectations and standards for effective performance?	Determine the percentage of employees who know what is expected of them for good performance and who can link their day-to-day behavior to organization outcomes. Ask employees how their performance outcomes are determined, through participation or prescription.
Standards linked to rewards	What percentage of executive compensation payouts are linked to the top five performance commitments? To what extent are bonuses and incentives tied to the interests of shareholders?	Determine the percentage of employees who receive regular performance reviews. Track the extent to which executive bonuses match strategic intent. Compare total shareholder return to CEO pay relative to peers over one and five years.

Indicators	Possible Indicators	How to Assess
Reward systems that drive behavior	To what extent do executive incentives reflect business strategy? To what extent do executives have their personal net worth tied to investor objectives (for example, with stock options)? To what extent do employees throughout an organization share in the gains of the organization? How much gap is there between the pay of CEO (senior leader) and the pay of employees throughout the company?	Examine the extent to which compensation systems tie to total shareholder return for long-term incentives. Track percentage of team members with salary at risk based on performance. Ensure that executives have personal ownership in the firm. Examine the depth of profit sharing or equity ownership throughout the organization.
Performance follow-up	To what extent do leaders doing follow-up focus on what is right more than what is wrong in their follow-up? To what extent do leaders help employees learn from mistakes rather than punish them? To what extent do leaders have timely performance conversations when things need improvement?	Survey the extent to which employees perceive leaders as qualified at follow-up. Probe when something has gone wrong to see how leaders respond.

CHAPTER 11

Information Processes

Investors Want Organizations That Use Information for Impact

Power, or the ability to influence others, comes from knowledge. Knowledge comes from information. When individuals or organizations access and use information that others don't have, they can make better decisions.

Having information is more than access to data; it requires knowing how to synthesize, interpret, and act on data. Organizations that create informed information processes go beyond reports, scorecards, analytics, and cloud data to intervene in decisions that will have positive impact. Information processes should be used to fulfill expectations outside the organization while creating meaning and purpose for those inside. Organizations that create information asymmetries for themselves should give investors increased confidence in future success. In this era of information ubiquity and the Internet, the information landscape continues to evolve rapidly. Investors should audit how well their targeted organizations manage the six information processes sketched in Figure 11.1. But before reviewing these processes, investors should be aware of the information trends that inform investor insights.

Trends in Information

Today's astoundingly rapid shifts in information technology provide both threat and opportunity for organizations.[1] With every hour, firms have more data to process, people have more access to data, and the speed of data transmission increases. As just one example, more data was created in any forty-eight-hour period in 2014 than by all of humanity during the preceding thirty thousand years. By 2020, this will happen every *hour*.[2] In 2010, global companies stored 7 exabytes of new data and consumers stored 6 exabytes. (One exabyte equals four thousand times the total

**Figure 11.1. Framework for Assessing
Organization's Information Processes**

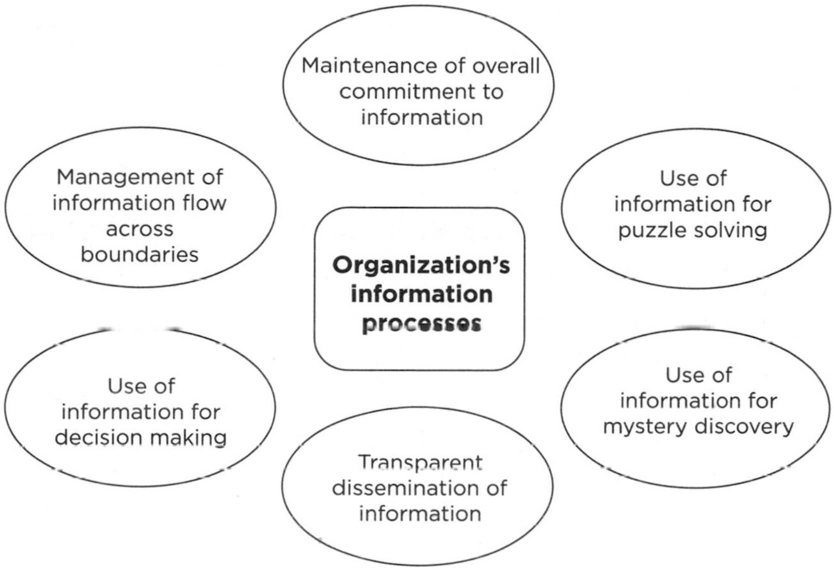

information in the U.S. Library of Congress.) In 2014, $600 will buy a disk drive that stores all the world's music. In 2014, there are three hundred million Tweets per day, thirty billion comments shared per month on Facebook, and a billion transistors for every person on the planet.

Because of these trends, nearly all investors will have access to the same traditional financial information. Without developing it on their own, however, they will not have a clear picture of the powerful asset of leadership, which makes the leadership capital index in this book a source of information asymmetry.

TRENDS IN SPEED AND ACCESS

Moore's law suggests that over the history of computing, the number of transistors on an integrated circuit (a surrogate for speed) doubles about every two years.[3] If that trend continues as technology changes, by the year 2025 computers will function at *6,500* times the speed of those we have in 2015. Essentially, the speed of information has gone up and cost has gone down. This speed of information affects people and investors. People visit a website less often if it is slower than a close competitor's by more than 250 milliseconds.[4]

Information is increasingly accessible to everyone. In 2000, 350 million people had Internet access and 750 million people had mobile phone access. In 2015, over 3 billion people had Internet access and 6 billion people had mobile phone access. Access makes the world smaller and its inhabitants closer to each other. Political trends in any one country rapidly have global impact, and social trends go viral and influence lifestyle choices around the world.

For investors, ability to access financial, intangible, and leadership information faster than a competitor becomes a major advantage.

INDUSTRY TRENDS DRIVEN BY INFORMATION TECHNOLOGY

Information trends shape nearly every industry:

- *3D printing:* Shoes, mobile phones, even full-sized motorcycles now can be printed rather than assembled.

- *News availability:* Some news websites publish more than a thousand articles a day. News is increasingly global and immediately accessible.

- *Cost savings:* By 2020, time and fuel savings through smart routing will reach $500 billion, and CO_2 emissions will be cut by 5% per year.

- *Video:* Six billion hours per month are spent on YouTube. Google purchased YouTube in 2006 for $1.65 billion. Revenues in 2015 will be over $4.5 billion. In 2015, YouTube is estimated to be worth $15 to $20 billion.

- *Transportation:* Self-driving cars developed by Google and Stanford University have traveled 100,000 miles with no accidents and will almost certainly enter the consumer market.

- *Identity recognition:* In 2000, Facebook had 1 billion photos. In 2010, 2.5 billion were posted per month. Technology and facial recognition allow someone to scan the Web to identify names of faces and then even the best friends of those they identify.

- *Internet of things (Industrial Internet):* We are transitioning from people talking to people about things to things talking to things about people. Intelligent machines can fix each other before they break. Sensors on planes signal to machines on the ground that repairs are needed. This eliminates 60,000 late flights per year.

- *Globalization of information:* Anthony Motua from Nairobi goes online and learns some stuff. He develops a crystal chip for the insole of his shoe to power his mobile phone. Illiterate seven-year-olds in Ethiopia are given preloaded and continually updated tablets from MIT Media Lab. In months, they are reciting the entire English alphabet and writing in complete sentences.

For investment firms such as BlackRock, PIMCO, Goldman Sachs, and the best sovereign wealth funds, information is a critical source of competitive advantage. These firms have a disciplined approach that creates information asymmetry—unique knowledge that offers a source of competitive advantage for the organization possessing it. The premise of the leadership capital index is that information about leadership will help investors make more informed decisions about firms in which they invest.

Just as investment firms need to learn to develop information for their use, they should also audit how organizations they invest in use and deploy information. Too much information may come from an over-abundance of charts, graphs, statistics, and data. Too little information means making decisions based on instinct instead of evidence. Some information is structured and found in reports; other information is unstructured and found in relationships. Both are important. The six information processes discussed in this chapter offer a structured way for investors to audit information processes.

Maintenance of Overall Commitment to Information

W. Edwards Deming updated an old saying to "In God we trust. All others must bring data."[5] Organizations have a range of choices about how they access and use data. Data has a time frame (past, present, and future) and a use referent (see Table 11.1).

As organizations move from reporting to scorecards to recommendations to predictions, they start to use data to shape future interventions. Traditionally, organizations had fragmented data sets that showed up in isolated reports about employees, customers, manufacturing processes, or financial performance. Many of these disparate data sets are being combined to create dashboards or scorecards that can be monitored to provide alerts about what is happening. Looking ahead, some leading companies use data to predict what will happen.

Much of this prediction process comes from "big data." For example, companies like Google, Amazon, and American Express have big data about customers. For these companies, data tells a story about customer purchasing patterns that can be used to target specific products to specific customers. The insights from this data allow companies to antici-

Table 11.1. Time Frame and Uses of Data

		Time Frame		
		Past	Present	Future
Use of Data	Intelligence and Insight	What happened? (reporting)	What is happening now? (scorecards, dashboards)	What will happen? (extrapolation)
	Intervention and Impact	How and why did it happen? (modeling)	What's the next best action? (recommendation)	What is the best or worst that can happen? (prediction)

Source: This chart is adapted from a Robert Morison presentation. Thomas Davenport, Jeanne Harris, Robert Morison, *Analytics at Work: Smarter Decisions, Better Results* (Boston: Harvard Business Review Press, 2010); Eric Siegel, *Predictive Analytics: The Power to Predict Who Will Click, Buy, Lie, or Die* (Hoboken, NJ: Wiley, 2013); Thomas Davenport, *Big Data at Work: Dispelling the Myths, Uncovering the Opportunities* (Boston, MA: Harvard Business Review Press, 2014).

pate what will happen and respond accordingly. For example, sentiment analyses make it possible to find out how social media reflect positive or negative attitudes about a company.[6] Companies more committed to current and future uses of data for intervention and impact are likely to have information processes that give investors greater confidence.

Investors can track an organization's commitment to uses of data. They can test the extent to which corporate leaders set the tone and influence the culture of analytics in the workplace. They can review the information strategy for the organization to see if it focuses on the past, present, or future. They can observe and ask if leaders demand data from others, because such demands for data are the most important factor to move information forward. They can observe how the leaders make decisions and whether the organization uses analytics to predict future employee and customer behavior. They can see whether the company uses separate data sets or integrated enterprise-wide data. They can review the budget allocated to analytics.

Investors also have to track the security of information. Recent data breaches at leading companies (such as Target, J.P. Morgan, Home Depot, SuperValu, and Verizon) indicate the seriousness of the need for information protection. Between 2005 and September 2014, more than 4,800 data breaches were reported.[7] Investors should monitor the extent to which organizations have implemented the latest information security disciplines to prevent these breaches.

Possible indicators:

- *Does the organization have an information bias and culture, so that people make decisions based on information?*
- *Does the organization have a strategy of how to access and use information?*
- *Does the organization invest in integrated information technology?*
- *Does the organization have state-of-the-art information security disciplines?*

Use of Information for Puzzle Solving

Gregory Treverton, a national security expert, distinguished between information for solving puzzles and information for resolving mysteries.[8] You can solve a puzzle and come up with a specific quantifiable answer. For example, finding Osama bin Laden meant solving a puzzle by having better information that led to a clear answer about where he lived. Leaders solve puzzles, make decisions, and move on. Mysteries, on the other hand, are a different matter. "[They] pose questions that have no definitive answers because their solution depends on a future interaction of many factors, known and unknown. A mystery really can't be answered; it can only be framed by identification of factors that interacted in the past and may in the future."[9] To continue the example, post-Afghanistan political transition is a mystery because it is not clear what will happen when the regime changes. As Millward Brown put it, solving puzzles delivers answers; exploring mysteries spawns fresh insights.[10]

Wayne Brockbank has distinguished between information for puzzle solving and for mystery exploration (see Table 11.2). A puzzle involves structured data, whereas a mystery revolves around unstructured data. When trying to assemble a puzzle, additional puzzle pieces (nuggets of information) will help make a complete picture. Additional information helps you make sense of the picture.

Investors should assess the extent to which organizations collect information to solve puzzles. Linear problem solving shows up in reports, scorecards, and dashboards; the structured information often involves spreadsheets, is organized into acceptable knowledge categories, and forms the basis of regular reports. Leaders who rely on structured information look for variances in patterns so that they can improve their decision making.

Increasingly, this structured information is coming from big data sources.[11] As applied to analytics, structured data works to explain more about why things happen. One firm was able to predict which employ-

Table 11.2. Types of Information: Puzzle versus Mystery

	Types of Information	
	Puzzle (structured information)	*Mystery (unstructured information)*
Nature of the Problem	· Not enough information	· Too much information
	· Discover facts	· Interpret patterns
	· Once found, information is readily interpreted	· Once found, information is difficult to interpret
	· More information clarifies	· More information muddles
	· Discovering simplicity	· Integrating complexity
	· Discovering reality	· Predicting reality
Environmental Assumptions	· Stable	· Unstable
	· Few components	· Many components
	· Simple	· Complex
	· More certain	· Uncertain
Information Assumptions	· Structured	· Unstructured
	· Predictable	· Unpredictable
	· Known	· Uncertain
Required Capabilities	· Disciplined investigator	· Identify patterns
	· Fact finders	· Knowledge integrators
	· Individual knowledge	· Collective knowledge
	· Framing powerful questions	· Answering existing questions

Source: Adapted from Wayne Brockbank. Wayne Brockbank has presented these types of information in various settings. One source of his presentation is found in *The Impact of Information,* Playbook for the RBL Institute (2014).

ees were more likely to leave, based on a series of factors (time on job, performance review, degree, career history, and manager). Another company was able to predict drivers of innovation (sharing of ideas, recruiting particular talent, experimenting on ideas, looking for quick wins, caring about the customer). Still another company defined the characteristics of an effective manager (clear vision, help with career development, technical grounding, communication, worry about team members, ability to coach). In each of these cases, structured information solved puzzles by analyzing how to improve retention, innovation, or management.

The presence and use of structured information gives investors confidence that leaders are on top of their business issues, recognize trends, and can solve existing problems. Investors can monitor the extent to which the firm has a strong analytics group with individuals who can apply advanced statistics to business problems. One investor asked company leaders what information they collected and monitored every week. This investor wanted to know if leaders were regularly monitoring key indicators of firm performance so that they could make quick updates when required.

Possible indicators:

- *To what extent does the organization have regular reporting mechanisms to monitor performance?*
- *To what extent does the organization solve problems with regular information?*

Use of Information for Mystery Discovery

Table 11.2 distinguishes between structured information for puzzle solving and unstructured information for mystery exploration. Investors clearly want to know whether firms use information to solve existing problems. But when dealing with a mystery, no one can address the problem directly; someone has to discover the pattern first—often a difficult job. The problem with mysteries is that sometimes leaders don't even know the right questions to ask to explore them. In the future, the nature of work will increasingly be identifying and investigating patterns in unstructured data.

Unstructured data cannot be readily put into spreadsheets. This information is often uncertain, unpredictable, unstable, changing, not readily usable, and not easily organized into knowable categories, and tends to reside in relationships more than numbers. In these cases, it is important to look for patterns in the complex data. Nonetheless, unstructured data is increasingly important as a source of a company's success. Walmart relies heavily on structured data from weekly reports about which products are selling for what price. But Walmart also relies heavily on personal visits from executives to stores, followed by a weekly "Walmart huddle" where participants look at the formal reports and listen to their fellows' informal experiences. Both structured (puzzle solving) and unstructured (mystery exploring) data are important to merchandise products.

Much of the unstructured data comes from social algorithms wherein leaders listen and spend time with customers, innovators, and industry leaders. Leaders who architect social algorithms create more successful firms. For example, a large financial service firm was receiving increasing regulatory pressure. To anticipate and shape the regulatory process, this firm hired one of the leading regulators, who brought insights about regulation into the firm. Another example of creating a unique social algorithm is when the CEO and CHRO worked together to get two of their top scientists who were working on somewhat related research protocols to sit down together to exchange ideas. The CEO had been unsuccessful getting the two scientists to talk to one another, as both felt their work was unrelated. So the CEO and CHRO orchestrated a big dinner and award ceremony to honor both scientists and had them sit next to one another. The real purpose of the award ceremony was to get the two top scientists to share ideas—and it worked perfectly. By the time they left the dinner table, the two scientists had outlined a protocol that ultimately led to a research breakthrough.

Some unstructured mystery information comes from big data sets that exist in photos, e-mail messages, web pages, videos, medical records, publications, and so forth. Other data comes from social algorithms wherein leaders join social networks and participate in hallway conversations, phone calls, town hall meetings, and other gatherings. Information is processed through thoughtful, focused, spontaneous, yet disciplined human interaction.

To help firms harness unstructured information from networks of relationships, it is necessary to share the information in a disciplined manner. The key challenge is putting science and discipline around unstructured information that has to be bundled and interpreted.

Investors should find out if the company diligently codifies, tracks, and uses hard information for decision making (as discussed in the section on puzzle solving). But leaders should also be part of the social fabric of the community. Investors could ask the extent to which leaders are encouraged to be involved in civic, industry, or other events where they can pick up signals about what is happening. This might include dinners, networking meetings, and other settings where they connect with thought leaders.

Possible indicators:

- *How much do leaders socially connect with thought leaders in their field?*
- *How well does the organization source information on unsolved problems or concerns in its field?*
- *How easily do people bring new ideas to the leadership team?*

Transparent Dissemination of Information

A number of years ago a leadership team prepared a strategy document. Each printed copy had a number, and employees accessing the strategy had to check it out and return it like a library book to ensure confidentiality. Not surprisingly, the strategy was never fully implemented. While some strategic choices are private (business restructuring, mergers, acquisitions, or downsizing, for example), keeping strategy under wraps is apt to be counterproductive. Unless strategic plans are broadly disseminated, they generally have limited impact. To ensure impact, both structured and unstructured information should be widely shared and used. Sharing information requires that organizations have processes for sharing the right information in the right way, even when it may be uncomfortable to absorb.

SHARING INFORMATION

Information comes in many forms. Online interactions continue to gain visibility, although currently 60% of employees prefer e-mail, compared to 8% who prefer Facebook to communicate with others.[12] Increasingly, companies are using more diverse forms of electronic information sharing, including Chatter, Twitter, LinkedIn, Yammer, Jive, and so forth. Companies create electronic water coolers where employees gather from a distance and share information. In addition to technology-enabled sharing, social settings continue to be viable ways of sharing information—annual leadership meetings where executives are encouraged to mingle and share ideas, town hall meetings where leaders interact with employees face to face or through technology, training forums where leaders meet in education events to learn from each other, and physical settings where leaders work in collaborative work environments. Information sharing is institutionalized by making it part of performance accountability, offering incentives to share bonuses across boundaries, hiring people who are inclined to share information, and weaving collaboration into the culture.

Organizations that share information smoothly are often called *learning organizations*. My colleagues and I have found that such organizations generated and generalized ideas with impact.[13] We found companies generated new ideas through continuous improvement, boundary spanning, competence acquisition, and experimentation activities. Companies generalized or moved ideas across time, business, or space boundaries by moving people across organization units, offering multifunctional learning forms, or relying on horizontal teamwork. Learning organizations were much more competitive over time than those where information was more closely held.[14]

Investors can monitor the extent to which leaders are inclined to share or hoard information. Some companies allow units to maintain a "not invented here" bias that precludes sharing. Information-sharing companies move ideas across boundaries, focus less on the person than on the idea, and encourage those who share ideas. One investor asked leaders for "one idea that they had borrowed from another leader in the firm." When leaders answered readily, it was a signal that the firm encouraged information sharing.

SHARING THE RIGHT INFORMATION

Some companies share information—but not necessarily the right information. The right information to share should improve business performance, as when innovation-driven companies source insights on technology developments so that their products and services lead the technology innovation curve. Most powerfully, companies work to manage information on their market brand and how the market brand becomes part of the company culture and shapes leadership behaviors. If the brand in the market (that is, in commercial advertisements) does not match the firm's internal reality, this information disconnect will eventually limit the company's success. Harley-Davidson encourages customers to be passionate about their experiences with their motorcycles and lifestyle by holding rallies, encouraging customers to wear Harley clothes (and tattoos), and sharing stories via YouTube. Frito-Lay invited customers to submit product videos about their preference for the product—information sharing so valuable that it led to the top-rated Super Bowl ad in 2009.

Sharing the right information also implies reducing the total volume of information, removing the low-value-added work that often clutters an information flow.[15] Current thinking on essentialism encourages leaders to simplify their work, sticking to things that really matter (markets), things they choose to do (passion), and things that match their skills (talents).[16] This process of simplification helps leaders focus on what matters most so that they can access the right information.

Investors should monitor the information that firms share. Is this information consistent with the firm's unique brand? Does the information have intellectual, social, and emotional appeal? Does external information match internal information? How well does the marketplace respond to the information?

SHARING BAD NEWS AND DISAGREEMENT

Inevitably, bad things happen to or within a company. Bad news might include missing financial guidance, having products or services that fall short of expectations or fail outright, or having employees who act inappropriately. Sometimes, leaders try to run and hide from these anomalies. Yet in case after case, when leaders run *toward* the bad news instead of away from it, they demonstrate willingness to face it, learn from it, and move on. Disagreements fall into a similar category—observations and opinions that differ from the norm are easy to sweep aside, hidden in an artificial consensus, but successful organizations encourage debate and dialogue so that alternative options are explored before reaching consensus.

One investor looked into information transparency in both good times and bad. In bad times he wanted leaders, rather than being defensive or blaming, to apply the principles of an effective apology: we missed, we are sorry, we learned, we will change, and then do it! He was less concerned about a company having bad news to share and more impressed when the bad news became a forum for learning.

Possible indicators:

- *How well does the organization share information, both electronically and socially?*
- *How well does the organization share the right information about what matters most?*
- *How well does the organization handle bad news and internal disagreements and learn from them?*

Use of Information for Decision Making

Recently I bought a new car. A few weeks later, a dutiful customer service call center called to solicit my experiences with the car. I was overall positive to the formal questions, but added some comments outside the formal survey. When I asked what would be done with the information I shared, the response was essentially nonexistent—a long silence, followed by a befuddled "We will get back to you," which they never did.

Whether information comes through structured puzzle solving or from unstructured mystery searching, to have impact it must lead to action. Structured information starts with questions that need to be answered; unstructured information raises questions that also need to be answered. In either case, information should be used to answer questions that lead to more informed decisions.

Clarifying decisions informs the type of information that should be collected. It is easy to go down the wrong track. For example, one company hired thoughtful industrial psychologists who studied turn-

Figure 11.2. Information for Decision Making

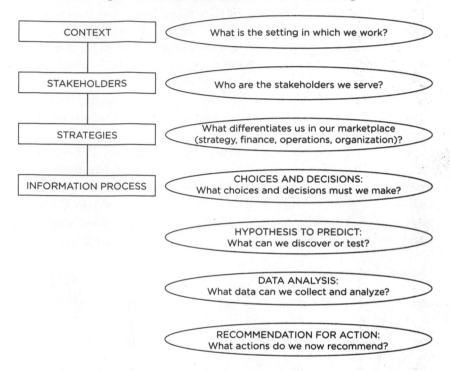

over to build a model of retention of senior people. When done, they had created a rigorous formula that would increase retention. But when asked what percentage of senior people who left the firm were "regrettable losses," the company's answer was 2% to 4%. So they had worked to solve a problem that was not really as significant as other problems facing the firm, such as entering new product categories, moving into new countries, shifting brand promises, and working with investors to meet their expectations.

Information should be developed to answer the right questions. These questions are the ones that help the business create and deliver on its strategy, meet promises to customers, and keep investor promises—all topics addressed in earlier chapters. Information does not start with data; rather, it starts with an understanding of the business questions that have to be answered and of the types of information that can help respond to those questions. Figure 11.2 reviews a process of going from context to information. *Context* defines the setting (industry, country, general business conditions) in which an organization operates. *Stakeholders* defines the key constituencies who have to be served and attended to (customers, investors, regulators, communities, and employees). *Strategies* defines how an organization wins. *Information processes* then helps specify the choices and decisions that need to be made given the context, stakeholders, and strategies, and the data required to make informed choices. Had the firm that hired the psychologists started with this logic, the information focus would have been not on executive turnover but on more urgent business challenges. Focus on decisions streamlines information. One senior leader said, "We are awash in data. Data is not our problem. We have more than enough data. We need insight that will help us appropriately intervene to succeed in the marketplace."

Investors should look for indications that a firm's information processes are connected to top business priorities. They should assess whether reports, scorecards, and dashboards provide information for making better decisions. They should ask leaders about the key questions they need to answer to help their business succeed, then explore the extent to which they source structured and unstructured information to answer these questions. Leaders who use information well often have strategic priorities that they need to resolve; if investors can see that these leaders are thoughtfully using information to respond to these priorities, they will have more confidence in the information processes.

Possible indicators:

- *Can executives prioritize key choices and decisions they need to make to be effective?*
- *Does the organization use the right information to make essential decisions?*

Management of Information Flow Across Boundaries

Information is not static; it continually flows or moves to connect people across boundaries through ideas. Organizations generally have four types of boundaries that information can traverse (or not): outside in, side to side, top to bottom/bottom to top, and global.[17] When information crosses these boundaries smoothly, the organization as a whole becomes more valuable than the parts.

OUTSIDE IN (CONTEXTUAL)

Information outside the organization can be brought inside. External expectations should shape both leadership brand and culture. Examples of accessing external information point to how companies solve customer expectations.[18] For example, SuperValu (a retail company) has stores located near U.S. college campuses and employs a lot of students—many of whom were posting on Yammer wondering why SuperValu didn't sell mini-refrigerators for small dormitory rooms. It seemed a natural and logical product to employees who live in dormitory rooms. SuperValu used this market input coming from Yammer and sold eight thousand mini-refrigerators to students, each with a $90 coupon inside for future purchases. In another example, Disney's "My Magic" wristband can store information on the name of a guest's child and birthday. The Disney characters have earplugs to get that information so that when little Lily comes close by, Cinderella says to her, "Happy birthday, Lily!" Driscoll's, the berry company, uses QR codes on its packaging so customers can scan the code on their smartphones, find information about the farm the berries came from, get information on the growing process, and provide feedback. Companies who encourage employees to act as customers (by blind shopping, making market research calls, or following up on customer complaints) and to share their experiences will help bring outside information inside the company. In these cases, investors can monitor the extent to which an organization accesses external information and turns it into internal organization actions.

SIDE TO SIDE (HORIZONTAL)

Organizations increasingly have to collaborate across silos to respond more quickly to market opportunities. In the auto industry, the cycle time from concept to commercialization of a new car used to be about seven years, as each functional area had to share knowledge over a boundary (from R&D to engineering to manufacturing to quality to marketing to sales to service). Some auto firms cut this cycle time to eighteen months by creating cross-function teams to share information simultaneously across boundaries. Investors can monitor how well information moves through informal groups, technology connections, rotational assignments, shared rewards, co-locations, or integrator roles.

TOP TO BOTTOM (VERTICAL)

The mental model of an organization as a pyramid is increasingly dysfunctional. When information moves rapidly from top to bottom and from bottom to top, an organization becomes a network.[19] Network organizations (discussed in Chapter 12) quickly share information across levels with town hall meetings, weekly blogs, chat rooms with employees, webinars, suggestion systems, formal ombudsman roles, and open-door practices. Investors can test the extent to which all employees understand and share the goals of the company.

GLOBAL

In our research on learning organizations, we found that most large global organizations generated exceptional ideas—somewhere, sometime, and someplace. The challenge was having a disciplined process to generalize these ideas across global boundaries so that successes in one location could be shared in others. Successful firms build disciplined processes to generalize ideas.

One company called this a *learning matrix* and identified key processes required for exceptional performance, along with the subpractices required for these processes. The company then identified geographic units where these exceptional practices were being deployed. With this information, its people were able to share top practices across geographic boundaries to encourage learning. Increasingly, global knowledge moves from emerging to mature markets, because managerial innovation often occurs in new settings. Investors interested in large company information flow can ask how well the organization moves experiences across country boundaries.

Investors should monitor how well information flows across these four boundaries in an organization. When organizations quickly and readily share information across these boundaries, they are likely to better solve puzzles and resolve mysteries in ways that lead to better decision making.

Possible indicators:

- *How well does the organization share information across outside-in boundaries?*
- *How well does the organization share information across side-to-side (horizontal) boundaries?*
- *How well does the organization share information across top-to-bottom (vertical) boundaries?*
- *How well does the organization share information across global boundaries?*

Conclusion

"I know something you don't know" has become a tag line, T-shirt slogan, rapper song, and fashion statement. In the information age, access to and use of information also helps organizations win.[20] With technological change, information moves faster and becomes more accessible. Organizations are defined by how well they turn information into action.[21] Investors can monitor how well leaders institutionalize processes that provide structured and unstructured information to make better decisions as well as how well information is shared across multiple boundaries. Table 11.3 presents indicators of these information processes that could go into a leadership capital index. By auditing information processes, investors can have more confidence in how their organization operates.

Table 11.3. Indicators for Information Practices

Indicators	Possible Indicators	How to Assess
Maintenance of overall commitment to information	Does the organization have an information bias and culture, so that people make decisions based on information? Does the organization have a strategy of how to access and use information? Does the organization invest in integrated information technology? Does the organization have state-of-the-art information security disciplines?	Examine recent key decisions and assess what information was used to make the decision. Review the information strategy to see if it meets the criteria of good information. Compare information budget per employee with that of competitors. Benchmark information security with latest information risk control practices.
Use of information for puzzle solving (structured information)	To what extent does the organization have regular reporting mechanisms to monitor performance? To what extent does the organization solve problems with regular information?	Review regular reports to see if they deal with current information. Audit the value of the reports generated each month.
Use of information for mystery discovery (unstructured information)	How much do leaders socially connect with thought leaders in their field? How well does the organization source information on unsolved problems or concerns in its field? How easily do people bring new ideas to the leadership team?	Audit the external social connections of key leaders. Determine if the organization has a reputation for thought leadership and new ideas. Ask leaders which problems are yet to be solved.

Indicators	Possible Indicators	How to Assess
Transparent dissemination of information	How well does the organization share information, both electronically and socially?	Audit the use of technology to share information. What percentage of employees use technology?
	How well does the organization share the right information about what matters most?	Determine how much priorities are shared throughout the organization. Ask employees what they think the priorities are.
	How well does the organization handle bad news and internal disagreements and learn from them?	Ask about times when something did not go well and audit how leaders responded.
Use of information for decision making	Can executives prioritize key choices and decisions they need to make to be effective?	Determine the alignment of strategies and decisions with information being generated.
	Does the organization use the right information to make essential decisions?	Examine the decision processes to see how people use information.
Management of information flow across boundaries	How well does the organization share information across outside-in boundaries?	Examine how well customer expectations are tied to employee actions.
	How well does the organization share information across side-to-side (horizontal) boundaries?	Find out how many people are on cross-functional teams.
	How well does the organization share information across top-to-bottom (vertical) boundaries?	Determine how well ideas are shared across regional and national boundaries.
	How well does the organization share information across global boundaries?	

CHAPTER 12

Work Processes

Investors Want Organizations That Govern Work to Cope with Increasing Change

The concept of *work*—the accomplishment of necessary tasks—has evolved over centuries. People have worked as isolated individuals and in small bands, in guild-sponsored associations, in factories, and in service and knowledge firms.[1] To get things done in large groups, people have evolved hierarchies based on principles of bureaucracy, which call for a clear structure for decision making and coordination of work, division of labor for specialized functional expertise and managerial control, and power and status based on position.[2]

In increasingly complex environments, organizations have been effective when they coordinate work through roles, control work through rules, and help define choices through routines.[3] Organizations that accomplish work have been studied by their morphology (shape and number of levels and key positions that define authority, specialization, and boundaries), their physiology (processes for planning, resource allocation, managing talent, ensuring accountability, and managing information), and their philosophy (building common purpose and values). It is not surprising that when asked to draw an organization, most people draw some version of the pyramid that visualizes these traditional principles for organizing work. Or that when asked to assess the quality of an organization, they tend to focus on number of levels, clarity of chain of command, or efficiency of process.

The environment for organizations is still complex, but the challenge of complexity pales before the challenge of coping with the astonishing pace of change in today's world. Changes are rapidly occurring in all aspects of the context of work:[4]

- *Social:* Transparency, expectations, lifestyle, globalization

- *Technological:* Information sharing, new tools and techniques (discussed in Chapter 11)

- *Economic:* Shrinking cycles, new industry definitions

- *Political:* Regulatory change, instability

- *Environment:* Social accountability

- *Demographic:* Multiple generations of employees, each with a view of how to approach work

To accomplish work in the face of unparalleled change, organizations have to change as fast as the world around them. Organizations that don't keep up will soon be extinct. This does not mean abandoning the benefits of hierarchy, but it does require building a capacity for rapid adaptation. The need for this change capacity has pushed the way work is accomplished to an inflection point. Just as products, services, and systems evolve, organizations are evolving to become more of a network than a hierarchy.[5] Many capture this network organization evolution as from-to: from hierarchy to flat structure, from fixed to flexible working hours, from hoarded to shared information, from command-and-control to coach-and-communicate leadership, from onsite to cloud technology, from vertical focus with silos to horizontal focus with co-creation, and from work at the office to work everywhere.[6] These transitions are occuring, but the from-to logic is dangerous because it may lose some of the benefits of the historic organization assumptions.

Instead of looking at organization work transitions (from–to), effective network organizations manage paradoxes (and also).[7] Successfully networked firms manage the inherent paradoxes of work, and by managing paradoxes they become more agile and flexible. This turns management into more of an art than science. At the risk of oversimplification, I see four paradoxes that leaders have to manage to accomplish work in network organizations:

- Inside–outside
- Individual–collective
- Centralized–decentralized
- Stable–flexible

For investors to discern how an organization accomplishes work, they should look at the way leaders approach the topic of paradox in general, manage these four paradoxes, and create a workplace that supports paradox management (see Figure 12.1).

Figure 12.1. Framework for Assessing Organization's Work Processes

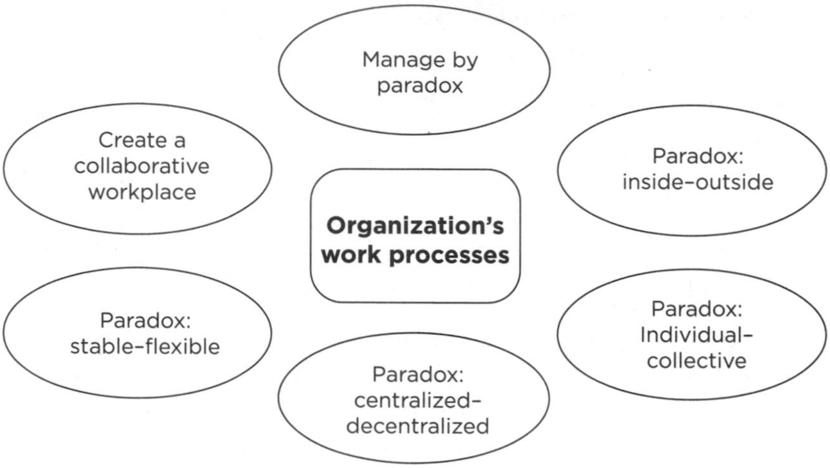

Manage by Paradox

Some of life's greatest challenges and opportunities for growth come from managing paradoxes. For example, parents love their children and want to guide them, but at the same time need to give them autonomy so they can grow through their own choices. Too much guidance (helicopter parenting) takes away opportunities to learn; too little guidance (latchkey parenting) takes away the discipline children need to grow. In a somewhat similar way, governments navigate the paradox between democracy, which encourages involvement, and autocracy, which offers a unified focus. In a republic, this paradox shows up with tensions between national policy and states' and individual rights. This control—freedom paradox also shows up at work, where leaders learn to simultaneously guide employees through control mechanisms and empower employees by permitting them to take risks.

As organizations face the challenge of accomplishing work at the pace of change, leaders need to embrace incompatible forces rather than choosing between them. Managing by paradox is essential in a volatile, uncertain, complex, and ambiguous world where the future is not predictable from the past.[8] Managing by paradox encourages debates before reaching conclusions, accepts differences as a way to discover new opportunities, and explores options rather than being locked into one solution. Managing in a world of paradoxes requires constant navigation to avoid rigidity, as well as a constant effort to maintain tension without

Figure 12.2. Paradoxes for Accomplishing Work

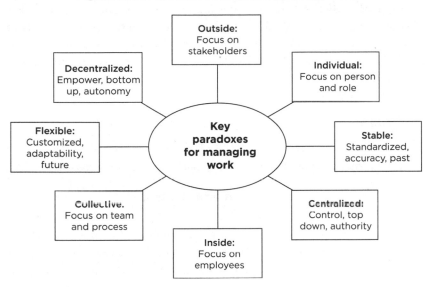

contention and to disagree without being disagreeable. When leaders accept and manage paradoxes, they create more agile and nimble
organizations.[9] Figure 12.2 outlines the desirable features of each of the
polar opposites involved in the paradoxes that confront organizations
today.

When facing paradoxes, average leaders ignore one of the polarities
and focus on a single solution. They have a hard time being consistently right. Poor leaders swing back and forth or demand both, and
often fail at either polarity. Great leaders acknowledge the paradoxes
and address them head-on. They accept and even clarify the options
as dualities, establishing a clear set of criteria for how to respond to
tensions. They encourage dialogue more than offer prescriptions, offer
menus of choice more than a single offering, create a shared resolution, and continue to adapt as situations change. As leaders grow—from
individual contributors to team leaders to managers of teams to directors of business units to executives in multiple business units to leading
global enterprises—the skills of managing paradox become ever more
important.

Investors can audit the extent to which a company uses paradox
management for accomplishing work. One investor likes to monitor the
extent to which leaders explore options before making decisions. He
likes to observe the continued cycle from broad exploration (divergent
and inductive thinking) to focused attention (convergent and deductive

thinking), then repeat the cycle over again. He likes to see meetings where people ask the "what if" questions before reaching consensus. He likes to see a devil's advocate take a contrarian view to make sure that other options are considered. In the spirit of paradox, too much consensus reduces available options; too little consensus reduces commitment.

Possible indicators:

- *Do leaders have the ability to see multiple sides of an issue?*
- *Do leaders address paradoxes but still make decisions?*
- *Do leaders encourage diverse points of view before reaching consensus?*

Paradox: Inside–Outside

A very common paradox is the focus on internal or external forces. Internally focused firms emphasize their history and who they have been; they focus on employee commitment and defining corporate culture as their norms and patterns, emphasize their values and strengths, and are driven by how to deliver profitability in the short term. At the extreme, leaders can get locked into their traditions, norms, and patterns, and they live in the past as a precursor to their present. They enjoy talking about what they have done and how they have done it. They react to today's demands and push for current results.

Externally focused firms emphasize customers and opportunities. By examining the outside world, firms anticipate what can be and look to develop new streams of profit for the long term. At the extreme, they are always anticipating opportunities in the future but never attaining them. They pander to customers and the latest fads without providing a real identity; they invest in a future that never seems to materialize; and they overpromise top-line growth from future opportunities. Table 12.1 sets out the positive aspects of each type of focus.

Too much internal focus limits innovation; too much external focus becomes pandering. Good leaders work to meld the inside and the outside. Investors can monitor the extent to which leaders take some of the following steps to manage the inside—outside paradox:

- *Frame future strategic goals as part of an evolution from the past.* That is, leaders should listen for the historical narrative of the strategy, but also see how it changes based on the requirements of the business.
- *Actively involve customers in cocreating strategy and innovation.* Leaders can include customers in key decision analysis forums, invite customers to review strategy initiatives, and observe and interview key customers to discover their unmet needs.

Table 12.1. Inside–Outside Paradox

Inside	Outside
Honor past history.	Create the future.
Focus on employee actions and employee commitment.	Focus on external stakeholders' expectations (customers, investors, regulators); customer service.
Build an internally focused corporate culture.	Build a market brand that shapes culture.
Articulate values and strengths.	Recognize the value of values, build strengths that strengthen others.
Do what is needed now; react.	Anticipate what is next; be proactive.
Emphasize short-term results and bottom-line profitability.	Seek long-term opportunities and top-line growth.

- *Symbolically let the past go.* Look for signs that leaders have let the past go by changing symbols, having events to bury the past, and changing customary phrases.
- *Invite customers to be more connected to employees.* This might include active customer participation in management processes like hiring, training, and communication but might also include employees acting as and spending time with customers, or having leaders respond directly to customer complaints.
- *Link the leadership behavior and corporate culture to the expectations of targeted customers.* Firm promises to customers should show up in the things leaders do.
- *Praise and celebrate customer responsiveness.* When employees react quickly to customers or anticipate what customers will want, leaders share news of what happened widely.
- *Connect employee engagement data to customer engagement scores and show the cause and effect.* Employee engagement is often a lead indicator of customer engagement; tracking the two measures simultaneously can provide advance notice and give the firm a chance to stave off potential problems.

As investors monitor and observe these types of activities, they can discern the extent to which the inside–outside paradox is managed.

Possible indicators:

- *To what extent do employees know the top 20% of customers and their buying criteria?*
- *What percentage of employees either visit with or act as customers of the firm?*
- *How much cocreation occurs with customers involved in key activities?*
- *How well do leaders create a narrative about the past, present, and future of the company?*

Paradox: Individual-Collective

The focus on individual talent (emphasized in Chapter 9) clearly matters. Attracting, motivating, and retaining more competent and committed employees would benefit any organization. But individuals who fail to work together as a team—no matter how gifted—will not live up to their potential value to the company. Individuals are parts; teams are wholes. Individuals are champions; teams win championships. Individuals try to maximize self-interest; teams succeed by selfless sacrifice to each other. Individuals often contribute through specialized skills and role; teams succeed by combining personal strengths into team unity. Table 12.2 sets out the advantages at both poles of the paradox.

In network organizations, teams exist in many forms. Formal teams such as the executive team have ongoing and regular meetings. Task forces and project teams focus on their particular objectives. Volunteer groups form naturally to accomplish work tasks. In complex and changing business settings, an increasing amount of work is performed through teams.

Obviously, it is great to have "A" players who have great personal skills. But individuals who do not work as a team suboptimize the whole. One investor told me, "We would rather have an A team than an A player." The best leaders surround themselves with great people, but also attend to the dimensions of a high-performing team (as discussed in detail in Chapter 6):

- *Purpose:* People share goals and understand why the team has been formed—and how it will define success.
- *Governance:* The membership of the team is clear, and people all feel free to contribute without automatically deferring to the leader.
- *Relationships:* Team members care for one another and manage the conflicts and differences that inevitably arise, without lasting ill-will.

Table 12.2. Individual–Collective Paradox

Individual	Collective
Parts	Whole
Personal: organization gets work done through gifted individuals (I succeed).	Team: organization gets work done through high-performing teams (we succeed).
Self-interested: focus on helping people build their personal talents.	Selfless and other service: focus on helping others build their talents.
Specialist with clear role.	Generalist with multiple skills.
Passion: inspire for opportunities ahead.	Processes: reengineer what can be improved.
Equity: people are treated differently based on what they produce.	Equality: everyone is treated the same.

- *Learning:* The team constantly learns from the past and improves its performance.

One venture capital investor said that he could discern the target organization's attention to teamwork by scrutinizing the term sheet on an investment offer. He felt that the term sheet was a negotiation, but also an indicator of how the organization managed teams and people. He looked for how the term sheet treated others, how the leadership allocated stock in the option pool, how they treated prior investors, and how many of their prior investors stayed with them in future deals.

Many investors examine the board as an exemplar of teamwork. Boards generally consist of eight to twelve people who are individually talented but need to come together to form collective insights about the organization. Investors can monitor how well the board performs as a team as a surrogate for teamwork within the organization. Do board members recognize their shared purpose (overseeing the firm, selecting the CEO, being stewards for the shareholders)? Do board members have the right talent (attracting the right mix of skills, serving the right length of time, holding staggered membership terms)? Do they make decisions and govern appropriately (finding middle ground between abdicating and controlling)? Do they have positive relationships with each other? Do they manage differences effectively (encouraging dissent and resolving rather than papering over their differences)? Does the board work to improve its process (doing feedback for board members, assessing board performance)?

Similar questions can be asked of the top leadership team and of other key teams throughout the organization. Leaders build leadership, and much of the creation of future leaders comes from participation in teams. For the long term, investors need to monitor collective teamwork as well as individual talent.

Possible indicators:

- *How well does the organization form teams to accomplish work?*
- *How well do teams operate against the criteria of a high-performing team?*
- *How well do individuals in key positions represent the best in their industry?*

Paradox: Centralized—Decentralized

In the history of organization design, most choices boil down to some version of centralization or decentralization of the way an organization is designed to deliver work.[10] These choices lead to pendulum swings from strong corporate control to strong local autonomy, and they determine the extent to which the firm focuses on global standards or local conditions. Companies riding this sort of pendulum often vacillate between top-line growth and bottom-line profitability. Table 12.3 sets out the advantages on each side of the paradox.

Leaders who manage the paradox of centralization and decentralization align the structure to fit the requirements of the business. The functional or more centralized organization structure is best at managing a single product or service line. BMW is an example of a company with a functional, single-product structure. When any organization begins, it usually has a functional organization based around a single business strategy. For example, when Google started in search, it used a functional organization. Nike, when it started with athletic footwear, was a functional organization. As companies become more complex and have multiple products and services in related businesses, they move to a divisional or multibusiness structure. Google and Nike now have multiple divisions reflecting their decentralized approach. Some companies become holding companies, operating completely unrelated stand-alone businesses with financial and accounting systems as forms of control. Holding companies have extreme decentralization (consider Berkshire Hathaway, Virgin, and Tata). Other companies shift to a matrix structure, whereby they try to gain the benefits of both centralized control

Table 12.3. Centralized–Decentralized Paradox

Centralized	*Decentralized*
Control: get things done with tight controls managed by rules and top-down directives.	Empowerment: get things done by giving employees opportunities and bottom-up influence.
Decision making from the top down: clear about who makes what decisions.	Decision consensus from the bottom up: process of defining who makes decisions.
Authority: encourage consistency, shared rules, dependence; discipline (nationalism).	Autonomy: encourage variation, self-rule, and independence; freedom (federalism).
Efficiency: build common platforms.	Effectiveness: adapt to local conditions.
Global reach: common processes worldwide, standardization.	Local connectedness: customized practices for each country, adaptation.
Differentiation.	Integration.

and decentralized autonomy. The challenge in a matrix is how to spread and balance scarce resources across the organization. IBM and P&G both are good examples of companies with a matrix structure.

Investors should assess the degree to which the organization structure matches the strategy. This alignment can be tracked by determining the breadth of the strategy and whether the focus is more on top-line innovation and growth or bottom-line profitability and efficiency. This strategy-structure alignment is simpler for smaller and less complex companies.

Most large and complex companies have some version of a matrix, whereby they seek the benefits of both centralization and decentralization. In these cases, investors should monitor management of this paradox closely. Investors might look at the organization chart—not because of the boxes but because of the signals the chart sends. Some organization charts are triangles, with traditional spans of control and governance guidelines that have delegated accountabilities cascading through the organization. Other organization charts might put customers or employees on top as a signal of what matters most.

Of course, the concept can be taken too far. One matrix organization

Table 12.4. Practical Paradox Management

Local Accountability Leaders	Global Strength Functions
Have direct responsibility for revenue growth and profitability; they own the P&L	Support the plant managers, who own the P&L
Run full multidisciplinary teams, with all functions reporting to them (with some exceptions)	Participate on all these teams
Make decisions and drive the growth of their businesses	Propose ideas, standards, processes, and the adoption of best practices to help the plants be successful
Welcome input and stay open to global strength recommendations	Provide input into business decisions to ensure alignment with broader objectives
Collaborate with one another to maximize synergies across the local businesses	Respond to the global nature of the businesses

mapped out the array of committees and teams it operated, revealing an incredible variety of roles and a corresponding lack of clear responsibility. It turned out that the leader in this organization had created such a tangle that far too many decisions were pushed up to him. An investor could see that the complexity slowed decision making and limited innovation.

Another organization did a clear job of defining roles for local and global operations. The leaders laid out the paradoxes and discussed how to manage them so they could quickly respond to both local adaptations and global efficiencies. Under the principle "local accountability and global strengths," the firm laid out plans shown in Table 12.4.

By managing the centralized–decentralized paradox, this organization was able to engage in an ongoing process of clarifying roles and responsibilities. One thoughtful investor said that when he looked at an organization structure, he sought answers to these questions:

- How do you manage decision rights for innovation?
- How do you allocate accountability for decision making?

- Who controls resources, and how are decisions made to move them?
- How do you integrate across areas of specialization?

When investors see that the organization appropriately aligns resources to business strategies and then manages the tensions inherent in centralized and decentralized settings, they have confidence in how work is accomplished.

Possible indicators:

- *To what extent does the organization structure align with business strategy?*
- *How effectively do leaders clarify roles and responsibilities for governance?*
- *How well do leaders encourage debate of trade-offs?*

Paradox: Stable—Flexible

Organizations that change too little calcify and become antiquated. Organizations that change too much lose their roots and act capriciously. Stability gives order; flexibility offers opportunity. Leaders have to manage the inherent paradox of stability and willingness to change.[11] When they do so, they both standardize and customize, build on the past and create the future, converge and diverge, and they grow both by evolution as well as by revolution.[12] Table 12.5 highlights the advantages on both sides.[13]

Knowing when to hold on and when to move on is a constant and evolving process. Investors can monitor the extent to which leaders:

- Hold onto principles that established their company and adapt practices to changing business requirements.
- Bring the outside in. Change that anticipates customer requirements should become the clarion call for when to move on.
- Have an ongoing dialogue about what works and what does not.
- Bring discipline to change. The precise approach to managing change matters little—leaders have dozens of them to choose from—but it's important to be disciplined about using it.
- Recognize what can be changed and what cannot be changed. Focusing on choices within control boosts the likelihood of success.
- Accept change as a positive and not a negative. While it is helpful to have common frameworks that guide discussions, it is also

Table 12.5. Stability-Flexibility Paradox

Stability	Flexibility
Establish standardized processes; accuracy.	Create customized solutions; adaptability.
Build on the past.	Create the future.
Be predictable, consistent, narrow.	Be adaptable, changeable, broad.
Manage costs through operational excellence and predictability.	Manage growth through innovation and creativity.
Support convergent thinking; exercise caution.	Advocate divergent thinking; encourage risk taking.
Gain scale.	Ensure speed.
Encourage evolutionary growth; one step at a time.	Encourage revolutionary growth; leap forward.

useful to evolve content of discussions based on the latest business requirements.

- Install valves on the flow of change. People and organizations have limits on the rate of change they can absorb, so it is best to stick with core principles while adapting to conditions with innovative practices.

As investors monitor these paradoxical choices of flexibility and stability, they can see how well the organization accomplishes work by maintaining a course and by adapting to a new course.

Possible indicators:

- *How well does the organization honor the past, by thanking predecessors, and create the future, by anticipating expectations?*
- *How well do leaders show the evolution of change efforts so that they build on each other?*
- *How well does the organization absorb new ideas?*

Create a Collaborative Workplace

The physical environment also sends signals about what work is done and how it is done. Today work may be done in an office, at home, in remote locations, in hotels, or in airports. In traditional office environments, work has shifted from managing personal space through cubicles to collaborative spaces with a focus on interaction, openness, and sharing—while at the same time allowing for privacy and solitude.[14]

The new workspace is organized around principles of variety and choice (flexibility in work arrangement), human connection (mix of private and public space), and social responsibility (social capital and environmental sustainability). A well-managed workspace enhances employee productivity and well-being and communicates a company's culture and identity.[15]

Managing workspace begins by categorizing the types of work being done, then creating a living office environment that enables effective procedures.[16] When the work activity matches the work setting, employees *want* to go to work there instead of seeing it as a place where they *have* to go to work.

Investors can assess the physical work setting casually by observing how work is organized, what messages are sent from workplace arrangements, and how work flows. These casual observations give a glimpse into how the work setting shapes the tasks of work. More formally, investors can do workplace audits to determine flexibility, social connection, and social responsibility woven into work arrangements. Investors can also survey employees to find out how their productivity and passion is triggered through work settings.

Work settings that match work *mode* to work *setting* model the paradoxes of work—and shape more agile organizations. In addition, investors can monitor the extent to which employees accomplish work outside formal work settings, at home and in remote locations. These technology-enabled work settings redefine the boundaries of work less as a place and more as a shared set of commitments.

Possible indicators:

- *How does the workplace match the work requirements?*
- *Does the employee workplace encourage employee productivity?*
- *Does the work setting reflect the organization's culture?*

Conclusion

An increasingly changing business context requires new modes for accomplishing work. Just as people develop predispositions, organizations develop routines. These routines often keep organizations from adapting to external challenges. Leaders who manage paradoxes and avoid getting locked into routines are able to create networked organizations that adapt to rapidly changing business contexts. Facing, understanding, and managing paradoxes enables organizations to anticipate and respond to change.

In the coming years, hierarchical organizations will probably be replaced by networked organizations because the latter more quickly adapt to change. Leaders who build networked organizations have a commitment and capacity to manage paradox. Paradoxes encourage dialogue that leads to more creative and innovative solutions. Managing paradox is more art than science, requires more questions than answers, explores options more than definitive directions, and encourages variety more than specificity. The indicators in Table 12.6 offer investors a diagnostic approach to assessing how work is accomplished.

Table 12.6. Indicators for Work Governance Practices

Indicators	Possible Indicators	How to Assess
Commitment to paradoxes of work	Do leaders have the ability to see multiple sides of an issue? Do leaders address paradoxes but still make decisions? Do leaders encourage diverse points of views before reaching consensus?	Observe management meetings to see the amount of debate before decisions. Survey employees on decision processes and amount of dialogue. Examine makeup of senior teams to measure diversity in their background.
Paradox: Inside-outside	To what extent do employees know the top 20% of customers and their buying criteria? What percentage of employees either visit with or act as customers of the firm? How much cocreation occurs with customers involved in key activities? How well do leaders create a narrative about the past, present, and future of the company?	Ask employees to name target customers and see if the answer is widely shared—and accurate. Ask employees to articulate customer buying criteria and compare with targeted customer criteria. Assess how many customers are involved in key management processes. Examine how well leaders connect the past to the future in describing goals.

Indicators	Possible Indicators	How to Assess
Paradox: Individual–collective	How well does the organization form teams to accomplish work? How well do teams operate against the criteria of a high-performing team? How well do individuals in key positions represent the best in their industry?	Survey members of the top teams on how well the team displays the characteristics of a high-performing team. Compare individuals in key positions against individuals in similar positions at top competitors (better, same, worse).
Paradox: Centralized– decentralized	To what extent does the organization structure align with business strategy? How effectively do leaders clarify roles and responsibilities for governance? How well do leaders encourage debate of trade-offs?	Assess the match (or mismatch) between the strategy and the formal structure. Survey employees to determine if they have clear decision rights based on their roles and responsibilities. Observe or survey to see if leaders seek second or alternative opinions before making decisions.
Paradox: Stable–flexible	How well does the organization honor the past by thanking predecessors and create the future by anticipating expectations? How well do leaders show the evolution of change efforts so that they build on each other? How well does the organization absorb new ideas?	Find out what proportion of their time leaders spend on the past compared to the future. Assess how leaders speak about their predecessors (positive or negative). Determine what percentage of revenue (and profits) are from products or services introduced in the last four years.
Creates a collaborative workplace	How does the workplace match the work requirements? Does the employee workplace encourage employee productivity? Does the work setting reflect the organization's culture?	Observe the workplace and summarize the signals and messages that it sends. Survey employees to determine if the workplace helps them be productive. Assess how frequently the workplace adapts to the type of work performed.

PART FOUR

Application and Action

Part 1 showed why and how leadership can be used to help realize full market value. Part 2 offered five elements of individual leaders that investors can assess as part of a leadership capital index. Part 3 proposed five elements of organization processes or human capital that investors can assess to determine leadership. Combined, these chapters offer the framework and logic for the leadership capital index.

Chapter 13 reviews the application and action plans to make this leadership capital index happen. Finally, Chapter 14 proposes questions and answers and offers tools for applying this material.

The Relevance and Use of a Leadership Capital Index

The true state of an organization today is found not in the financials (balance sheet or income statement) nor in the intangible processes (strategic planning, brand, manufacturing, customer service) but in the hearts and minds of those who lead it. Assessing these personal imprints will be a primary investor challenge of the next decade. Today, investors primarily value a firm by looking at its financial performance and intangible assets—but regulatory reporting requirements make financial insights universally available, so they provide little advantage to an investor. Intangibles also are becoming easier to perceive and measure. The next evolution of investor value will be in assessing the quality of leadership.

Unfortunately, that is apt to be a difficult task. As one investor vividly explained to me, most investment management firms operate in ways that are basically feudal, so investors often have no direct personal experience of modern leadership. Investors nonetheless have a strong sense that leadership matters. A leader in the private equity market told me, "If we have an 'A' investment but a 'C' management, we don't make money. But if we have an 'A' management and a 'C' investment, we will make money." Another prominent investor said, "We recognize the importance of leadership. It is the only source of leverage for our investment. But we are just not very good at assessing it. We try psychological testing, and they come back well, but still fail. We try reference checking, and they are good, but the leader fails. We hire people we have worked with before, but this limits our talent pool and leaves us doing what we have always done."

At the end of one of the investor focus groups my colleagues and I ran, a leading investor said, "If I knew what we talked about in this discussion, I would pay even more attention to leadership." His point was that while investors often intuitively recognize that leadership matters, they don't have a rigorous or predictable way to assess leadership.

With this book, I provide the framework, dimensions, elements, and indicators of such a tool.

Relevance of Leadership Capital Index

Investors who understand and assess leadership effectively will make better investment decisions, so the leadership capital index will reward the undeniable effort involved in using and refining it.

The task is both simple and complex. For an investor, a leadership audit starts with a compelling question: To what extent does this firm have the quality of leadership that will lead to future intangible and tangible results? A simple answer would be investors' first impressions of a CEO's personal style. This might come from sizing up the CEO in meetings or in the media and making judgments based on these observations. Persuasive as such judgments can be, however, their relation to actual results often seems little better than a lucky (or unlucky) guess.

By contrast, this leadership capital index identifies specific attributes of effective leaders, in terms of both individual proficiencies they demonstrate and the organization processes they create. It takes in the whole cadre of top leadership rather than just the top leader in the company. Instead of having confidence in one person or even a team of proficient people, this index will give investors confidence in the quality of leadership within a possible investment. This logic is laid out in Figure 13.1.

Figure 13.1. Evolution of Approaches to Assessing Quality of Leadership

		From individual leader to collective leadership	
		Individual leader or isolated organization practice	Collective leadership or integrated organization practices
Audit approach	**Intuition and impression**	1 Chemistry with top leader	2 Confidence in individuals at the top
	Leader proficiencies	3 Thorough assessment of top individual	4 Team of leaders
	Human capital processes	5 Assessment of an isolated organization practice	6 Assessment of integrated and multiple organization practices

Table 13.1 sets out details for each evolutionary step for leadership capital. In many cases, when investors examine leadership, they often rely on Cell 1 or 2: they meet with a top leader and team—and gain or

Table 13.1. Approaches to Measuring Leadership

	Approach to leadership assessment	Investor action: To do this assessment, an investor . . .	Good news: Why this approach gives more insight on quality of leadership	Bad news: What is missing from this approach
1	Chemistry with top leader	Meets with top leader and forms personal impression of ability	Goes beyond public data to have a personal interaction with leader	Top leader not enough; first impressions on style can be misleading.
2	Confidence in individuals at the top	Meets with top leadership team to form impression of their abilities	Goes beyond individual leader and observes team	First impressions of many individuals may still be biased.
3	Thorough assessment of top leader	Hires a firm or personally does a thorough review of the senior leader	Gains more confidence in the senior leader; especially if using a holistic model of leadership proficiency	Focused on key individual, who may or may not be present for the long term; does not look at systems.
4	Assessment of a team of leaders	Does a thorough leadership proficiency assessment of each member of the top team	Learns about the proficiencies of the next generation of leaders and how they might complement each other	Identifies talents of individuals and their teamwork, but not the infrastructure they create.
5	Assessment of isolated organization practice	Look at a pet organization practice (such as compensation or work structure) to evaluate quality of the organization	Recognizes that organization systems outlive individuals and create performance	Looks at best practice, not best system.
6	Assessment of integration of organization practices	Performs a more thorough organization audit of key processes	Examines organization processes that create an integrated system	No direct information on adaptability of organization processes to the future.

lose confidence in their skills as a result. By using the insights on leadership proficiency outlined in Part 2 (Chapters 3 through 7), investors can vastly improve their assessment of the top leader (Cell 3) and the top leadership team (Cell 4). No one individual leader is likely to have all the leadership proficiencies, but the collective leadership team can complement each other to give investors more confidence in the team of leaders. Further, if investors use the insights from Part 3 (Chapters 8 through 12), they will also be able to audit human capital or organization processes, improving their confidence in the isolated (Cell 5) and integrated (Cell 6) organization processes leaders have created. The message is simple: Investors who have relied on individual leaders or isolated organization practices to assess leadership can better value leadership with the comprehensive and rigorous approach embedded in the leadership capital index.

The complete leadership capital index offers investors a disciplined lens to look at individual and collective leaders and isolated and integrated organization practices. Will this index guarantee investor success? No. Will it mitigate risk? Yes. Will it give investors more confidence in their decision making? Yes.

Content of a Leadership Capital Index

This book turns the intuitive insight that leadership is important into a more rigorous diagnosis. While assessing leadership is still more art than science, doing so based on a careful plan helps investors anticipate future organization success. Quality of leadership need not remain a random mystery—it can be an assessable set of personal actions and organization processes.

Figure 13.2 summarizes the application of the leadership capital index. Leadership capital supplements financial and intangible assessments. It has two domains: *personal leadership traits*, which represent who leaders are, what they know, and how they act, and *human capital systems*, which represent organization processes that shape leadership.

Drawing on and synthesizing an extensive literature on the personal traits of effective leaders, the leadership capital index suggests five elements of personal leadership. Investors may assess the effectiveness of senior leaders based on their competence at:

- Building personal proficiency
- Articulating strategy
- Executing strategy
- Managing people now and for the future
- Maintaining the organization's leadership brand

Figure 13.2. Overall Flow

Investor: What is the value of the firm?
Answer:

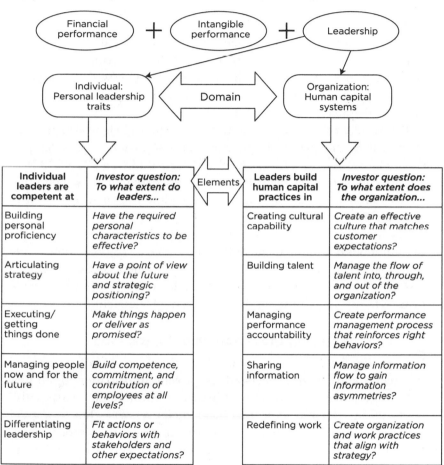

Individual leaders are competent at	Investor question: To what extent do leaders...	Elements	Leaders build human capital practices in	Investor question: To what extent does the organization...
Building personal proficiency	*Have the required personal characteristics to be effective?*		Creating cultural capability	*Create an effective culture that matches customer expectations?*
Articulating strategy	*Have a point of view about the future and strategic positioning?*		Building talent	*Manage the flow of talent into, through, and out of the organization?*
Executing/ getting things done	*Make things happen or deliver as promised?*		Managing performance accountability	*Create performance management process that reinforces right behaviors?*
Managing people now and for the future	*Build competence, commitment, and contribution of employees at all levels?*		Sharing information	*Manage information flow to gain information asymmetries?*
Differentiating leadership	*Fit actions or behaviors with stakeholders and other expectations?*		Redefining work	*Create organization and work practices that align with strategy?*

For each of these five elements of personal leadership, investors can identify and track specific indicators of what leaders should be, know, and do to be effective. These assessments will enable investors to determine the quality of individual leaders in organizations where they might invest.

Drawing on and synthesizing literature and experiences about how leaders build human capital processes, the leadership capital index suggests five elements of human capital practices. Investors can assess how well an organization conceives and manages these five critical organization processes:

- Creating cultural capability
- Building talent
- Managing performance accountability

- Sharing information
- Redefining work

When leaders create and embed these human capital processes, they build organization capabilities that outlast their individual competencies. When investors track specific indicators of how well the targeted organization performs on these five processes, they have more confidence in the quality of leadership.

Figure 13.2 offers investors a more through and rigorous approach to measuring the quality of leadership. This approach moves from personal observations of a leader (Cell 1 of Figure 13.1 and Table 13.1) to a more complete assessment (Cell 6). Investors who acknowledge that leadership matters can now be more disciplined in their approach to assessing it.

Creating a leadership capital index offers deeper insights into why organizations deliver financial results and create intangible value. While some may argue that Figure 13.2 misses some elements of personal leadership or human capital processes, the index offers a minimum viable process for bringing order to the assessment of leadership.

Applying the Leadership Capital Index

Investors tend to be comfortable with existing measures on income statements and balance sheets, which provide information about how well a firm makes decisions about managing cash. Some analysts also try to find leadership indicators in financial reports—but to a great extent this is a mirage. Financial reports are designed to report financial information. Leadership audits need to access and assess leadership information. The leadership capital index requires investors, or their surrogates, to learn about individual leadership and human capital processes from additional data sources. The indicators suggested for each of the ten elements of the leadership capital index often come from these sources:

- Observation
- Interviews

- Actions and behaviors
- Surveys and reports

OBSERVATION

Investors who visit an organization can pick up many leadership signals as they observe the leadership team, employees, and work setting. One senior leader who relied heavily on traditional financial and market analytics made a different assumption about organization issues: "I will know the quality of organization, leadership, and people when I visit a plant. In less than sixty minutes, I can sense and feel how things are going." While personal perceptions may be biased or skewed, most of us can sense the ambiance or culture of an organization—from a retail store to a corporate office—in the course of a visit. More rigorous observations can be made when investors or others observing leadership have an explicit template of what they are looking for. Having a leadership capital index with specific elements of personal leadership and human capital processes helps investors observe and recognize quality of leadership. Investors have suggested the following types of observation:

- Meet with the CEO and team at least three times before making an investment, so as to observe the consistency of leadership behavior.

- Observe the leader in different settings to watch the response to customers, to communities, to employees, to competitors, and to the top team, so as to assess the adaptability of the leader in different settings.

- Observe the leader meeting with the top team, watching for facilitation of dialog, focused decision making, and the personal skills involved in strategy, execution, and talent management.

- Observe the leader's physical setting to determine the signals sent by how the office is organized and how it is managed.

INTERVIEWS

Investors can attempt to capture the quality of leadership within an organization with interviews that are structured or unstructured, personal or group, formal or informal. They can include the top leader or stakeholders to the leader (board members, peers, subordinates, customers, and so forth) to assess the response to different audiences. The value of a leadership capital index is that the interviews are not random conversations but structured inquiries about personal leadership and human capital processes. The following are some types of interviews that have been reported:

- One-on-one interviews with leaders, where investors personally meet with company leaders to discover how they think about leadership and organization.

- Group interviews with representative targeted employees who can offer unique insights into the leadership questions raised in this book.

- Group interviews with leaders from three or four firms in the same industry invited to form a focus group and talk about the future of the industry, so the investor can see how each responds not only to the trends but also to each other.

- Correspondence, wherein the investor asks leaders to write letters about what they want for their company and for themselves. The resulting letters highlight the leaders' personal strengths and focus.

ACTIONS AND BEHAVIORS

Everything leaders do reflects their quality of leadership. Their actions show up in leadership speeches, video conferences, e-mail messages, or other communication mechanisms. How leaders promote themselves and others becomes an indicator of their personal skills.

Where leaders spend time is often a major indicator of their commitments. By tracking a leader's calendar, investors can often discern how much attention leaders pay to the human capital processes described in this index. Again, having a leadership capital index ensures that investors are paying attention to the array of activities a leader may pursue.

SURVEYS AND REPORTS

Investors can review existing reports generated within a company to track leaders' inclinations. These reports might include minutes of senior meetings, regular (daily, weekly, monthly) business performance scorecards or reports, or employee surveys. By tracking these information sources, investors can see what leaders pay attention to and how they are perceived by others. Increasingly, these reports are likely to be embedded in social media outside the company.

For each of these data sources, it is important to have a framework of what to look for. Without a framework, it is only natural for personal biases to shape an observer's data collection and insights. The ten elements of the leadership capital index fall short of being the ultimate tool, but even this minimum viable process offers a robust and disciplined way to assess quality of leadership.

Implications of a Leadership Capital Index

As introduced in Chapters 1 and 2, a leadership capital index moves investment decisions from past financial data to anticipated future business opportunity. The research from investors suggests that leadership matters but is not easy to discern. A leadership capital index will have dramatic implications for many organization stakeholders.

IMPLICATIONS FOR INVESTORS

This book is primarily targeted to active, long-term, firm-focused investors who want to go beyond publicly available financial information to insights that allow them to develop information asymmetries and so reduce their investment risks. When sovereign wealth, private equity, venture capitalist, hedge, or other fund managers consider investments, the additional insights provided from the leadership capital index should increase their confidence in both equity and debt investments. By assessing the quality of leadership, investors mitigate risk and improve their likelihood of getting desirable returns. If investors can move from a 5% to 10% confidence in leadership to a 35% to 40% confidence in leadership, they can make dramatic improvements in their investment portfolio. With the leadership capital index, I would envision sovereign wealth fund managers both offering guidance on leadership assessment and expecting leadership assessments as part of their investment criteria.

IMPLICATIONS FOR REGULATORS

As discussed in Chapter 2, many groups observe and regulate investment decisions. The leadership capital index can offer additional insights to ratings firms as they offer more thorough and predictive models of firm performance. Just as Moody's and S&P rate firms' ability to repay financial obligations, the leadership capital index will rate the ability of firms to deliver on financial promises. Proxy advisory firms can offer more insights about firms they might invest in, based on the quality of leadership within the organization. Regulatory agencies can begin to discover and create leadership safety nets to ensure continuity of investment choices.

IMPLICATIONS FOR BOARDS OF DIRECTORS

As discussed in Chapter 1, boards have fiduciary responsibility to oversee a firm's performance. Selecting the CEO and managing the human capital processes are key factors in firm performance. The leadership capital index offers boards a more thorough approach to selecting a top leader, managing senior leadership, and building leadership bench strength. One board member said that such an index would help his board in selecting future board members as well. As part of regular strategic, risk, and talent assessments, boards might discuss a firm's leadership capital scores.

IMPLICATIONS FOR C-SUITE EXECUTIVES AND SENIOR LEADERS

Senior executives have responsibilities both to investors (to present their organization's current and future performance) and to employees (to develop future leaders). One company that has maintained investor confidence invites investors, once or twice a quarter, to spend time with the management team. Some of this time is structured, with financial reports and strategic presentations, but some of it is unstructured, so that investors can interact more informally with leaders in the organization. In one company this half-day meeting went something like this:

- CFO kick-off
- SVP presentations of fifteen to twenty minutes each, in which they talk about whatever the investor wants to discuss
- CEO conclusion—one hour at the end

By structuring and holding such investor meetings, the company helped investors learn more about how each of the leaders thought, and the two groups began to build mutual respect and liking. In addition, in monthly investor calls or periodic road shows to investors, senior executives could add a disciplined dialogue about the quality of leadership that complements financial and intangible presentations.

Senior leaders also have the primary stewardship for building future leaders. The leadership capital index will help them see gaps and opportunities for future leadership expenditures. Most leaders have done personal leader 360-degree assessment so they can improve their personal leadership skills; the leadership capital index is an organization leadership 360-degree assessment for how to upgrade leadership throughout the organization.

IMPLICATIONS FOR THOSE CHARGED WITH DEVELOPING LEADERS

HR professionals should be architects, building better leadership throughout an organization. The leadership capital index offers them analytics and insights on how they can deliver better leadership. Too often HR professionals focus on activities, not outcomes. If quality of leadership is a desired outcome from HR activities, the leadership capital index offers a disciplined approach to delivering this outcome. When HR specialists or consultants in learning, development, or leadership see their work through the value they create to investors, they shift their thinking from activities they offer to outcomes they deliver.

Organization development (OD) professionals also have recognized that their success often comes from changing individual leaders, collective leadership, and organization processes. OD professionals who use a systems approach to organization diagnosis will find this leadership capital index helpful for both diagnosis and improvement.

I also assume that those committed to teaching and researching leadership will find the leadership capital index a unique and rigorous approach to the propagation and science of leadership.

IMPLICATIONS FOR KEY ORGANIZATION PROCESSES

In Chapter 2, I suggested that a leadership capital index would provide further insights into risk, governance, social responsibility, and reputation processes. With a quality of leadership element added to each of these processes, they become more robust. Uncertainty and variability of leadership shapes other risk factors. Better controls on leadership help shape the governance of other organization processes. Leadership sustainability becomes a predictor of social responsibility. A firm's overall reputation is often predicated on its leadership reputation—something a leadership capital index would capture. Each of these organization processes could be informed by the leadership capital index. Leadership complements key organization processes.

Conclusion

This book attempts to answer an apparently straightforward question: How much is a firm worth? The answer quickly becomes very complex, especially when including leadership as one of the determinants of value. Most investors know that leadership matters but are not sure how to make fine gradations. The leadership capital index may be good both at separating the extremely good from bad leaders and also at making more refined gradations among the strengths and weaknesses of leaders who are in the middle. The quality of leadership on the ten factors can vary by organization and by person.

Figure 13.2, with its two domains and ten elements (five for individual and five for organization), may not be completely relevant in every setting—and the specific elements may not always be easily assessable. But the overall framework allows investors to have more confidence in the quality of leadership of firms they choose to investigate. With the leadership capital index, investors include people and not just markets or products and technologies as part of their investment equation. Investing in people may become as viable as investing in products or markets.

The leadership capital index offers investors and others a more robust and comprehensive way to determine the quality of leadership. The index is not the end point, but it is a useful beginning of more thoughtful and rigorous conversations that lead to insights into leadership.

CHAPTER 14

Putting the Leadership Capital Index into Practice

As I prepared the ideas in this book, I received a stream of responses. The most common and optimistic comment is essentially, "Studying leadership through investor expectations is a very good and breakthrough idea."

I also got some questions and skepticism. I can respond to some of these directly with ideas and tools.

QUESTION: *Where do I find leadership measures in the financial reporting data?*
ANSWER: You won't. Financial reporting data are often the outcomes of a host of management choices about investments in strategy, product, operations, and so forth. Leadership is another investment that should drive these financial results. The leadership capital index offers disciplined insights into the quality of leadership.

QUESTION: *Don't investors, particularly active investors, already take leadership into account?*
ANSWER: Yes. Most investors *say* that leadership matters, but most have rather narrow and disorganized views of effective leadership, in large part because they have not been trained in the science of leadership. After decades of research in leadership, I decided it was time to cull those insights into a leadership capital index that gives investors a more thorough and rigorous way to assess leadership.

QUESTION: *How do you know that your two domains (individual and organization) and ten elements (five in each) and indicators are accurate?*
ANSWER: I don't. One of the unique approaches in this work is to acknowledge that this work is a minimum viable process (MVP) or Leadership Capital Index 1.0, realizing that 2.0 and 3.0 will follow. But without the blueprint in this book, we cannot begin this assessment journey.

This work explores the mystery of leadership in a more structured way (using the ideas from the information in Chapter 11). Having reviewed the proposed two domains, ten elements, and hundreds of indicators with leadership scholars, I am comfortable that this is a significant leap forward in realizing the market value of leadership.

QUESTION: *What would an investor actually do to apply your ideas? How would this really work?*

ANSWER: Investors come with many intents and approaches. The leadership capital index supplements financial (earnings, income statement, balance sheet) and intangible (strategy, brand, information systems, operational processes) insights and enables active investors to gain more rigorous insights into the domains and elements of leadership.

For example, a private equity investor may screen two hundred firms to identify forty that meet financial and intangible investment criteria, but then need to do deeper analyses of those firms to select the twenty that they will ultimate invest in. Going from two hundred to forty may depend much more on financial and intangible audits. But going from forty to twenty should include a thorough leadership audit using the leadership capital index.

I could propose four stages of this assessment, the first two being rather superficial, the last two being much more thoughtful, using this index.

- Stage 1: Leadership general observations. At this stage investors (or others) realize that leadership matters in sustainable firm performance. They include generic and generalized observations about "leadership" when probing deeper into the firm. This might include making judgments about the CEO and/or top team based on casual interviews or observations. As many have pointed out, these impressionistic views of talent are often biased and risky.

- Stage 2: Leadership domain awareness. At this stage, investors (or others) recognize both individual and organizational domains of "leadership." In the individual domain, the investor is worried about both the top leader and the top leadership team. In the organization domain, the investor recognizes that the "organization" (broadly and generically defined at this point) affects long-term success. This awareness leads to observations and some light probing such as "Tell me about your leadership team" or "How effective is your organization?" These queries at least acknowledge the impact of individual competencies and organization capabilities as domains of interest.

- Stage 3: Leadership element assessment. At this stage, investors (or others) have a more thorough and robust way of conceiving both individual and organizational domains. The five elements in Part 2 (Chapters 3 through 7) define individual competence; the five elements in Part 3 (Chapters 8 through 12) define organization capability or human capital. A more thorough leadership capital assessment may now be made by asking these ten questions. This assessment is proposed in Table 2.3 and repeated here (Table 14.1) because it offers a significant step forward in realizing the market value of leadership. The leadership capital index assessment at this stage is comprehensive, but not as detailed as an investor might prefer.

- Stage 4: Leadership item assessment. At this stage, investors (or others) may probe more deeply into each of the ten elements. In each chapter on each element, I have offered five or six specific items that may indicate quality of leadership for element. This assessment would include twenty-eight items for the five elements of the individual domain (Table 14.3) and twenty-nine items for the five elements of the organization domain (Table 14.4). These items could then be assessed by tracking the indicators offered in each chapter. In total, I offer over 250 indicators that investors may select to determine these items, domains, and overall leadership capital. These results can be plotted onto a chart to capture the quality of leadership for either the top leader, leadership team, or organization capabilities (Figure 14.1).

The summary of these four stages is in Table 14.5. As investors move from stages 1 and 2 to stages 3 and 4, they can begin to implement a more comprehensive and disciplined approach to leadership.

In addition to using the leadership capital index for active investors, organization leaders can also use the insights from this assessment when they communicate with investors. In monthly or quarterly investor calls or in road shows for investors, organizations are well advised to dedicate 10 to 15 percent of these investor conversations to the quality of leadership. By having a consistent and reliable metric of leadership, companies could give investors increasing confidence in the quality of leadership that would likely affect intangibles and financial performance over time. I envision companies providing regular and rigorous leadership reports to investors as part of their reporting practices.

QUESTION: *How much impact will these insights from the leadership capital index actually have on market value?*

ANSWER: I don't know at this point. We do know that leadership affects financial performance of a company, and we know that investors care about but cannot fully measure leadership. This book is a starting point, presenting our leadership capital index as a minimum viable process that will be advanced. For example, we envision further research to show the amount of intangible value created by these ten leadership elements over time.

Table 14.1. Leadership Capital Index: Individual Assessment with Five Elements

Element	Top leader		Top leadership team	
	To what extent does our **top leader** ...	RATING Low (1) to high (10)	To what extent does our **senior leadership team** ...	RATING Low (1) to high (10)
Personal proficiency	Have the required personal characteristics to be effective?		Have the required personal characteristics to be effective?	
Strategist	Have a point of view about the future and strategic positioning?		Have a point of view about the future and strategic positioning?	
Executor	Make things happen or deliver as promised?		Make things happen or deliver as promised?	
People manager	Build competence, commitment, and contribution of employees at all levels?		Build competence, commitment, and contribution of employees at all levels?	
Leadership brand	Fit actions or behaviors with stakeholder and other expectations?		Fit actions or behaviors with stakeholder and other expectations?	
	TOTAL:		TOTAL:	

Table 14.2. Leadership Capital Index: Organization Capability Assessment with Five Elements

Element	To what extent do leaders . . .	RATING Low (1) to high (10)
Cultural capability	Create an effective culture that matches customer expectations?	
Talent management	Manage the flow of talent into, through, and out of the organization?	
Performance accountability	Create a performance management process that reinforces right behaviors?	
Information flow	Manage information flow to gain information asymmetries?	
Work processes	Create organization and work practices that align with strategy?	
	TOTAL:	

Table 14.3. Leadership Capital Index: Individual Domain with Five Elements and Twenty-Eight Items

Element	Top leader — To what extent does our **top leader** possess . . .	RATING: Low (1) to high (10)	Top leadership team — To what extent does our **senior leadership team** possess . . .	RATING: Low (1) to high (10)
Personal proficiency	Relevant past experience and performance		Relevant past experience and performance	
	Physical presence and vitality		Physical presence and vitality	
	Sense of personal well-being and identity		Sense of personal well-being and identity	
	Ability to make others feel better and multiply their work		Ability to make others feel better and multiply their work	
	Strong values and ethical judgment		Strong values and ethical judgment	
	Ability to learn, be resilient, grow, and show grit		Ability to learn, be resilient, grow, and show grit	
	Personal proficiency total:	= ÷6 =	**Personal proficiency total:**	= ÷6 =
Strategist	Understand external drivers		Understand external drivers	
	Position the organization for the future		Position the organization for the future	
	Turn aspiration to action through systems		Turn aspiration to action through systems	
	Engage and communicate with employees		Engage and communicate with employees	
	Manage the process of strategy creation		Manage the process of strategy creation	
	Strategist Total:	= ÷5 =	**Strategist Total:**	= ÷5 =

(continued)

Table 14.3. (continued)

Element	To what extent does our top leader possess... (Top leader)	RATING: Low (1) to high (10)	To what extent does our senior leadership team possess... (Top leadership team)	RATING: Low (1) to high (10)
Executor	Recognize and create need for execution		Recognize and create need for execution	
	Focus on priorities		Focus on priorities	
	Ensure clear accountability		Ensure clear accountability	
	Manage decision making or governance		Manage decision making or governance	
	Influence others to mobilize commitment		Influence others to mobilize commitment	
	Adapt quickly		Adapt quickly	
	Executor Total:	= = ÷6	**Executor Total:**	= = ÷6
People manager	Have a positive people philosophy and behavior		Have a positive people philosophy and behavior	
	Know and trust his/her people		Know and trust their people	
	Attend to his/her personal succession		Attend to their personal succession	
	Coach and mentor others		Coach and mentor others	
	Excel at communication		Excel at communication	
	Understand and use teams		Understand and use teams	
	People Manager Total:	= = ÷6	**People Manager Total:**	= = ÷6
Leadership brand	Customer expectations : Have leadership brand		Customer expectations : Have leadership brand	
	Strategic goals: Match to strategy		Strategic goals: Match to strategy	
	Life cycle: Fit with organization stage		Life cycle: Fit with organization stage	
	Community: Have strong community reputation		Community: Have strong community reputation	
	Values: Embody organization values		Values: Embody organization values	
	Leadership Brand Total:	= = ÷5	**Leadership Brand Total:**	= = ÷5

Table 14.4. Leadership Capital Index: Organization Capability Human Capital Assessment with Five Elements and Twenty-Nine Items

Element	To what extent do our leaders . . .	RATING Low (1) to high (10)
Cultural Capability: **Create an effective culture that supports strategic capability**	Focus attention on culture?	
	Prioritize key capabilities needed to win?	
	Create a clear intellectual agenda about a shared cultural message?	
	Establish a behavioral agenda with employee actions aligned to culture?	
	Embed process agendas with HR practices aligned with culture?	
	Cultural Capability TOTAL:	= ÷ 5 =
Talent Management: **Manage the flow of people**	Demonstrate overall commitment to talent management?	
	Bring people **in:** Acquire new talent into the organization?	
	Move people **through:** Develop current talent?	
	Move people **through:** Prepare future successors?	
	Move people **through:** Build commitment?	
	Take people **out:** Manage retention of key people?	
	Take people **out:** Remove poor performers?	
	Talent Management TOTAL:	= ÷ 7 =
Performance Accountability: **Reinforce desired behavior**	Demonstrate and overall commitment to performance accountability?	
	Engage in positive accountability conversation?	
	Establish clear standards of what makes good performance?	
	Link standards to rewards?	
	Create reward systems that drive behavior?	
	Follow up on performance?	
	Performance Accountability TOTAL:	= ÷ 6 =

(continued)

Table 14.4. (continued)

Element	To what extent do our leaders . . .	RATING Low (1) to high (10)
Information Flow: **Use information** **for impact**	Demonstrate an overall commitment to information?	
	Use information for puzzle solving (structured information)?	
	Use information for mystery discovery (unstructured information) ?	
	Demonstrate information transparency?	
	Rely on information for decision making?	
	Manage the flow of information across boundaries?	
	Information Flow TOTAL:	= ÷ 6 =
Work Processes: **Organize to cope** **with increasing** **change**	Demonstrate commitment to managing paradoxes of work?	
	Manage paradox: inside versus outside?	
	Manage paradox: individual versus collective?	
	Manage paradox: centralized versus decentralized?	
	Manage paradox: stability versus change?	
	Create a collaborative workplace?	
	Work Processes TOTAL:	= ÷ 6 =

Figure 14.1: Leadership Capital Index: Profile for Top Leader

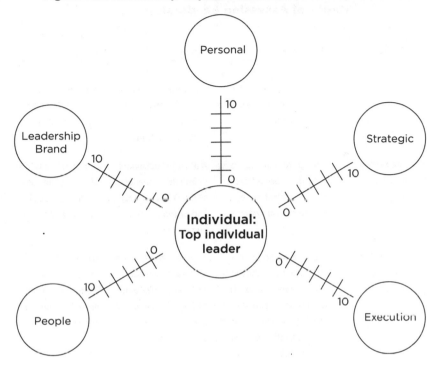

Note: The center circle could be top leadership or organization capability, depending on the audit used.

Table 14.5. Leadership Capital Index: Stages of Assessing Leadership

	Stage	Assumption	Activity	Implications and tools
1	Leadership general observations	Realize that leadership makes a difference in firm performance.	Include a generic view of "leadership" as an issue for investors looking at a firm.	Not a rigorous assessment; high risk of leadership failure
2	Leadership domain assessment	Recognize that leaders as individuals are different from organization or human capital systems.	Ask about behaviors of individual leaders, of the leadership team, and organization or human capital systems.	Better recognition of dimensions of leadership, but little rigor in audit
3	Leadership element assessment	Create a model of effective leadership with five elements related to leaders and leadership and five elements related to organization or human capital systems.	Audit the five elements of individual leaders and leadership teams and the five elements of organization capabilities.	Moderate audit of leaders and leadership; could result in Figures 13.3 and 13.4
4	Leadership item assessment	Leadership elements can be further assessed by identifying the five or six items identified in each chapter.	For each of the ten elements of leadership, identify five or six items that could be assessed.	Use the instruments in Chapter 14

NOTES

Introduction

1. The term "leadership capital index" has been used to describe political leadership style and how effectively the leader can attain and wield authority. These political efforts are thoughtful applications in the public sector that capture political goodwill. This focus has not been on investors or private firms. Mark Bennister, Paul 't Hart, and Ben Worthy, "Leadership Capital: Measuring the Dynamics of Leadership," December 15, 2013 (http://ssrn.com/abstract=2510241); Mark Bennister, Paul 't Hart, and Ben Worthy, "Assessing the Authority of Political Office-Holders: The Leadership Capital Index," *West European Politics* (2014), 1–24.

Chapter 1

1. The criticism of financial stress test was a major theme in Davos discussions by world economic leaders in 2014. This included comments from Axel Weber, CEO of UBS (http://www.irishtimes.com/business/economy/world/stress-tests-could-reignite-debt-crisis-davos-hears-1.1664196); Huw van Steenis, head of European financial services research at Morgan Stanley (http://www.cnbc.com/id/101359028); and Laura Noonan, "Data Dumps and Pig Farms; Inside Europe's Stress Tests," January 23, 2014 (http://www.reuters.com/article/2014/01/23/us-europe-stresstests-preview-idUSBREA0M08C20140123).

2. CEO/C-Suite Studies, *Leading Through Connections: Insights from the Global Chief Executive Officer Study* (IBM, 2012).

3. See work on the minimum viable product in software by: Eric Ries, Venture Hacks interview: "What Is the Minimum Viable Product?" Startup Lessons Learned, March 23, 2009, (http://www.startuplessonslearned.com/2009/03/minimum-viable-product.html); Eric Ries, "Minimum Viable Product: A Guide," Startup Lessons Learned, August 3, 2009 (http://www.startuplessonslearned.com/2009/08/minimum-viable-product-guide.html); Jon Radoff, "Minimum Viable Product Rant," John Radoff's Internet

Wonderland, May 4, 2010 (http://web.archive.org/web/20140323181121/http://radoff.com/blog/2010/05/04/minimum-viable-product-rant/).

4. There are good summaries of the overall valuation process: James Catty, *The Professional's Guide to Fair Value* (New York: Wiley, 2006); Tim Koller, Marc Goerhart, David Wessels, *Valuation: Measuring and Managing the Value of Companies*, 5th ed. (New York: Wiley; McKinsey & Company, 2010); Aswath Damodaran, *Investment Valuation: Tools and Techniques for Determining Value* (New York: Wiley, 2001); Rawley Thomas and Benton Gup, *The Valuation Handbook: Valuation Techniques from Today's Top Practitioners* (New York: Wiley, 2010); Michael Mard, James Hitcher, and Steven Hyden, *Valuation for Financial Reporting* (New York: Wiley, 2010).

5. Scott Baker, Nicholas Bloom, and Steven Davis, "Measuring Economy Policy Uncertainty," *Chicago Booth Research Paper* 13-02 (2013).

6. Nanette Byrnes and David Henry, "Confused about Earnings?" *Business Week,* November 26, 2001.

7. Baruch Lev, *Intangibles: Management, Measuring, and Reporting* (Washington, DC: Brookings Institute, 2001). In particular, Lev examined the ratio of capital market value of companies compared to their net asset value of the S&P 500, which has risen from 1 to more than 6 in the twenty-five years from 1990 to 2015.

8. Allan Webber interviewing Baruch Lev, "New Math for a New Economy," *Fast Company,* January–February 2000.

9. Baruch Lev, *Winning Investors Over: Surprising Truths about Honesty, Earnings Guidance, and Other Ways to Boost Your Stock Price* (Boston: Harvard Business Press, 2011).

10. Robert G. Eccles, Robert H. Herz, E. Mary Keegan, and David M. H. Phillips, *The Value Reporting Revolution* (New York: Wiley, 2001), 4–6.

11. Roland Burgman and Robert Eccles, "The Creation, Valuation, and Disclosure of Intellectual Assets through Enhanced Business Reporting," part of Enhanced Business Reporting consortium.

12. Accenture team: John Ballow, Robert Thomas, Eric Noren, Paul Herring, *Getting a Truer Picture of Shareholder Value* (Accenture report in *Outlook*, volume 2, 2005).

13. Ernst & Young, "Measures That Matter" (Ernst & Young, 1997), p. 3.

14. Others have studied intangibles, including: Mergermarket and RHR International, "Private Equity Firms Increase Deal Success by Focusing on Human Capital, Says RHR International," *Human Capital in Private Equity*, April 2007, http://www.businesswire.com/news/home/20070419005864/en/Private-Equity-Firms-Increase-Deal-Success-Focusing#.UubhU7Tn_IU; Spencer Stuart and National Venture Capital Association, *Emerging Best Practices for Building Next Generation of Venture-Backed Leadership* (Spencer Stuart and National Venture Capital Association, 2010); Ian C. MacMillan, R. Siegel, and P. N. S. Narasimha, "Criteria Used by Venture Capitalists to Evaluate New Venture Proposals," *Journal of Business Venturing* 1, no. 1: 119–128 (New York: Elsevier Science Publishing, 1985); Boris Groysberg, Paul Healy, Nitin Nohria,

and George Serafeim, "What Factors Drive Analyst Forecasts?" *Financial Analysts Journal* 67, no. 4 (July–August 2011).

15. BilanciaRSI and AIAF Working Group "Mission Intangibles," "The Value of Intangibles to Overcome the Systemic Crisis," *I Quaderni AIAF*, March 2010 (http://www.thevaluegroup.de/fileadmin/documents/Quaderno_AIAF_145-The_value_of_intangibles_to_overcome_the_systemic_crisis.pdf).

16. Andrew Sherman, *Harvesting Intangible Assets: Uncover Hidden Revenue in Your Company's Intellectual Property* (New York: AMACON, 2011).

17. Baruch Lev, *Intangibles: Management, Measurement, and Reporting* (Washington, DC: The Brookings Institute, 2001); Baruch Lev, "Intangible Assets: Concepts and Measurements," *Encyclopedia of Social Measurement* 2 (2005); Baruch Lev and Suresh Radhakrishnan, "The Valuation Organizational Capital," in *Measuring Capital in the New Economy*, ed. C. Corrado, J. Haltiwanger, and D. Sichel, *Studies in Income and Wealth*, vol. 65 (Chicago: The University of Chicago Press, 2005), 73–99.

18. Dave Ulrich and Norm Smallwood, *Why the Bottom Line Isn't: How to Build Value Through People and Organization* (New York: Wiley, 2003).

19. Gretchen Morgenson, "BlackRock Agrees to End Wall Street Analysis Previews," *New York Times*, January 8, 2014.

20. Ian C. MacMillan, R. Siegel, and P. N. S. Narasimha, "Criteria Used by Venture Capitalists to Evaluate New Venture Proposals," *Journal of Business Venturing* 1, no. 1: 119–128 (New York: Elsevier Science Publishing, 1985).

21. Boris Groysberg, Paul Healy, Nitin Nohria, and George Serafeim, "What Factors Drive Analyst Forecasts?" *Financial Analysts Journal* 67, no. 4 (July–August 2011).

22. T. Kiessling and M. Harvey, "The Human Resource Management Issues During a Global Acquisition: The Target Firm's Top Management Team and Key Managers," *International Journal of Human Resource Management* 17, no. 7 (2006); M. Harvey and M. Novicevic, "The Challenges Associated with the Capitalization of Managerial Skills," *International Journal of Human Resource Management* 16, no. 8 (2005); M. Harvey and R. Lusch, "A Systematic Assessment of Potential Strategic Alliance Partners," *International Business Review* 4, no. 2 (1995).

23. Nicholas Bloom and John van Reenen, "Management Practices Across Firms and Countries," *Quarterly Journal of Economics* 122, no. 4: 1351–1408 (Harvard College and the Massachusetts Institute of Technology, 2007).

24. See our summary of leadership in Dave Ulrich and Norm Smallwood, "What Is Leadership?" in *Advances in Global Leadership*, vol. 7, ed. William Mobley, Ming Li, and Ying Wang (Emerald Publishing Group, 2012).

25. Ethan Mollick, "People and Process, Suits and Innovators: The Role of Individuals in Firm Performance," *Strategic Management Journal* 33, no. 9 (2012): 1001–1015.

26. S. J. Zaccaro, "Trait-Based Perspectives of Leadership," *American Psychologist* 62, no. 1 (2007): 6–16; B. J. Hoffman, D. J. Woehr, R. Maldagen-Youngjohn, and B. D. Lyons, "Great Man or Great Myth? A Quantitative

Review of the Relationship between Individual Differences and Leader Effectiveness," *Journal of Occupational and Organizational Psychology* 84, no. 2 (2011): 347–381.

27. Competency theorists include Richard E. Boyatzis, *The Competent Manager: A Model for Effective Performance* (New York: Wiley, 1982); Lyle Spencer and Signe Spencer, *Competence at Work: Modes for Superior Performance* (New York: Wiley, 1993).

28. Dave Ulrich, Norm Smallwood, and Kate Sweetman, *Leadership Code: Five Rules to Live By* (Boston: Harvard Business Press, 2008).

29. F. E. Fielder, "A Theory of Leadership Effectiveness," in *Advances in Experimental Social Psychology*, ed. L. Berkowitz (New York: Academic Press, 1964); P. Hersey and K. H. Blanchard, "An Introduction to Situational Leadership," *Training and Development Journal* 23 (1969): 26–34; V. H. Vroom and A. G. Jago, "Situation Effects and Levels of Analysis in the Study of Leader Participation," *Leadership Quarterly* 6 (1995): 169–181.

30. Robert B. Kaiser, Robert Hogan, and S. Bartholomew Craig, "Leadership and the Fate of Organizations," *American Psychologist* 63, no. 2 (2008): 96.

31. A summary in the UK of the impact of leadership and leadership training on performance was done by John Burgoyne, Wendy Hirsh, and Sadie Williams, Research Report PR 560, *The Development of Management and Leadership Capability and Its Contribution to Performance: The Evidence, the Prospects and the Research Need* (Department for Education and Skills, 2004).

32. Studies of engagement are too numerous to mention, but a summary can be found: S. Fleck and I. Inceoglu, "A Comprehensive Framework for Understanding and Predicting Engagement," in *Handbook of Employee Engagement: Perspectives, Issues, Research and Practice*, ed. S. L. Albrecht (Cheltenham, UK: Edward Elgar, 2010), 31–42; Theresa Welbourne and Steven Schlater, "Engaged in What? Role Theory Perspectives for Enhancing Engagement Research and Practice" (working paper, University of Nebraska–Lincoln, 2014). Some specific studies include A. J. Rucci, S. P. Kirm, and R. T. Quinn, "The Employee-Customer-Profit Chain at Sears," *Harvard Business Review* (January–February 1998): 84–97. Barber found the same in one hundred retail stores in the UK: L. Barber, S. Hayday, S. Bevan, *From People to Profits*, IES Report 355 (Brighton: Institute for Employment Studies, 1999).

33. W. Glenn Rowe, "Creating Wealth in Organizations: The Role of the Strategic Leader," *Academy of Management Executive* 15, no. 1 (2001).

34. Edgar Schein, *Leadership and Organizational Culture* (4th ed.) (San Francisco: Jossey Bass, 2010); Daniel Denison, Robert Hoojberg, Nancy Lane, and Colleen Lief, *Leading Culture Change in Global Organizations: Aligning Culture and Strategy* (San Francisco: Jossey Bass, 2012).

35. Dave Ulrich and Wayne Brockbank, *HR Value Proposition* (Boston: Harvard Business Press, 2006).

36. John Kotter and James Heskett, *Corporate Culture and Performance* (New York: Free Press, 2011).

37. There are five significant studies on leadership and its impact on performance: S. Lieberson and J. F. O'Connor, "Leadership and Organizational Performance: A Large Study of Corporations," *American Sociological Review* 37 (1972): 117–130; Nan Weiner, "Situational and Leadership Influence on Organizational Performance," Proceedings of the Academy of Management (1978); A. B. Thomas, "Does Leadership Make a Difference in Organizational Performance?" *Administrative Science Quarterly* 33 (1988): 388–400; N. Wasserman, N. Nohria, and B. N. Anand, "What Does Leadership Matter? The Contingent Opportunities View of CEO Leadership," Harvard Working Paper no. 02-04 (2001); Alison Mackey , "How Much Do CEOs Influence Firm Performance—Really?" September 1, 2005, http://papers.ssrn.com/sol3/papers.cfm?abstract_id=816065. These results are summarized in the following table:

Affects	Lieberson and O'Connor	Weiner	Thomas	Wasserman, Nohria, Anand	Mackey
Year affect	1.8%	2.4%	5.6%	2.6%	1.0%
Industry affect	28.5%	20.5%	n/a	n/a	18.0%
Corporate affect	22.6%	45.8%	82.2%	25.5%	29.5%
CEO affect	14.5%	8.7%	5.7%	14.7%	12.9%
Error	32.6%	22.6%	5.4%	50.9%	38.5%

Using ROA as dependent variable

38. Jack Zenger, "Great Leaders Can Double Profits, Research Shows," *Forbes*, January 15, 2015, http://www.forbes.com/sites/jackzenger/2015/01/15/great-leaders-can-double-profits-research-shows/.

39. R. D. Ireland and M. A. Hitt, "Achieving and Maintaining Strategic Competitiveness in the 21st Century: The Role of Strategic Leadership," *Academy of Management Executive* 13, no. 1 (1999): 43–57; Glen Rowe, "Creating Wealth in Organizations: The Role of Strategic Leadership," *Academy of Management Executive* 15, no. 1 (2001).

40. Alison Mackey, "The Effect of CEOs on Firm Performance," *Strategic Management Journal* 29, no. 12 (2008): 1357–1367.

41. Dave Ulrich, Jon Younger, Wayne Brockbank, and Mike Ulrich, *HR from the Outside In* (New York: McGraw-Hill, 2012).

42. Dave Ulrich, Justin Allen, Norm Smallwood, Wayne Brockbank, and Jon Younger, "Building Culture from the Outside In," *Strategic HR Review* 8, no. 6 (2009): 20–27.

43. Dave Ulrich and Norm Smallwood, *Leadership Brand* (Boston: Harvard Business Press, 2009).

44. An excellent study and report by Deloitte reports a 15.7% premium on effective leaders and a 19.8% discount on ineffective leaders. This work confirms the importance of leadership in driving shareholder value; see Deloitte, *The Leadership Premium: How Companies Win the Confidence of Investors* (2012).

45. Dave Ulrich, Norm Smallwood, and Michael Ulrich, "The Leadership Gap: Assessing Leadership Is Investors' Most Glaring Weakness When Making Investment Decisions," *CFA Magazine*, January–February 2012.

Chapter 2

1. This story comes from personal correspondence with Nick Holley.

2. Dave Ulrich and Norm Smallwood, "What Is Talent?," *Leader to Leader* 12 (2012): 55–61.

3. Ceridian, Human Capital White Paper, Ceridian UK Ltd, 2007, http://www.ceridian.co.uk/hr/downloads/HumanCapitalWhitePaper_2007_01_26.pdf.

4. Those who follow our work may recall that in *The Leadership Code* my colleagues and I separate talent manager (which focuses on managing people for today) and human capital developer (which focuses on investing in people for tomorrow). Here I have combined these two talent-related leadership skills for simplicity in developing the leadership capital index. Both focus on the underlying ability of a leader to manage people; investors who see this skill in leaders will have more confidence in the firm's ability to deliver intangible and tangible value. To follow up with that book, see Dave Ulrich, Norm Smallwood, and Kate Sweetman, *Leadership Code: Five Rules to Live By* (Boston: Harvard Business Press, 2008).

5. These studies include Laurie J. Bassi and Daniel P. McMurrer, "A Capital Investment," *Learning and Performance,* February 2009; Chartered Institute of Personnel & Development (CIPD), "Human Capital Evolution—Developing Performance Measures," *Human Capital Panel Report,* Summer 2007; Greg Filbeck and Diane Preece, "Fortune's Best 100 Companies to Work For: Do They Work for Shareholders?" *Journal of Business Finance & Accounting* 30 (June 2003): 771–797; Hay Group, "What Makes the Most Admired Companies Great: Reward Program Effectiveness," December 2008; McBassi & Company, Human Capital Capability Scorecard Human Capital Management (HCM) Index and Factor Definitions, 2007; Mercer, The Value of People—Insights into Human Capital, 2006; PriceWaterhouseCoopers, Managing People in a Changing World: Key Trends in Human Capital: A Global Perspective—2008, *Human Resource Services,* Saratoga, 2008; Ingrid Smithey Fulmer, Barry Gerhart, and Kimberly Scott, "Are the 100 Best Better? An Empirical Investigation of the Relationship Between Being a 'Great Place to Work' and Firm Performance," *Personnel Psychology* 56 (2003): 965–993.

6. Reviews of the human capital metrics and financial performance can be found in: Ingrid Smith Fulmer and Robert Ployhart, "Our Most Important Asset: A Multidisciplinary/Multilevel Review of Human Capital Valuation for Research and Practice," *Journal of Management* 40 (2014): 371–398, doi:10.1177/0149206313511271; A. J. Nyberg, T. P. Moliterno, D. Hale, and D. P. Lepak, "Resource-Based Perspectives on Unit-Level Human Capital: A Review and Integration," *Journal of Management* 40 (2014): 316–346.

7. American National Standards Institute (ANSI) and Society for Human Resource Management (SHRM), *Cost per Hire,* 2012.

8. Kim Heldman, *Project Manager's Spotlight on Risk Management* (San Francisco: Jossey-Bass, 2005); "ISO 31000," http://en.wikipedia.org/wiki/ISO_31000/; ISO Guide 73:2002 defines risk.

9. Robert S. Kaplan, "Risk Management and the Strategy Execution System," *Balanced Scorecard Report,* November–December 2009; Robert S. Kaplan and Anette Mikes, "Managing the Multiple Dimensions of Risk," *Balanced Scorecard Report,* July–August 2011; Robert S. Kaplan and Anette Mikes, "Managing the Multiple Dimensions of Risk," *Balanced Scorecard Report,* September–October 2011.

10. The Committee of Sponsoring Organizations of the Treadway Commission, Enterprise Risk Management—Integrated Framework, September 2004.

11. David Cooper, *Leadership Risk: A Guide for Private Equity and Strategic Investors* (New York: Wiley, 2010).

12. David Larcker and Brian Tayan, *Corporate Governance Matters: A Closer Look at Organizational Choices and Their Consequences* (Saddle River, NJ: FT Press, 2011).

13. Paul Coombes and Mark Watson, Global Investor Opinion Survey 2002: Key Findings, McKinsey Company, 2002, http://www.eiod.org/uploads/Publications/Pdf/II-Rp-4-1.pdf.

14. Freer Spreckley first articulated the triple bottom line in a publication called "Social Audit—A Management Tool for Co-operative Working"; John Elkington, *Cannibals with Forks: The Triple Bottom Line of 21st Century Business* (Mankato, MN: Capstone Publishing, 1997).

15. Sustainability Accounting Standards Board (SASB), presentation by Jean Rogers, executive director, November 13, 2012.

16. For more information on socially responsible investing, visit http://www.responsible-investor.com/; Kent Baker and John Nofsinger, eds., *Socially Responsible Finance and Investing: Financial Institutions, Corporations, Investors, and Analysts* (New York: Wiley, 2012), part of Robert K. Kolb series.

17. Neil Harrison, *Sustainable Capitalism and the Pursuit of Well Being* (London: Routledge, 2014).

18. Gary Davies, with Rosa Chun, Rui Vinhas da Silva, and Stuart Roper, *Corporate Reputation and Competitiveness* (London: Routledge, 2002); Gary Davies, Rosa Chun, Rui Vinhas da Silva, and Stuart Roper, "A Corporate Character Scale to Assess Employee and Customer Views of Organization Reputation," *Corporate Reputation Review* 7 (2004): 125–146.

Table 2.2

a. Eric Flamholtz, *Human Resource Accounting: Advances in Concepts, Methods, and Applications* (2nd ed.) (San Francisco: Jossey-Bass, 1985); Wayne Cascio, *Costing Human Resources: The Financial Impact of Behavior in Organizations* (3rd ed.) (Boston: PWS-Kent Pub. Co, 1991).

b. John Boudreau, "Utility Analysis for Decisions in Human Resource Management," in *Handbook of Industrial and Organizational Psychology,* vol. 2 (2nd ed.), ed. Marvin D. Dunnette and Leaetta M. Hough (Palo Alto, CA: Consulting Psychologists Press: 1991), 621–745; J. W. Boudreau and P. M. Ramstad, *Beyond HR: The New Science of Human Capital* (Boston, MA: Harvard

Business School Publishing, 2007); W. F. Cascio and J. W. Boudreau, *Investing in People* (2nd ed.) (Upper Saddle River, NJ: Pearson, 2011).

c. M. A. Huselid, "The Impact of Human Resource Management Practices on Turnover, Productivity and Corporate Financial Performance," *Academy of Management Journal* 38, no. 3 (1995): 635–672; M. A. Huselid and B. E. Becker, "Bridging Micro and Macro Domains: Workforce Differentiation and Strategic Human Resource Management," *Journal of Management* 37, no. 2 (2011): 421–428.

d. J. Delaney and M. A. Huselid, "The Impact of Human Resource Management Practices on Perceptions of Organisational Performance," *Academy of Management Journal* 39, no. 4 (1996): 949–969.

e. Dr. Bassi's studies of human capital and market value are lengthy and thoughtful; "Corporate Investments in Human Capital: Accounting for and Measuring Its Impact" (Brookings Institution); Laurie Bassi and Daniel McMurrer, "How's Your Return on People?" *Harvard Business Review* (March 2004); Laurie Bassi and Daniel McMurrer, "Maximizing Your Return on People," *Harvard Business Review* 85, no. 3 (2007); Laurie Bassi, Ed Frauenheim, Dan McMurrer, and Larry Costello, *Good Company: Success in the Workplace* (San Francisco: Berrett-Koehler, 2011); Laurie Bassi, Rob Carpenter, and Dan McMurrer, *HR Analytics Handbook* (Brooklyn, NY: McBassi & Company, 2012).

f. Laurie J. Bassi and Daniel P. McMurrer, "A Capital Investment," *Learning and Performance* (Brooklyn, NY: February 2009); Laurie Bassi, Paul Harrison, Jens Ludwig, and Daniel McMurrer, "The Impact of U.S. Firms Investments in Human Capital on Stock Prices" (Brooklyn, NY: June 2004).

g. Mark van Clieaf, "How Is Your Organization Capital Performance?" MVC Associates, www.mvcinternational.com; Mark van Clieaf, "Are Boards and CEOs Accountable for the Right *Level* of Work?" *Ivey Business Journal* (May/June 2004); Mark van Clieaf, "Levels of Work and Internal Pay Equity: More Defensible Than Executive Compensation Surveys," *Executive Compensation Strategies* (2005); Mark van Clieaf, "The Opportunity for 'Strategic Governance' at Investee Companies to Create Long Term Value"; presentation to CFA Society of Chicago, April 24, 2014; Mark van Clieaf, "Designing Investee, Company Metrics, Incentives, Leadership, to Create Long Term Value" (presentation to CFA Society of Chicago, April 24, 2014).

h. UBS, Ascent Project Equity Research: Human Capital Management (HCM), presentation provided by UBS.

i. The market value of being a great company to work for was also demonstrated in a study that focused on employee satisfaction, one of the key indicators of great companies to work for. Alex Edmans, "Does the Market Fully Value Intangibles? Employee Satisfaction and Equity Prices" (working paper, Wharton School, University of Pennsylvania, 2008).

j. CIPD, *View from the City: How Can Human Capital Reporting Inform Investment Decisions,* prepared by CIPD, 2010, https://www.cipd.co.uk/hr -resources/research/human-capital-management-inform-decisions.aspx.

k. See the summary of the work in David Creelman and Laurie Bassie, *Reporting on Human Capital: The Drama, the Guidelines, and the Future* (Toronto: Creelman Research, 2013).

l. American National Standards Institute (ANSI) and SHRM, *Cost-per-Hire Standard,* 2012, https://www.shrm.org/HRStandards/PublishedStandards/Documents/11-0096%20HR%20Standards%20Booklet_WEB_revised.pdf; American National Standards Institute (ANSI) and SHRM, *Performance Management American National Standard,* 2012, https://www.shrm.org/HRStandards/Documents/12-0794%20Performance%20Mngmt%20Standard_Interior_viewonlyFNL_rvsd10-4-13.pdf.

m. Ingrid Smithey Fulmer, Barry Gerhart, and Kimberly Scott, "Are the 100 Best Better? An Empirical Investigation of the Relationship between Being a 'Great Place to Work' and Firm Performance," *Personnel Psychology* 56 (2003): 965–993.

n. Hay Group, In a League of Their Own: How the World's Most Admired Stay Ahead of the Game, 2007; Hay Group, What Makes the Most Admired Companies Great: Reward Program Effectiveness, December 2008.

o. Jerry Amernic, "The Impact of Human Capital Management on Shareholder Value," *Drake Business Review* 1 (2009): 31–34, http://www.workforce.com/articles/about-the-human-capital-index-study.

p. Mercer, The Value of People—Insights into Human Capital, 2006.

q. PriceWaterhouseCoopers, Managing People in a Changing World: Key Trends in Human Capital: A Global Perspective—2008; *Human Resource Services, Saratoga,* 2008; PriceWaterhouseCoopers, Reward: A New Paradigm? September 2008.

r. The ROI Institute (www.roiinstitute.net) has produced a number of books and tools for measuring human capital, including: Jack Phillips, Patti Phillips, and Rebecca Ray, *Measuring Leadership Development: Quantify Your Program's Impact and ROI on Organizational Performance* (New York: McGraw-Hill, 2012).

Chapter 3

1. The foundation article for this work is found in Jim Loehr and Tony Schwartz, "The Making of a Corporate Athlete," *Harvard Business Review,* January 2001; subsequent updates of the work are at https://www.hpinstitute.com/research-press/hpi-in-the-news.

2. Rick Wartzman, "Conditioning the Corporate Athlete," *Bloomberg Businessweek,* May 22, 2008, http://www.businessweek.com/stories/2008-05-22/conditioning-the-corporate-athletebusinessweek-business-news-stock-market-and-financial-advice.

3. Boris Groysberg, Andrew McLean, and Nitan Nohria, "Are Leaders Portable?," *Harvard Business Review* 84, no. 5 (May 2006): 92–100; Boris Groysberg, *Chasing Stars: The Myth of Talent and the Portability of Performance* (Princeton, NJ: Princeton University Press, 2011).

4. Daniel Goleman, *Emotional Intelligence: Why It Can Matter More Than IQ*

(New York: Bantam Books, 2005); Travis Bradberry, Jean Greaves, and Patrick Lencioni, *Emotional Intelligence 2.0* (San Diego: TalentSmart, 2009); Peter Salovey, John Mayer, and David Caruso, "Emotional Intelligence: Theory, Findings, and Implications," *Psychological Inquiry* (2004): 197–215; J. D. Mayer, P. Salovey, and D. R. Caruso, "Emotional Intelligence: New Ability or Eclectic Traits?" *American Psychologist* 63 (2008): 503–517; Adam Grant, "The Dark Side of Emotional Intelligence," *Atlantic Monthly*, January 2, 2014.

5. Timothy R. Clark, *The Leadership Test: Will You Pass?* (Oxford, UK: Oxonian Press, 2009); Timothy R. Clark, *The Employee Engagement Mindset: The Six Drivers for Tapping Into the Hidden Potential of Everyone in Your Company* (New York: McGraw-Hill, 2012).

6. Malcolm Gladwell discusses the importance of connectors in building social movements.

7. Liz Wiseman and Greg McKeown, *Multipliers: How the Best Leaders Make Everyone Smarter* (New York: HarperBusiness, 2010).

8. Martin Seligman, *Authentic Happiness: Using the New Positive Psychology to Realize Your Potential for Lasting Fulfillment* (New York: Free Press, 2002); Martin Seligman, "Can Happiness Be Taught?" *Daedalus* 133, no. 2 (Spring 2004): 80–87, doi:10.1162/001152604323049424; Christopher Peterson and Martin E. P. Seligman, *Character Strengths and Virtues* (Oxford, UK: Oxford University Press, 2004); Martin Seligman, *Flourish: A Visionary New Understanding of Happiness and Well-Being* (New York: Free Press, 2011).

9. B. L. Fredrickson and M. Losada, "Positive Affect and the Complex Dynamics of Human Flourishing," *American Psychologist* 60, no. 7 (2005): 678–686; B. L. Fredrickson, *Positivity: Top-Notch Research Reveals the 3-to-1 Ratio That Will Change Your Life* (New York: Crown, 2009); B. L. Fredrickson, "Updated Thinking on Positivity Ratios," *American Psychologist*, July 15, 2013.

10. Shawn Achor, "The Happiness Advantage: Linking Positive Brains to Performance," TED Talk, Bloomington, IN, May 14, 2011, http://www.youtube .com/watch?v=GXy__kBVq1M&feature=youtube_gdata_player.

11. Kenneth P. De Meuse, Guangrong Dai, and George S. Hallenbeck, "Learning Agility: A Construct Whose Time Has Come," *Consulting Psychology Journal: Practice and Research* 62, no. 2 (2010): 119–130.

12. Victoria Swisher, *Becoming an Agile Leader* (Lominger International, a Korn/Ferry Company, 2012).

13. Linda Tischler, "17 Career Lessons from Ideo's David Kelley," *Fast Company*, February 4, 2009, http://www.fastcompany.com/1150457/17-career -lessons-ideos-david-kelley. This idea is also in Ryan Babineaux and John Krumboltz, *Fail Fast, Fail Often: How Losing Can Help You Win* (New York: Tarcher/Penguin, 2013).

14. Dori Meinert, "Creating an Ethical Culture," *HR Magazine*, April 2014.

15. Ibid.; Warren Bennis and Robert Thomas, *Leading for a Lifetime: How Defining Moments Shape Leaders of Today and Tomorrow* (Boston: Harvard Business Review Press, 2007).

Chapter 4

1. Ronald Jonash and Tom Sommerlatte, *The Innovation Premium: How Next Generation Companies Are Achieving Peak Performance and Profitability* (New York: Basic Books, 2010). Innovation premium has also become an annual feature of *Forbes* in which Gibb Dyer and Hal Gregerson rank the most innovative companies and show their increased market value: http://www.forbes.com/sites/innovatorsdna/2013/08/14/an-faq-on-the-innovation-premium/.

Chapter 5

1. The percentage of behavior tied to habit varies by study, ranging from 50% to 95%; see Charles Duhigg, *The Power of Habit: Why We Do What We Do in Life and Business* (New York: Random House, 2012); Tony Schwartz, "Six Keys to Changing Almost Anything," *HBR* Blog, January 17, 2011; Schwartz suggests that only 5% of choices are consciously chosen, and 95% habits; James Claiborn and Cherry Pedrick, *The Habit Change Workbook: How to Break Bad Habits and Form Good Ones* (New Harbinger, 2001); M. J. Ryan, *This Year I Will . . . : How to Finally Change a Habit, Keep a Resolution, or Make a Dream Come True* (New York: Broadway Books, 2006); Mark F. Weinstein, *Habitually Great: Master Your Habits* (Author, 2009); Jack Hodge, *The Power of Habit: Harnessing the Power to Establish Routines That Guarantee Success in Business and Life* (Bloomington, IN: Author, 2003).

2. The term "flywheel" has been used to describe the heavy start-up efforts for any new initiatives; James Collins, *Good to Great: Why Some Companies Make the Leap—and Others Don't* (New York: Harper Business, 2001).

3. Simon Sinek, *Start with Why: How Great Leaders Inspire Everyone to Take Action* (New York: Portfolio Trade, 2011).

4. Categories of resistance to change are laid out nicely in Noel Tichy, *Managing Strategic Change: Technical, Political, and Cultural Dynamics* (New York: Wiley, 1983); Warren Bennis, Kenneth Benne, and Robert Chin, *The Planning of Change* (New York: Holt Rinehart, 1985); Warner Burke, Dale Lake, and Jill Payne, *Organization Change: A Comprehensive Reader* (San Francisco: Jossey-Bass, 2008).

5. Daryl Conner, *Managing at the Speed of Change* (New York: Random House, 1993); Daryl Conner, *Leading at the Edge of Chaos: How to Create the Nimble Organization* (San Francisco: Wiley, 1998); Richard Beckhard, *Organization Development: Strategies and Models* (New York: Addison-Wesley 1969); Richard Beckhard and Reuben T. Harris, *Organizational Transitions: Managing Complex Change* (Reading, MA: Addison-Wesley, 1987); Richard Beckhard and Wendy Pritchard, *Changing the Essence: The Art of Creating and Leading Fundamental Change in Organizations,* vol. 10 (San Francisco: Jossey-Bass, 1992).

6. See the Conner Partners' glossary of Change Thinking at http://www.connerpartners.com/uncategorized/glossary#sthash.ecJiSfm3.dpuf.

7. Some excellent recent work on decision making comes from extensive work by Bain & Company: Marcia Blenko, Michael Adams, and Paul Rogers,

Decide and Deliver: Five Steps to Breakthrough Performance in Your Organization (Boston: Harvard Business Press, 2010).

8. The focus on mobilizing commitment comes from our work with the GE Change Acceleration Process (CAP), where we asked users of the CAP toolkit to define which of the seven processes (see Table 5.1) was most critical to making change happen. We validated with other companies working on change.

9. Thoughtful colleagues have written about influence: Allan Cohen and David Bradford, *Influence without Authority* (New York: Wiley, 2005); Roger Fisher and Alan Sharp, *Getting It Done: How to Lead When You Are Not in Charge* (New York: HarperBusiness, 1999); Robert Cialdini, *Influence: The Psychology of Persuasion* (New York: HarperBusiness, 2006).

10. The importance of adapting as a key to success is nicely laid out in Tim Harford, *Adapt: Why Success Always Starts with Failure* (Picador, 2012). The underlying theories of learning are laid out in Chris Argyris, *Knowledge for Action: A Guide to Overcoming Barriers to Organizational Change* (San Francisco: Jossey-Bass, 1993); Chris Argyris, *On Organization Learning* (New York: Wiley, 1999); Donald Schon, *The Reflective Practioner: How Professionals Think in Action* (New York: Basic Books, 1984).

11. These failure-to-success stories, and others, are laid out in http://blogs .static.mentalfloss.com/blogs/archives/20336.htm.

12. Robert Goldman and Stephen Papson, *Nike Culture: The Sign of the Swoosh* (London: SAGE Publications, 1998), 49.

Chapter 6

1. S. Kerr and J. M. Jermier, "Substitutes for Leadership: Their Meaning and Measurement," *Organizational Behavior and Human Performance* 22 (1978): 375–440; S. Kerr, C. A. Schriesheim, C. J. Murphy, and R. M. Stogdill, "Toward a Contingency Theory of Leadership Based upon the Consideration and Initiating Structure Literature," *Organizational Behavior and Human Performance* 12 (1974): 62–82.

2. We are not about to start to synthesize this vast literature of human performance at work. Others have done thoughtful integrations of much of this work: M. Attridge, "Measuring and Managing Employee Work Engagement: A Review of the Research and Business Literature," *Journal of Workplace Behavioral Health* 24, no. 4 (2009): 383–398; M. S. Christian, A. S. Garza, and J. E. Slaughter, "Work Engagement: A Quantitative Review and Test of Its Relations with Task and Contextual Performance," *Personnel Psychology* 64, no. 1 (2011): 89–136; Gallup Consulting, State of the American Workplace: Employee Engagement Insights for U.S. Business Leaders, 2013, http://www .gallup.com/strategicconsulting/157451/state-american-workplace-2008-2010 .aspx; W. H. Macey, B. Schneider, K. M. Barbera, and S. A. Young, *Employee Engagement: Tools for Analysis, Practice, and Competitive Advantage* (London: Wiley-Blackwell, 2009).

3. One of the best summaries of the engagement work for individuals, organizations, and nations is this report: David McLeod and

Nita Clarke, *Engaging for Success: Enhancing Performance through Employee Engagement,* prepared for the Office of Public Information, Information Policy Team (n.d.), http://www.engageforsuccess.org/ideas-tools/employee-engagement-the-macleod-report/#.U_PnSmPp-3M.

4. Work on the erosion in engagement around the globe is summarized in a study by Mercer, "What's Working around the World: Global Insights on Employee Engagement," http://107.22.238.165/mercer-wwaw/; M. Gatenby, C. Rees, E. Soane, and C. Truss, *Employee Engagement in Context* (London: Chartered Institute of Personnel and Development C, 2009); Towers Perrin-ISR, *The ISR Employee Engagement Report* (2006); Accenture, "An Accenture Point of View on Employee Engagement—What It Is, Why It Matters, How You Can You Change It" (2008).

5. Liz Wiseman, "Smart Leaders Get More Out of the Employees They Have," *Harvard Business Review* blog, August 20, 2012.

6. Douglas McGregor, *The Human Side of Enterprise* (New York: McGraw-Hill, 1960).

7. Some of the thoughtful work on servant leadership was based on these works: Robert Greenleaf, *The Power of Servant-Leadership* (Oakland, CA: Berrett-Koehler, 1998); Robert Greenleaf and Larry Spears, eds., *Servant Leadership: A Journey into the Nature of Legitimate Power and Greatness* (Mahwah, NJ: Paulist Press, 2002); Robert Greenleaf, *The Servant-Leader Within: A Transformative Path* (Mahwah, NJ: Paulist Press, 2003); Ken Blanchard, *Servant Leader* (Nashville, TN: Thomas Nelson, 2003).

8. Some of the thoughtful work on authentic leadership was crafted and synthesized with some of the following: Bill George, *Authentic Leadership: Rediscovering the Secrets to Creating Lasting Value* (San Francisco: Jossey-Bass, 2004); David Irvine and Jim Reger, *The Authentic Leader: It's About Presence, Not Position* (DC Press, 2006); William Gardner, Bruce Avolio, and Fred Walumbwa, eds. *Authentic Leadership Theory and Practice, Volume 3: Origins, Effects and Development* (Bingley, UK: Emerald Group Publishing, 2005).

9. Bruce Avolio and William Gardner, "Authentic Leadership Development—Getting to the Root of Positive Forms of Leadership," *The Leadership Quarterly* 16, no. 3 (2005): 315–338; William L. Gardner, "The Power of Positive Tinkering," *Workforce,* September 12, 2013, http://www.workforce.com/articles/9352-the-power-of-positive-tinkering; Jennifer Robison, "The Business Benefits of Positive Leadership," *Business Journal,* May 10, 2007, http://businessjournal.gallup.com/content/27496/Business-Benefits-Positive-Leadership.aspx; Tom Rath, "The Impact of Positive Leadership," *Business Journal,* May 13, 2004, http://businessjournal.gallup.com/content/11458/Impact-Positive-Leadership.aspx.

10. Kim Cameron, *Positive Leadership: Strategies for Extraordinary Performance* (Oakland, CA: Berrett-Koehler, 2012); Kim Cameron, *Practicing Positive Leadership: Tools and Techniques That Create Extraordinary Results* (Oakland, CA: Berrett-Koehler, 2013); Jane Dutton and Gretchen Spreitzer, *How to Be a Positive Leader: Small Actions, Big Impact* (Oakland, CA: Berrett-Koehler, 2014);

Adam Grant, *Give and Take: Why Helping Others Drives Our Success* (New York: Penguin, 2014).

11. The personal, organizational, and societal benefits of trust can be seen in Stephen M. R. Covey, *The Speed of Trust: The One Thing That Changes Everything* (New York: Free Press, 2008); David Horsager, *The Trust Edge: How Top Leaders Gain Faster Results, Deeper Relationships, and a Stronger Bottom Line* (New York: Free Press, 2012); William Ouchi, "Markets, Bureaucracies, and Clans," *Administrative Science Quarterly* 25 (1980): 129–141; Oliver Williamson, *Markets and Hierarchies: Analysis and Antitrust Implications* (New York: Free Press, 1975).

12. Steven M. R. Covey (ibid.) identified thirteen behaviors that enhance trust: talk straight, demonstrate respect, create transparency, right wrongs, show loyalty, deliver results, get better, confront reality, clarify expectation, practice accountability, listen first, keep commitments, and extend trust. The academic literature on trust has been nicely summarized in Kurt Dirks and Donald Ferrin, "Trust in Leadership: Meta-Analytic Findings and Implications for Research and Practice," *Journal of Applied Psychology* 87, no. 4 (2002): 611–628. Trust in marriage has been a key factor for success: John Gottman and Nan Silver, *The Seven Principles for Making Marriage Work: A Practical Guide from the Country's Foremost Relationship Expert* (New York: Harmony, 2000); John Gottman and Nan Silver, *What Makes Love Last? How to Build Trust and Avoid Betrayal* (New York: Simon & Schuster, 2013). Trust in teams has been nicely captured in Carl Larson and Frank LaFasto, *Teamwork: What Must Go Right/ What Can Go Wrong* (Newbury Park, CA: Sage, 1989).

13. The interesting research is showing that next-generation parents are taking their responsibility seriously. High-level indicators of teenage drug use, alcoholism, and smoking are declining overall as parents spend time with their children, attend to their education, and help their children find hobbies (http://www.cdc.gov/alcohol/fact-sheets/underage-drinking.htm). "Tiger moms" and "helicopter parents" may intrude and hover over their children, but in general the children are being raised to be successful.

14. The leadership coaching "profession" has grown exponentially in the last twenty years. There are some wonderful summaries of coaching logic: Marshall Goldsmith, Laurence Lyons, and Sarah McArthur, eds., *Coaching for Leadership: Writings on Leadership from the World's Greatest Coaches* (Hoboken, NJ: Pfeiffer, 2012); Dave Ulrich and Jessica Johnson, "Demystifying the Coaching Mystique," in eds. Marshall Goldsmith, Laurence Lyons, and Sarah McArthur, *Coaching for Leadership: Writings on Leadership from the World's Greatest Coaches* (Hoboken, NJ: Pfeiffer, 2012); Marshall Goldsmith and Mark Reiter, *What Got You Here Won't Get You There* (New York: Random House, 2007).

15. Dave Ulrich, "A Brief Trek Towards the Next Agenda for Coaching," in eds. Goldsmith, Lyons, and McArthur, *Coaching for Leadership*.

16. John Whitmore, *Coaching for Performance* (Boston, MA: Nicholas Brealey Publishing, 2009).

17. Peter Wilson, *Make Mentoring Work* (Australia: Major Street Publishing, 2012), 304.

18. My son and I indulged our personal passion for basketball and calculated these scoring averages from statistics available at NBA.com.

19. Patrick Lencioni, *The Advantage: Why Organizational Health Trumps Everything Else in Business* (San Francisco: Jossey-Bass, 2012); Patrick Lencioni, *The Five Dysfunctions of a Team: A Leadership Fable* (San Francisco: Jossey-Bass, 2002).

20. Characteristics of high-performing teams can be found in Richard Hackman, *Leading Teams: Setting the Stage for High Performance* (Boston: Harvard Business Press, 2002); Jon Katzenbach and Douglas Smith, *The Wisdom of Teams: Creating the High Performance Organization* (New York: Harper Business, 2006); Jon Katzenbach, *The Discipline of Teams: A Mindbook-Workbook for Delivering Small Group Performance* (New York: Wiley, 2001); S. W. J. Kozlowski and D. R. Ilgen, "Enhancing the Effectiveness of Work Groups and Teams," *Psychological Science in the Public Interest* 7 (2006): 77–12.

21. Howard Schultz and Joanne Gordon, *Onward: How Starbucks Fought for Its Life without Losing Its Soul* (Emmau, PA: Rodale Books, 2012).

Chapter 7

1. References on the nature vs. nurture debate: Leadership and Evolutionary Psychology, 21st Annual SIOP Convention, Dallas 2006. This symposium presented four papers on the topic of evolutionary psychology, or nature vs. nurture. See also Andrew Solomon, *Far from the Tree: Parents, Children, and the Search for Identity* (New York: Scribner, 2013); Matt Ridley, *Nature via Nurture: Genes, Experience, and What Makes Us Human* (New York: HarperCollins, 2003); J. T. Neill, "Nature vs Nurture in Intelligence" (2004; last updated April 2005), http://www.wilderdom.com/personality/L4-1IntelligenceNatureVsNurture.html; Stephen J. Ceci and Wendy M. Williams, eds. *The Nature–Nurture Debate: The Essential Readings* (Malden, MA: Blackwell Publishing, 1999); Dale Goldhaber, *The Nature-Nurture Debates: Bridging the Gap* (New York: Cambridge University Press, 2012); B. Kolb, R. Gibb, and T. E. Robinson, "Brain Plasticity and Behavior," *Current Directions in Psychological Science* 12 (February 2003).

2. John C. Flanagan, "The Critical Incident Technique," *Psychological Bulletin* 54, no. 4 (July 1954).

3. David McClelland, "Testing for Competence Rather Than Intelligence," *American Psychologist* 28 (1973): 1–14; S. Horton, "The Competency Movement," in eds. S. Horton, A. Hondeghem, and D. Farnham, *Competency Management in the Public Sector: European Variations on a Theme* (Brussels: IOS Press, 2002), 3–15; Richard Boyatzis, *The Competent Manager: A Model for Effective Performance* (New York: Wiley, 1982).

4. Dave Ulrich, Jack Zenger, and Norm Smallwood, *Results-Based Leadership* (Boston: Harvard Business Review Press, 1999).

5. Erin Wilson Burns, Lawrence Smith, and Dave Ulrich, "Competency

Models with Impact: Research Findings from the Top Companies for Leadership," *People and Strategy,* November 30, 2012.

6. Dave Ulrich, *HR from the Outside In.*

7. We are indebted to Dick Beatty for this insight.

8. There are many works on the power of branding: Duane Knapp, *The Brand Promise* (New York: McGraw-Hill, 2008); Klaus Schmidt and Chris Ludlow, *Inclusive Branding: The Why and How of a Holistic Approach to Brands* (Basingstoke, UK: Palgrave Macmillan, 2002); David Aaker and Erich Joachimsthaler, *Brand Leadership: The Next Level of the Brand Revolution* (New York: Free Press, 2000); David Aaker, *Brand Portfolio Strategy: Creating Relevance, Differentiation, Energy, Leverage, and Clarity* (New York: Free Press, 2004).

9. These ideas on evolution of brand are laid out in Ulrich and Smallwood, *Leadership Brand*; Dave Ulrich and Norm Smallwood, "Building a Leadership Brand," *Harvard Business Review* 85, no. 7/8 (2007): 92.

10. Life cycle work is captured by many psychologists, but often illustrated by Erik Erickson, *Identity and the Life Cycle* (New York: Norton, 1994); Erick Erickson and Joan Erickson, *The Life Cycle (Completed)* (New York: Norton, 1998); Daniel Levinson, *The Seasons of a Man's Life* (New York: Ballantine Books, 1986); Gail Sheehy, *Passages: Predictable Crises of Adult Life* (New York: Ballantine Books, 2006).

11. Larry Greiner, "Evolution and Revolution as Organizations Grow," *Harvard Business Review* 50, no. 4 (1972); Ichak Adizes, *Corporate Lifecycles: How and Why Corporations Grow and Die and What to Do about It* (Carpinteria, CA: The Adizes Institute, 1990); Ichak Adizes, *Managing Corporate Lifecycles* (New York: Prentice Hall, 1999); Rodolphe Durand, *Organizational Evolution and Strategic Management* (Thousand Oaks, CA: SAGE Publications, 2006).

12. Paul Hersey and Ken H. Blanchard, *Management of Organizational Behavior: Utilizing Human Resources,* 2nd ed. (New York: Prentice Hall, 1972); Paul Hersey and Ken H. Blanchard, *Management of Organizational Behavior: Utilizing Human Resources,* 3rd ed. (New York: Prentice Hall, 1977).

13. Geert Hofstede and Michael H. Bond, "Hofstede's Culture Dimensions: An Independent Validation Using Rokeach's Value Survey," *Journal of Cross-Cultural Psychology* 15 (1984): 417–433; Geert Hofstede and Michael H. Bond, "The Confucius Connection: From Cultural Roots to Economic Growth," *Organizational Dynamics* 16, no. 4 (1988): 4–21; Geert Hofstede, *Culture's Consequences: Comparing Values, Behaviors, Institutions and Organizations across Nations* (2nd ed.) (Thousand Oaks, CA: SAGE Publications, 2001); Geert Hofstede, Gert Jan Hofstede, and Michael Minkov, *Cultures and Organizations: Software of the Mind,* revised and expanded 3rd ed. (New York: McGraw-Hill, 2010).

14. Robert House, Paul Hanges, Mansour Javidan, and Peter Dorfman, eds., *Culture, Leadership, and Organizations: The GLOBE Study of 62 Societies* (Thousand Oaks, CA: SAGE Publications, 2004); Robert House, Peter Dorfman, Mansour Javidan, Paul Hanges, and Mary Sully de Luquem,

Strategic Leadership across Cultures: GLOBE Study of CEO Leadership Behavior and Effectiveness in 24 Countries (Thousand Oaks, CA: SAGE Publications, 2013).

15. Dave Ulrich, ed., *Leadership in Asia: Challenges, Opportunities, and Strategies from Top Global Leaders* (New York: McGraw-Hill, 2010); Dave Ulrich and Robert Sutton, eds., *Asian Leadership: What Works* (New York: McGraw-Hill, 2010); Chris Rowley and Dave Ulrich, eds., *Leadership in Asia Pacific: A Global Research Perspective* (London: Routledge, 2013).

16. We have done this same exercise in other settings with similar results, with customer receiving the most points and with country receiving 15 to 20 points.

17. Dave Ulrich and Wendy Ulrich, *The Why of Work* (New York: McGraw-Hill, 2010).

18. Dave Ulrich, "The Value of Values," talk given at Utah Valley University on winning the 2010 Kirk Englehardt Business Ethics award; Dave Ulrich, "The Value of Values," posted on Thinker's 50, July 30, 2014.

19. Deloitte, *Culture of Purpose: A Business Imperative*, 2013, http://www.deloitte.com/assets/Dcom-UnitedStates/Local%20Assets/Documents/us_leadership_2013corebeliefs&culturesurvey_051613.pdf.

20. Perry Pascarella and Mark Frohman, *The Purpose-Driven Organization: Unleashing the Power of Direction and Commitment* (San Francisco: Jossey-Bass, 1989).

21. Deloitte, *Culture of Purpose: Building Business Confidence and Driving Growth*, 2014.

Chapter 8

1. Curt Coffman and Kathie Sorenson, *Culture Eats Strategy for Lunch* (Highlands Ranch, CO: Liang Addison Press, 2013); Charles B. Handy, *Understanding Organizations* (Oxford, UK: Oxford University Press, 1976); Edgar Schein, *Organizational Culture and Leadership: A Dynamic View* (San Francisco: Jossey-Bass, 1992).

2. Scott Keller and Colin Price, *Beyond Performance: How Great Organizations Build Ultimate Competitive Advantage* (New York: Wiley, 2011); J. P. Kotter and James L. Heskett, *Corporate Culture and Performance* (New York: Free Press, 1992).

3. These data on cultural surrogates and firm performance come from a presentation by Jeffrey Pfeffer, professor at Stanford Business School, in a conference in Brazil HSM in 2013.

4. Rajendra Sisodia, Jagdish Sheth, and David Wolfe, *Firms of Endearment: How World Class Companies Profit from Passion and Purpose,* 2nd ed. (Upper Saddle River, NJ: Pearson Education, 2014).

5. The resource-based view of organizations has a more academic tradition in work by J. B. Barney, "Firm Resources and Sustained Competitive Advantage," *Journal of Management* 17, no. 1 (1991): 99–120; R. Makadok, "Toward a Synthesis of the Resource-Based View and Dynamic-Capability Views of Rent Creation," *Strategic Management Journal* 22, no. 5 (2001): 387–

401; D. G. Sirmon, M. A. Hitt, and R. D. Ireland, "Managing Firm Resources in Dynamic Environments to Create Value: Looking Inside the Black Box," *Academy of Management Review* 32, no. 1 (2007): 273–292; J. B. Barney, "Is the Resource-Based Theory a Useful Perspective for Strategic Management Research? Yes," *Academy of Management Review* 26, no. 1 (2001): 41–56; B. Wernerfelt, "The Resource-Based View of the Firm," *Strategic Management Journal* 5, no. 2 (1984): 171–180.

6. Approaching organizations as core competencies has been captured in work by Prahalad and Hamel: C. K. Prahalad and Gary Hamel, "The Core Competence of the Corporation," *Harvard Business Review,* May–June 1990, 79–91.

7. Scott Keller and Colin Price, *Beyond Performance: How Great Organizations Build Ultimate Competitive Advantage,* 1st ed. (Hoboken, NJ: Wiley, 2011); see also Scott Keller and Colin Price, "Organizational Health: The Ultimate Competitive Advantage," *McKinsey Quarterly,* June 2011, mckinsey.com; Aaron de Smet, Bill Schaninger, and Matthew Smith, "The Hidden Value of Organizational Health—and How to Capture It," *McKinsey Quarterly,* April 2014.

8. A. E. Reichers and B. Schneider, "Climate and Culture: An Evolution of Constructs," in *Organizational Climate and Culture,* ed. B. Schneider (San Francisco: Jossey-Bass, 1990); D. M. Rousseau, "The Construction of Climate in Organizational Research," in *International Review of Industrial and Organizational Psychology,* ed. C. L. Cooper and I. Robertson (London: Wiley, 1988).

9. The process approach to organization may be seen in the balanced scorecard work: Dave Norton and Robert Kaplan, "The Balanced Scorecard: Measures That Drive Performance," *Harvard Business Review,* January–February 1992; David Norton and Robert Kaplan, *The Strategy-Focused Organization: How Balanced Scorecard Companies Thrive in the New Business Environment* (Boston: Harvard Business Review Press, 2000); David Norton and Robert Kaplan, *Strategy Maps: Converting Intangible Assets into Tangible Outcomes* (Boston: Harvard Business School Press, 2014). It is also found in process management work: Howard Smith, Peter Fingar, *Business Process Management: The Third Wave* (Tampa, FL: Meghan-Kiffer Press, 2006); Markus Kohlbacher, "The Effects of Process Orientation: A Literature Review," *Business Process Management Journal* 16, no. 1 (2010): 135–152.

10. HR value proposition and HR transformation books.

11. Edgar Schein, *Organizational Culture and Leadership: A Dynamic View* (San Francisco: Jossey-Bass, 1992); T. E. Deal and A. A. Kennedy, *Corporate Cultures: The Rites and Rituals of Corporate Life* (Reading, MA: Addison-Wesley, 1982).

12. Kim Cameron and Robert E. Quinn, *Diagnosing and Changing Organizational Culture: Based on the Competing Values Framework* (New York: Prentice Hall, 1999; reprinted by Wiley, 2011).

13. The concept of mindset comes from cognitive psychology and is called

automatic thoughts, schema, or mental models: P. DiMaggio, "Culture and Cognition," *Annual Review of Sociology* (1997): 23263–23287, doi:10.1146/annurev.soc.23.1.263. In organizations, we have talked about shared mindset, or culture, being the shared cognitions in an organization: Dave Ulrich and Dale Lake, *Organization Capability: Competing from the Inside Out* (New York: Wiley, 1990).

14. Daniel Denison, *Corporate Culture and Organizational Effectiveness* (New York: Wiley, 1990).

15. Russell Ackoff, *Re-Creating the Corporation: A Design of Organizations for the 21st Century* (New York: Oxford University Press, 1999); Russell Ackoff, *Redesigning the Future: A Systems Approach to Societal Problems* (New York: Wiley, 1974).

16. Chartered Institute of Internal Auditors, *Culture and the Role of Internal Audit: Looking Below the Surface,* 2014, http://www.iia.org.uk/policy/culture-and-the-role-of-internal-audit/.

17. Jay Galbraith, *Designing Organizations: Strategy, Structure, and Process at the Business Unit and Enterprise Level,* 3rd ed. (San Francisco: Jossey-Bass, 2014); Gregory Kessler and Amy Kates, *Leading Organization Design: How to Make Organization Design Decisions to Drive the Results You Want* (San Francisco: Jossey-Bass, 2010).

18. Dave Ulrich and Norm Smallwood, "Capitalizing on Capabilities," *Harvard Business Review,* June 2014; Igor Ansoff, *Corporate Strategy: An Analytic Approach to Business Policy for Growth and Expansion* (New York: McGraw-Hill, 1965); Dave Ulrich and Dale Lake, *Organizational Capability: Competing from the Inside/Out* (New York: Wiley, 1990); Kim Ruyle, Robert Eichinger, and David Ulrich, *FYI: For Strategic Effectiveness* (Los Angeles: Korn Ferry, 2007); David J. Collins, "Research Note: How Valuable Are Organizational Capabilities?" *Strategic Management Journal,* Winter 1994, 143–152.

19. Charles O'Reilly, III, "Variations in Decision Makers' Use of Information Sources: The Impact of Quality and Accessibility of Information," *Academy of Management Journal* 25 (1982): 756–771; Charles O'Reilly, "The Use of Information in Organizational Decision Making: A Model and Some Propositions," in *Research in Organizational Behavior,* ed. L. L. Cummings and B. M. Staw (Greenwich, CT: JAI Press, 1983), 5:103–139.

20. David Foster Wallace graduation talk to 2005 graduating class at Kenyon College, http://online.wsj.com/news/articles/SB122r178211966454607.

21. Dave Ulrich, Ron Ashkenas, Todd Jick, and Steve Kerr, *The GE Work-Out: How to Implement GE's Revolutionary Method for Busting Bureaucracy and Attacking Organizational Problems* (New York: McGraw-Hill, 2002).

Chapter 9

1. Ed Michaels, Helen Handfield-Jones, and Beth Axelrod, *The War for Talent* (Boston: Harvard Business Press, 2001).

2. David Creelman and John Boudreau, "When Investors Want to Know

How You Treat Your People," *Harvard Business Review* blog, February 10,2105, https://hbr.org/2015/02/when-investors-want-to-know-how-you-treat-people.

3. Dave Ulrich and Justin Allen, "Talent Accelerator: Understanding How Talent Delivers Performance for Asian Firms," *South Asian Journal of HRM* (2014); Dave Ulrich and Justin Allen, Talent Accelerator: Secrets for Driving Business Growth in Asia, manuscript prepared for Singapore Ministry of Manpower, published by The RBL Group, 2013; Dave Ulrich and Mike Ulrich, *Marshalling Talent* (Montreal: Academy of Management, 2010); Dave Ulrich and Michael Ulrich, "Marshalling Talent: A Collaborative Approach to Talent Management," in *The Talent Management Handbook,* Lance Berger and Dorothy Berger (New York: McGraw-Hill, 2010).

4. The Hackett Group Research Alert, 2007.

5. William W. Lewis, *The Power of Productivity: Wealth, Poverty, and the Threat to Global Stability* (Chicago: University of Chicago Press, 2014).

6. Dick Beatty, a thought leader in HR analytics, uses these overall productivity measures to track strategic use of HR. He has presented them in a number of forums.

7. James L. Heskett, W. Earl Sasser, Jr., and Leonard A. Schlesinger, *The Service Profit Chain: How Leading Companies Link Profit and Growth to Loyalty, Satisfaction, and Value* (New York: Free Press, 1997); Anthony Rucci, Steven Kirn, and Richard Quinn, "The Employee-Customer-Profit Chain at Sears," *Harvard Business Review,* January-February 1998, 82–99; Dave Ulrich, Richard Halbrook, Dave Meder, and Mark Stuchlik, "Employee and Customer Attachment: Synergies for Competitive Advantage," *Human Resource Planning* 14, no. 2 (1991): 89–102.

8. "Nearly Seven in Ten Businesses Affected by a Bad Hire in the Past Year, According to CareerBuilder Survey," CareerBuilder, December 13, 2012, http://www.careerbuilder.com/share/aboutus/pressreleasesdetail.aspx?sd =12/13/2012&sc_cmp1=cb_pr730-&siteid=cbpr&id=pr730&ed=12/31/2012.

9. Robin Kessler, *Competency-Based Interviews: How to Master the Tough Interview Style Used by the Fortune 500* (Pompton Plains, NJ: Career Press, 2012); M. A. McDaniel, D. L. Whetzel, F. L. Schmidt, and S. Maurer, "The Validity of the Employment Interview: A Comprehensive Review and Meta-Analysis," *Journal of Applied Psychology* 79 (1994): 599–617; Mark Murphy, *Hiring for Attitude: A Revolutionary Approach to Recruiting and Selecting People with Both Tremendous Skills and Superb Attitude* (New York: McGraw-Hill, 2011).

10. Rick Kennedy, "When Customers Help Select Staff," *HR Magazine* 57, no. 12 (2012).

11. Laurie Miller, "ASTD 2012 State of the Industry Report: Organizations Continue to Invest in Workplace Learning," ASTD, November 8, 2012, http://www.astd.org/Publications/Magazines/TD/TD-Archive/2012/11/ ASTD-2012-State-of-the-Industry-Report.

12. We found that high-potential employees could be identified by looking at the 4 A's: ambition, ability, agility, and achievement. Jessica Johnson and

Dave Ulrich, "Winning Tomorrow's Talent Battle: What Really Matters," RBL working paper, *Leadership Excellence* 30, no. 6 (June 2013).

13. The relative weighting of these three development approaches has generally been 70-20-10; Cynthia McCauley and Morgan McCall, *Using Experience to Develop Leadership Talent: How Organizations Leverage On-the-Job Development* (Hoboken, NJ: Pfeiffer, 2014). We have argued that the emerging ratio might be 50-30-20, with an increased focus on training and outside-of-work learning: Kate Sweetman, Dave Ulrich, Norm Smallwood, "Results Based Learning," *CLO Magazine*, 2014; Dave Ulrich and Norm Smallwood, "What Is Talent?" *Leader to Leader*, Winter 2012.

14. Justin Allen and Dave Ulrich, *Talent: Asia's Critical Resource and Potential Export*, report prepared for Singapore Ministry of Manpower, published by The RBL Group, 2013.

15. Michael Lombardo and Robert Eichinger, *Eighty Eight Assignments for Development in Place* (Greensboro, NC: Center for Creative Leadership, 1989).

16. This leadership training figure comes from a study, Deloitte Consulting LLP and Bersin by Deloitte, *Global Human Capital Trends 2014: Engaging The 21st-Century Workforce*, 2014, http://dupress.com/wp-content/uploads/2014/03/GlobalHumanCapitalTrends2014.pdf; for total training, see Laurie Miller, ASTD 2012 State of the Industry Report: Organizations Continue to Invest in Workplace Learning, ASTD, November 8, 2012, http://www.astd.org/Publications/Magazines/TD/TD-Archive/2012/11/ASTD-2012-State-of-the-Industry-Report.

17. Allen and Ulrich, *Talent: Asia's Critical Resource.*

18. Mark Huselid, Richard Beatty, and Brian Becker, "'A Players' or 'A Positions,'" *Harvard Business Review,* December 2005.

19. Dave Ulrich, "Intellectual Capital = Competence * Commitment," *Sloan Management Review,* Winter 1998. I have since used the equation: competence * commitment * contribution. Commitment focuses on behavioral engagement; contribution on emotional engagement. This formula has appeared in Dave Ulrich and Norm Smallwood, "What Is Talent?" *Leader to Leader,* Winter 2012.

20. Aon Hewitt, Trends in Employee Engagement, 2011, http://www.aon.com/attachments/thought-leadership/Trends_Global_Employee_Engagement_Final.pdf.

21. Aon Hewitt, 2013 Trends in Global Employee Engagement: 4 out of 10 Employees Are Not Engaged, 2013, http://www.aon.com/attachments/human-capital-consulting/2013_Trends_Global_Engagement_Report.pdf; Gallup, Majority of American Workers Not Engaged in Their Jobs, http://www.gallup.com/poll/150383/majority-american-workers-not-engaged-jobs.aspx.

22. A Towers Perrin study finds that 21% are engaged on their job, 71% enrolled (partially engaged) or disenchanted (partially disengaged), and 8% disengaged; Towers Perrin, Employee Engagement/Global Workforce Study, http://employeeengagement.com/towers-perrin-employee-engagement/.

23. Right Management, Employee Engagement: Maximizing

Organizational Performance, 2009, http://www.rightmanagement.ca/en/thought-leadership/research/employee-engagement-maximizing-organizational-performance.pdf; Tim Clark, *The Employee Engagement Mindset: The Six Drivers for Tapping into the Hidden Potential of Everyone in Your Company* (New York: McGraw-Hill, 2012); Clark reports that in the average organization, only about 25% are engaged.

24. Ulrich and Ulrich, *The Why of Work.*

25. Jack Phillips and his colleagues have written some exceptional books on the financial impact of talent management activities: Jack Phillips and Patricia Pulliam Phillips, *ROI at Work* (Alexandria, VA: ASTD, 2006); Jack Phillips, *Return on Investment in Training and Performance Improvement Programs* (London: Routledge, 2011); Jack Phillips and Patricia Pulliam Phillips, *Proving the Value of HR: How and Why to Measure ROI* (Alexandria, VA: SHRM, 2012).

26. There are excellent works on retention strategies: Beverly Kaye and Sharon Jordan-Evans, *Love 'Em or Lose 'Em: Getting Good People to Stay* (Oakland, CA: Berrett-Koehler, 2014); Beverly Kay and Julie Winkle Giulioni, *Help Them Grow or Watch Them Go: Career Conversations Employees Want* (Oakland, CA: Berrett-Koehler, 2012).

27. Watson Wyatt study referenced in Entrepreneur, "How to Create a Winning Employee Retention Strategy," n.d., http://www.entrepreneur.com/article/76456.

28. Anne Tsui, *A Multiple-Constituency Approach to Managerial Effectiveness: A Theoretical Framework and an Exploratory Study,* dissertation, UCLA, 1981.

29. Some of these ideas are in Linda Hill and Lowell Kent Lineback, *Being the Boss: The 3 Imperatives for Becoming a Great Leader* (Boston: Harvard Business Press, 2011).

30. Jac Fitz-enz, *The New HR Analytics: Predicting the Economic Value of Your Company's Human Capital Investments* (New York: AMACOM, 2010); Lauri Bassi, *HR Analytics Handbook* (Golden, CO: McBassi & Company, 2012); Wayne Cascio and John Boudreau, *Investing in People: Financial Impact of Human Resource Initiatives* (Upper Saddle River, NJ: Pearson Education, 2011).

Chapter 10

1. Aon Hewitt, The Current State of Performance Management and Career Development, 2010, http://www.aon.com/attachments/thoughtleadership/Hewitt_Survey_Results_PerfMgmtCareerDevS V10.pdf.

2. E. E. Lawler, "Performance Management: Creating an Effective Appraisal System," working paper, Center for Effective Organizations, University of Southern California, 2010, http://ceo.usc.edu/working_paper/performance_management_creatin.html.

3. Michael West, James Gutherie, Jeremy Dawson, Carol Borrill, and Matthew Carter, "Reducing Patient Mortality in Hospitals: The Role of Human Resource Management," *Journal of Organizational Behavior* 27 (2006): 983–1002.

4. R. Sumlin, "Performance Management: Impacts and Trends," white

paper, Development Dimensions International, http://www.ddi.com/pdf/ OCWP06.pdf (26 March 2004).

5. Society for Human Resource Management, Performance Management Survey, 2000, http://www.shrm.org/research/surveyfindings/documents/ performance%20management%20survey.pdf.

6. David Rock, "Give Your Performance Management System a Review," HBR Blog Network, June 14, 2013, http://blogs.hbr.org/2013/06/ give-your-performance-manageme/.

7. Jackie Morton, "Making the Most of Your Performance Management Software," TalentSpace Blog, May 12, 2014, http://www.halogensoftware.com/ blog/making-the-most-of-your-performance-management-software.

8. WorldatWork, Sibson, and Synygy, *A WorldatWork Survey Brief: Survey of WorldatWork Members*, August 2004, http://www.worldatwork.org/waw/ adimLink?id=17173&nonav=yes.

9. In talking about performance, there are many terms I could choose. Performance *appraisal* generally refers to the process and assessment of performance (called review, evaluation); performance *management* helps ensure that goals are met (called leadership, systems, planning); performance *improvement* emphasizes how to improve results (alignment, engineering, behavior modification). I pick performance accountability to capture the above, with a focus on how to ensure that promised performance occurs.

10. Mercer, *2013 Global Performance Management Survey Report: Global Results*.

11. Ibid.

12. Carol Dweck, *Mindset: The New Psychology of Success* (New York: Ballantine Books, 2007).

13. John R. Baldwin and James Chowhan, *The Impact of Self-Employment on Labour-Productivity Growth: A Canada and United States Comparison*, August 28, 2003, http://ssrn.com/abstract=1387882 or http://dx.doi.org/10.2139/ ssrn.1387882.

14. We are indebted to Charlie Tharp for the perceptive insight that reward systems are primarily communication tools that signal what matters most.

15. Steve Kerr, *Reward Systems: Does Yours Measure Up?* (Boston, MA: Harvard Business Press, 2008); Steve Kerr, "Do Your Company's Incentives Reward Bad Behavior?" HBR Blog Network, August 27, 2014.

16. This data comes from a presentation by Charlie Tharp.

17. "CEOs Earn 354 Times More Than Average Worker," CNN Money, April 15, 2013, http://money.cnn.com/2013/04/15/news/economy/ceo-pay -worker/; Deborah Hargreaves, "Can We Close the Pay Gap?," *New York Times*, March 29, 2014, http://opinionator.blogs.nytimes.com/2014/03/29/ can-we-close-the-pay-gap/?_php=true&_type=blogs&_r=0.

18. Dave Ulrich and Norm Smallwood, *Leadership Sustainability: Seven Disciplines to Achieve the Changes Great Leaders Know They Must Make* (New York: McGraw-Hill, 2013).

19. Marshall Goldsmith and Howard Morgan, "Leadership Is a Contact Sport: The 'Follow Up' Factor in Management Development," *Strategy + Business* no. 36 (Fall 2004).

Chapter 11

1. I am grateful to Wayne Brockbank for summarizing these trends in information. His ideas influence much of this chapter and many of the ideas in this book.

2. Eric Schmidt and Jared Cohen, *The New Digital Age: Transforming Nations, Businesses, and Our Lives* (New York: Vintage, 2014); Victor Mayer-Schonberger, *Big Data: A Revolution That Will Transform How We Live, Work, and Think* (New York: Eamon Dolan/Mariner Books, 2014).

3. Gordon E. Moore, "Cramming More Components onto Integrated Circuits," *Electronics Magazine*, 1965, 4; "Excerpts from a Conversation with Gordon Moore: Moore's Law" (video transcript), Intel Corporation, 2005, 1, http://large.stanford.edu/courses/2012/ph250/lee1/docs/Excepts_A_Conversation_with_Gordon_Moore.pdf; "1965—'Moore's Law' Predicts the Future of Integrated Circuits," Computer History Museum, 2007, http://www.computerhistory.org/semiconductor/timeline/1965-Moore.html.

4. "For Impatient Web Users, an Eye Blink Is Just Too Long to Wait," *New York Times*, February 29, 2012, http://www.nytimes.com/2012/03/01/technology/impatient-web-users-flee-slow-loading-sites.html?pagewanted=all&_r=0.

5. Trevor Hastie, Robert Tibshirani, and Jerome Friedman, *The Elements of Statistical Learning*, 2nd ed. (Secaucus, NJ: Springer, 2009).

6. Matthew Russell, *Mining the Social Web: Data Mining Facebook, Twitter, LinkedIn, Google+, GitHub, and More* (Sebastopol, CA: O'Reilly Media, 2013).

7. "Data Breaches," Identity Theft Resource Center, http://www.idtheft center.org/id-theft/data-breaches.html.

8. Gregory Treverton, "Risks and Riddles," *Smithsonian Magazine,* June 2007. These ideas were picked up and popularized by Malcolm Gladwell in "Open Secrets," January 2007, http://gladwell.com/open-secrets/.

9. Ibid.

10. Millward Brown, "Point of View: Solving Puzzles Delivers Answers; Solving Mysteries Delivers Insights," http://www.millwardbrown.com/docs/default-source/insight-documents/points-of-view/MillwardBrown_POV_Solving_Puzzles_Delivers_Answers.pdf.

11. Thomas Davenport and Jill Dyché, "Big Data in Big Companies," International Institute for Analytics, 2013, http://www.sas.com/resources/asset/Big-Data-in-Big-Companies.pdf.

12. Barry Gill, "E-mail: Not Dead, Evolving," *Harvard Business Review,* June 2013.

13. Arthur Yeung, Dave Ulrich, Stephen Nason, and Mary Ann Von Glinow, *Organization Learning Capability: Generating and Generalizing Ideas with Impact* (New York: Oxford University Press, 1999).

14. There are many works on learning organization: Peter Senge, *The*

Fifth Discipline: The Art and Practice of the Learning Organization (New York: Doubleday, 2006); Michael Marquardt, *Building the Learning Organization: Achieving Strategic Advantage through a Commitment to Learning* (Boston, MA: Nicholas Brealey America, 2011).

15. Ulrich, Ashkenas, Jick, and Kerr, *The GE Work-Out.*

16. Greg McKeown, *Essentialism: The Disciplined Pursuit of Less* (New York: Crown Business); Ron Ashkenas, *Simply Effective: How to Cut through Complexity in Your Organization and Get Things Done* (Boston, MA: Harvard Business Review Press, 2009).

17. Dave Ulrich, Ron Ashkenas, Todd Jick, and Steve Kerr, *Boundaryless Organization: Breaking the Chains of Organization Structure* (San Francisco: Jossey-Bass, 1995).

18. These examples come from a presentation on information by Wayne Brockbank.

19. Robert Cross and Andrew Parker, *The Hidden Power of Social Networks: Understanding How Work Really Gets Done in Organizations* (Boston, MA: Harvard Business Review Press, 2004).

20. Carlota Perez, *Technological Revolutions and Financial Capital* (Northhampton, MA: Edward Elgar, 2003); James Gleick, *The Information: A History, a Theory, a Flood* (New York: Vintage, 2012).

21. Jay Galbraith, *Organization Design* (Boston, MA: Addison-Wesley, 1977).

Chapter 12

1. Histories of work can be found in Alfred Chandler, Jr., *The Visible Hand: The Managerial Revolution in American Business* (Cambridge, MA: Belknap Press, 1993); Alfred Chandler, Jr., *Strategy and Structure: Chapters in the History of the American Industrial Enterprise* (Cambridge, MA: MIT Press, 1969); Peter Drucker, *The Practice of Management* (New York: Harper Business, 2006); Richard Donkin, *The History of Work* (New York: Palgrave MacMillan, 2010).

2. Oliver Williamson, *Markets and Hierarchies: Analysis and Antitrust Implications* (New York: Free Press, 1983); William G. Ouchi, "Markets, Bureaucracies, and Clans," *Administrative Science Quarterly* 25 (1980): 129–141; William G. Ouchi, "The Relationship between Organizational Structure and Organizational Control," *Administrative Science Quarterly* 22 (1977): 95–113.

3. Gary Hamel, *The Future of Management* (Boston, MA: Harvard Business Review Press, 2007); Gary Hamel, *What Matters Now: How to Win in a World of Relentless Change, Ferocious Competition, and Unstoppable Innovation* (San Francisco: Jossey-Bass, 2012).

4. Lynda Gratton, *The Shift: The Future of Work Is Already Here* (New York: HarperCollins Business, 2011); Thomas Malone, *The Future of Work: How the New Order of Business Will Shape Your Organization, Your Management Style, and Your Life* (Boston, MA: Harvard Business Review Press, 2004); Jeanne Meister and Karine Willyerd, *The 2020 Workplace: How Innovative Companies Attract, Develop, and Keep Tomorrow's Employees Today* (New York: HarperBusiness, 2010).

5. There are many terms for this evolving organization, including lattice organization, the spider's web, the holonic enterprise, and the virtual corporation; David Skyrme, "The Virtual Corporation," October 1995, Minor revisions August 1999, http://www.skyrme.com/insights/2virtorg.htm.

6. Jacob Morgan, "The Evolution of Work," *Forbes*, September 9, 2013, http://www.forbes.com/sites/jacobmorgan/2013/09/10/the-evolution-of-work/; "What's Next: Future Global Trends Affecting Your Organization; Evolution of Work and the Worker," The Economist Intelligence Unit, SHRM Foundation, February 2014, http://www.shrm.org/about/foundation/shaping thefuture/documents/2-14%20theme%201%20paper-final%20for%20web.pdf.

7. Paul Evans, "A Duality-Based Interpretation of and Prospective for Strategic Human Resource Management," in eds. Patrick Wright, Lee Dyer, John Boudreau, and George Milkovich, *Research in Personnel and Human Resources Management* (Greenwich, CT: JAI Press, 1998); Charles Handy, *The Age of Paradox* (Boston, MA: Harvard Business Review Press, 1995); Kim Cameron and Robert E. Quinn, *Diagnosing and Changing Organization Culture: Based on the Competing Values Framework* (San Francisco: Jossey-Bass, 2011); Robert E. Quinn, *Beyond Rational Management: Mastering the Paradoxes and Competing Demands of High Performance* (San Francisco: Jossey-Bass, 1988).

8. Judith Hicks Stiehm and Nicholas W. Townsend, *The U.S. Army War College: Military Education in a Democracy* (Philadelphia, PA: Temple University Press, 2002), 6; Nathan Bennett and James Lemoine, "What VUCA Means for You," *HBR Blog*, January 2014, http://hbr.org/2014/01/what-vuca-really -means-for-you/ar/1 .

9. A nice summary of the power of managing paradox is in Fiona Sutherland and Aaron Smith, "Duality Theory and the Management of Change-Stability Paradox," *Journal of Management and Organization* 17 (2011): 534–547.

10. Discussions of centralized versus decentralized organizations are found in Paul Lawrence and Jay Lorsch, *Organization and Environment: Managing Differentiation and Integration* (Cambridge, MA: Harvard Business School Press, 1986); Gregory Kessler and Amy Kates, *Leading Organization Design: How to Make Organization Design Decisions to Drive the Results You Want* (San Francisco: Jossey-Bass, 2010); Jay Galbraith, Diane Downey, Amy Kates, *Designing Dynamic Organizations: A Hands on Guide for Leaders at All Levels* (New York: AMACOM, 2001); William Ouchi, *M Form Society: How Teamwork Can Capture Competitive Edge* (Boston, MA: Addison-Wesley, 1984).

11. Moshe Farjoun, "Beyond Dualism: Stability and Change as a Duality," *Academy of Management Review* 35, no. 2 (2010): 202–225.

12. Noel Burchell and Darl Kolb, "Stability and Change for Sustainability," *University of Auckland Business Review* 8, no. 2 (2006): 33–41.

13. Christopher Worley, Thomas Williams, and Edward Lawler, *The Agility Factor: Build Adaptable Organizations for Superior Performance* (San Francisco: Jossey-Bass, 2014); Amanda Sethi, *The Agility Advantage. How to Identify and Act on Opportunities in a Fast-Changing World* (San Francisco: Jossey-Bass, 2014);

Wendell French, Cecil Bell, and Robert Zawacki, *Organization Development and Transformation: Managing Effective Change* (New York: McGraw-Hill, 2004); Dave Ulrich, Dale Lake, Jon Younger, and Wayne Brockbank, "Change Insights," *NHRD Network Journal* 5, no. 3 (July 2012): 10–19.

14. Christine Congdon, Donna Flynn, and Melanie Redman, "Balancing 'We' and 'Me': The Best Collaborative Spaces Also Support Solitude," *Harvard Business Review*, October 2014, https://hbr.org/2014/10/balancing-we-and-me-the-best-collaborative-spaces-also-support-solitude.

15. "Work Life," *Why Magazine*, n.d., http://www.hermanmiller.com/why/work-life.html.

16. Rick Duffy and Don Goeman, "The New Office Landscape: Why Variety and Choice Are Good for Work Environments," *See Magazine*, Fall 2004.

INDEX

ABOUT THE AUTHOR

Ranked as the number one management guru by *BusinessWeek*, profiled by *Fast Company* as one of the world's top ten creative people in business, and recognized on Thinkers50 as one of the world's leading business thinkers, Dave Ulrich has a passion for ideas with impact. In his writing, teaching, and consulting, he continually seeks new ideas that tackle some of the world's thorniest and longest-standing challenges.

His best-selling books and popular speeches set the corporate agenda. He has influenced thinking about organizations by defining organizations as bundles of capabilities (in *Organizational Capability*) and has worked to delineate capabilities of learning (in *Organizational Learning Capability*), collaboration (in *The Boundaryless Organization*), talent management (in *The Why of Work*), and culture change (in *GE Work-Out*). His work has articulated the basics of effective leadership (in *Leadership Code*), connected leadership with customers (in *Leadership Brand*), and synthesized how to ensure that leadership aspirations turn into actions (in *Leadership Sustainability*). He has shaped the HR profession and been called the "father of modern HR" by focusing on HR outcomes, governance, competencies, and practices (in *Human Resource Champions, Transformation, Competencies for the New HR,* and *HR from the Outside In*).

Ulrich is the Rensis Likert Professor of Business at the University of Michigan and cofounder of the RBL Group (www.rbl.net). From this body of work, he has received numerous profiles, accolades, and lifetime honors. Passionate about learning and perennially curious, Ulrich is one of the most in-demand business speakers worldwide. So far, he has worked in eighty-seven countries and consulted for half of the Fortune 200.

He gives back to the profession and others, having served as Editor of *Human Resource Management* for ten years and donated time to the *Rise of HR,* an anthology focused on what's next for HR professionals. He works as a trustee and adviser to universities and other professional groups. At the peak of their careers, he and his wife took a three-year sabbatical to run a mission for their church.

He and his wife, Wendy, have three children and eight grandchildren, and they get their greatest joy when their grandkids' eyes light up at seeing them and when they want them to read a book or simply go on a walk together.